go and sin no more

Mark Garver

Go and Sin No More
ISBN: 979-8-9894852-5-3

Copyright © 2024 Mark Garver

Published By:
Garver Ministries
All rights reserved.
Printed in USA

Garver Ministries
Madison, AL 35758

acknowledgements

First and foremost, I want to sincerely thank the Lord for the illumination given to me on this subject. It has been a blessing in my own life and in the lives of many others. I remember what the Lord told me while my wife and I were praying, "It's for you and it's for them."

What started out as a simple rewrite of material has bloomed into the wonderful book that I had always envisioned. "Go and Sin No More" is the title that the Lord gave me years ago and I trust this book will be a blessing in the lives of many. I would like to thank everyone who helped me to obey and get this message out.

I want to thank my wife, Rhonda, who has always helped me in every way in the ministry. She is my support and my sounding board, and the best editor ever.

I want to thank Doris for her special anointing to help me "get the Word out," just like the Lord said she would do so many years ago. I want to thank Wesley for the great cover design and all his input. I want to thank my Admin staff, Bethany, Daniel, and Jacque, for all their hard work in making this book all that it was supposed to be. And thank you to those who read it and helped create the questions at the end of each chapter, as well as those who inspired me to do this book in this way.

-   **Pastor Mark Garver**

contents

chapter 1: breaking free from sin

We all deal with sin. It's our enemy, and it's everywhere. It comes to every one of us, believers and unbelievers alike, to tempt us and trap us in a life we do not want. In fact, the Bible guarantees that we will all confront temptation and sin. So, it's not if sin comes, but what we'll do when it does come.

If you think this only applies to really bad sins, like sexual sins, that's just not true. All sin puts us in bondage, but the good news is that Jesus set us free! He set you free from every evil force of darkness that would try to hold you captive. This means that the only thing that can keep you bound is you! How do you get free and stay free? You must be convinced that Jesus set you free and then receive all that Jesus has provided for you, so you can walk in this freedom. How can you be convinced? The Word of God will do the convincing, so don't take my word for it. Take God's Word for it. Take God at His Word.

Let's look at what the Bible has to say about walking free from bondage. Throughout His

Word, God has made it very clear that in order for His promises to belong to us, we must believe and receive them as our own. So, together, let's take hold of His Word that promises us freedom from sin.

GOD SAYS YOU ARE FREE

The first step in receiving from God is to know His will in the matter. Some people think it's hard to know His will, but that's just not true. It's easy once you know what the Bible has to say because the Word of God is the will of God.

In other words, if we want to know God's will on any matter, all we need to do is check out what the Bible has to say about it. The Bible contains 66 books of God's thoughts and ways. It's a manual, a guidebook, written to tell us how to successfully live on this Earth. The Holy Spirit supernaturally moved on holy men of old to write the Bible, so every word written is quick, alive, and contains the power needed to bring it to pass (Hebrews 4:12). This is no ordinary book; this is God talking directly to you and me.

For those who say, "But if God's will is His Word, then what difference does it make whether or not I believe it?" The answer is simple. The will of God is not automatically done in our lives just because it's His will. If that were true, everyone would be born again because the Bible says it's God's will that none should perish or be lost, but that all would receive salvation (2 Peter 3:9). Unfortunately, people perish every day and go to Hell because they never made Jesus their Lord and Savior. The bottom line is that even though God's will is given to us in His Word, you and I must still choose whether or not to believe His Word and then, act on His Word. If we choose to believe God's promises, then our faith in God's Word will bring His promises to pass in our lives.

So, what is God's will regarding freedom from sin? Does God want you free from sin, bad habits, and whatever else trips you up and binds you; or does God send sin to test you, so you'll become a better and stronger person? God's Word has the answer.

Psalm 91:3 (NKJV) **Surely He shall deliver you from the snare of the fowler and from the perilous pestilence.**

God wants to deliver you and set you free. Does this scripture say that maybe or sometimes God will deliver you? No. It says surely, absolutely, and without a doubt God will deliver you. It's a definite promise. From what will He deliver us? It says, "from the snare of the fowler," which means from every trap the enemy sets. And what is the biggest trap of the enemy? Sin! It doesn't matter how long you've been trapped or held captive, or what sin it is because God has promised to deliver you from them all if you will follow Him.

It's so important we understand that sin is never "Your cross to bear." Remember, it's God who wants you free from sin; but sadly, I've heard people mistakenly say that some of us have sins to bear since the Bible does say, "Take up your cross and follow Jesus." Matthew 16:24 does say that, but it's not talking about sin. When you study it out, your cross to bear is laying down your way of doing things and picking up His way of doing things.

In the chapters that follow, we'll talk more about how sin is a two-fold problem that involves both the devil and your human flesh. That's why God sent Jesus to defeat the devil and deliver you from sin, which includes things that have happened in your past that hold you in bondage and make you think or act wrong. God wants you completely delivered from it all!

John 10:10 says that Jesus came to give us abundant life, which is a good and satisfying life. He wants us to have a good marriage, a good family life, and to do well at our job. God wants us to succeed at all we do.

If you're dealing with a bad habit, He wants to deliver you. If you struggle with depression, or oppression, or with bondage in any area of your life, God wants to deliver you. If you continually go from relationship to relationship, or can't keep a job because you think the last six bosses just didn't understand you, the common denominator here is you, so maybe you need God to deliver you from yourself, and He will. Whatever you need fixed in your life, God wants to fix it. He wants to deliver you.

Even if you've been a Christian for a long time and fell into sin, God will deliver you. If you were a minister who made a mistake and got into sin, God will deliver you. If you were just born again yesterday, but sinned today, God will deliver you. If you aren't born again at all, God will deliver you, too, if you will turn to Him. No matter your circumstances, God wants to free you from whatever bondage you have in your life.

James 1:17 (NKJV) says, "Every good gift and every perfect gift...comes down from the Father..." Ephesians 2:10 (AMPC) says that God has "prearranged" a plan for you to walk in the good life. God is so good, and He only wants good for you, so begin to put God's goodness to work in your life right now by saying, "God shall deliver me from the snare of the fowler. He will deliver me out of the devil's hands. And God will deliver me from myself if that's what it takes."

Let's look at another promise of deliverance.

> **2 Timothy 4:18** **And the Lord shall deliver me from every evil work, and will preserve me unto his heavenly kingdom: to whom be the glory for ever and ever. Amen.**

Isn't that good? God is again promising to deliver you, to free you from every evil work. So, no matter what fleshly temptation the devil uses to entice you, God has given you a "get out of jail free" card. Did you hear that? God said He will get you out of the bondage you're in and deliver you from every evil work. Just think about that! God not only promises to get you out of sin, but He has also set you in heavenly places in Christ Jesus (Ephesians 2:6), which means you can live like a king right now on the Earth, ruling and reigning over the works of devil.

In 2 Peter 2:9 (NKJV) it says, "The Lord knows how to deliver the godly out of temptations...." Aren't you glad God knows how to deliver you? Aren't you happy to know you're not stuck in sin, that He's provided you an escape to freedom? On our own, we may not know how to get out and stay out of bondage, but God knows, and He's made a way for us to be free from any sin that tries to track us like a dog tracks a racoon.

TREED BY THE DEVIL

Back in Illinois, where I'm from originally, my dad would go raccoon hunting with his coon dog, Bud. I know that sounds like some make-believe detail from a movie, but it's the truth; and it makes a real point about how the devil tries to harass Christians.

My dad would start out hunting by turning Bud loose in the woods to pick up the scent of a raccoon. When Bud was on the trail, he would let out a certain bark to let my dad know he had found a raccoon. Then, when Bud's bark changed, my dad knew that he had treed that raccoon. "Treed" is a hunting term used to describe how Bud had trapped the raccoon up a tree, where it had no way of escape and was about to meet a bullet and become a fur hat.

In this same way, the devil tries to trap Christians, so they feel treed. Maybe you feel bound by sin or bad habits with no way out, feeling like your life is over, but the good news is, you are no raccoon, and you don't have to stay treed. There is a way out because God knows how to deliver you from every temptation the devil throws at you; but, again, the first step to freedom is to believe you can be free, and that He has delivered you from every evil work and trap the devil has set for you.

Do you believe this? Do you accept what God's Word says? If so, activate your faith by confessing, "I don't want to sin, and I don't have to sin!"

GO AND SIN NO MORE

Jesus once told a woman that she didn't have to sin anymore, and it changed her life. We read about this woman in John 8. She was caught in the act of adultery and brought to Jesus by the religious leaders to test what He would do. These angry accusers reminded Jesus that the law of Moses required this woman be stoned and asked Jesus what He had to say about her sin. Jesus told them that whoever was without sin should cast the first stone. One by one, her accusers left without saying a word. Then, when Jesus was the only one who remained with the woman, He asked her, "Woman, where are your accusers? Did no one condemn you?" (Verse 10). She said, "No one, Lord;" Jesus said, "Neither do I condemn you; go and sin no more" (Verse 11).

These are powerful words that Jesus spoke. In fact, when He said, "Go and sin no more" to this woman, I believe He was also speaking these words to us. Jesus is saying to every one of us today, "Neither do I condemn you for your sin but go and sin no more." I believe Jesus was communicating Heaven's desire for each and every one of us, so we would know that it's possible to live a sin free life and to go and sin no more!

God doesn't want you tied to anything that keeps you down or holds you captive. God wants you free from everything that tries to bind you, no matter how big or small it is.

GUILT AND CONDEMNATION

Just as much as God wants you free from sin, He also wants you free from the guilt sin causes. Guilt leads to condemnation and God doesn't want you feeling condemned. He didn't set you free from sin so you could continually worry about your former lifestyle of sin and carry that baggage of guilt with you everywhere you go. No, when God sets you free, you are free indeed!

In the encounter between Jesus and the woman caught in adultery, you'll recall that Jesus did not condemn her, and He is not condemning you and me. After we've repented and God has forgiven our sins, condemnation should be nowhere near us.

> **Romans 8:1** **There is therefore now no condemnation to those who are in Christ Jesus who do not walk according to the flesh, but according to the Spirit.**

Now, if you're feeling convicted, that's something entirely different. Conviction and condemnation are not the same. When you're living in sin and the Spirit of God deals with you to change something in your life, or He points out and highlights sin in your life, that's conviction. You should actually be happy when you feel convicted because that's the Holy Spirit talking and trying to help you turn from it. So, when you feel convicted, deal with the conviction immediately by asking God to forgive you and then, make a change by no longer doing what you were doing.

Again, condemnation is a feeling of guilt, and that never comes from God. Jesus did not condemn the woman caught in adultery, and He's not condemning you and me. Jesus bore your guilt and shame, so you wouldn't have to feel condemned. Condemnation always comes from the devil and from religious people who try to make you feel guilty and unworthy.

Let me say it this way. Conviction is when the Holy Ghost says, "Stop it! Don't do that! That will pull you away from the Father." Condemnation is when the devil or other people say things that cause you to feel guilty or ashamed and thinking, "I'm just a rotten worm. I'm just a sinner." But if you're born again, you're no longer a sinner because you have received God's amazing grace and have become a child of God, a joint heir with Jesus. You have royal blood flowing through your veins; you've got the DNA of God Almighty Himself on the inside of you because you're a new creature in Christ Jesus.

If you're born again and have asked God to forgive you of your sins, He has forgiven and forgotten them. The Bible says that when God forgives, He forgets and removes your sins is as far as the east is from the west (Psalm 103:12). If you have not yet received Jesus as your Lord and Savior, you're probably dealing with sin morning, noon, and night, but your life can be turned around in an instant once you're born again, so don't tolerate guilt and condemnation for another minute. If you have not yet made Jesus the Lord of your life, turn to Page 263 right now and pray a prayer that will change your life forever.

Religion, sometimes, likes to tell people that guilt and condemnation are good for them, but that's a lie. Guilt and condemnation will separate us from God, and there's nothing worse than that. If you're feeling guilty or condemned by sin, you won't go boldly into God's presence where you can receive help in your time of need.

GET SMART

Whether you've never met Jesus Christ, you're newly born again, or you've been in the family of God for years, you will never grow past the temptation to sin. As long as you are alive on this Earth, you will have many opportunities to resist sin. That's why it's so important for us to be aware that sin comes to us all; and if we let our guard down, the devil will be right there to put us back into bondage. Whenever we think we're smarter than the devil or that we don't need to keep our flesh under, we set ourselves up for a big fall. It's called pride, and it comes before destruction.

Whether you've had an occasional problem, a continual problem, or don't think you have a problem with sin at all, this message is for you. If you live in a body on this Earth, you need this message if you want to live in victory and be healthy, wealthy, and wise.

So, the next question becomes, "How can I get free and stay free from sin?" The Bible answers this question and so much more, which we'll look at in the chapters that follow.

Chapter
One
Questions

1. What scripture promises that God will deliver you from every evil work? Explain it.

2. Who tempts us to sin? Who delivers us from sin?

3. What is the difference between conviction and condemnation?

4. **What is condemnation; who condemns us, and why?**

5. **What is conviction, who convicts us, and why?**

Chapter
One
Confessions

✷ **The Lord will deliver me from every trap of the enemy.** (Psalm 91:3)

✷ **Who the Son sets free is free indeed, so I am free in Christ Jesus.** (John 8:36)

✷ **Condemnation cannot live in me because I am in Christ Jesus and walk in the spirit and not the flesh.** (Romans 8:1)

✷ **The Lord will deliver me from every evil work and keep me safe in His Heavenly Kingdom** (2 Timothy 4:18)

✷ **I am born again and because I walk uprightly, God knows how to deliver me out of every temptation and evil work. I am delivered!** (2 Peter 2:9)

chapter 2: truth about temptation

The more we understand what sin is and how it works, the better equipped we will be to break free from its control. Most people don't like to talk about sin; and yet, understanding how it works and what it is will give us the advantage and the power to get free from it, because turning on the lights will always chase away the darkness.

Let's begin by asking ourselves some very important questions about sin and then, searching God's Word to find, in more detail, the answers.

- **Where did sin come from?**

- **Is sin God's way of testing us?**

- **How does sin work?**

- **How can we stay away from sin altogether?**

WHO IS THE TEMPTER?

Many people believe that God uses sin, temptation, and the evils of this world to test us, but that's just not the case. The Bible clearly tells us where they come from, and it's not from God.

Temptation and sin never come from God. It's important to be rock solid on this truth because if we don't know the origin of something, we won't know who we're fighting against. We know we shouldn't fight against God, so when people think the temptation to sin came from God, as a test, they don't know whether to roll over and accept it or resist it. They'll even change the way they talk when they think it's from God and go all King James saying, "Mine heart is saddened that I have fallen into sin and failed the test that God hath sendeth me." It sounds religious, but it's so wrong.

Let's settle this once and for all by seeing what the Word of God has to say about it.

> **James 1:13 (NKJV)** Let no one say when he is tempted, "I am tempted by God", for God cannot be tempted by evil, nor does He Himself tempt anyone.

> **1 Thessalonians 3:5 (NKJV)** For this reason, when I could no longer endure it, I sent to know your faith, lest by some means the tempter had tempted you, and our labor might be in vain.

God has never tempted your flesh to sin, but the devil has been the tempter from the beginning. Did you get that? Temptation to sin only comes from one source: the devil; he is the one who tempts us.

Notice what James has to say about it.

> **James 1:12-15 (NKJV)**
>
> 12 Blessed is the man who endures temptation; for when he has been approved, he will receive the crown of life which the Lord has promised to those who love Him.

> **¹³ Let no one say when he is tempted, "I am tempted by God"; for God cannot be tempted by evil, nor does He Himself tempt anyone.**
>
> **¹⁴ But each one is tempted when he is drawn away by his own desires and enticed.**
>
> **¹⁵ Then, when desire has conceived, it gives birth to sin; and sin, when it is full-grown, brings forth death.**

Did James say that God tests us with temptation and sin? No. It says the exact opposite. James said, "Let no one say when he is tempted, 'I am tempted of God;'" and then went on to say, "God cannot be tempted with evil, nor does He Himself tempt anyone." Verse 14 gives us even more detail saying, "But each one is tempted when he is drawn away by his own desires [lusts] and enticed." Notice that last phrase, "When he is drawn away by his own desires [lusts] and enticed." We will talk more about this later because lusts and enticements have much to do with sinning or not sinning; but for now, let's focus on who is tempting and enticing us.

In 1 Thessalonians 3:5, it says that it is the tempter, the devil. He's the culprit. The title of tempter belongs to him alone, and he will tempt you every chance he gets and in every way he can. The devil is the one who coaxes us to sin and probably does a happy dance when we fall for his plan.

Let's look at some scriptures that clearly identify the devil as the tempter.

> **Matthew 4:3 (NKJV)** **Now when the tempter came to Him [Jesus], he said, "If You are the Son of God, command that these stones become bread."**

> **2 Corinthians 11:3** **But I fear, less by any means, as the serpent beguiled Eve through his subtlety, so your minds should be corrupted from the simplicity that is in Christ.**

Who tempted Jesus and Eve? The serpent. Who was the serpent? The devil. We can clearly see that it's not God who is tempting us; it's the devil. God will never tempt you at any time, in any place or in any way to sin. We must recognize that temptation and sin are weapons the enemy uses to trick, defeat, and get us off track; and it's up to us to refuse to let the enemy influence us in that way.

TEST OR TEMPTATION?

Even after some folks become convinced that God will not tempt them, they begin to ask if God will test them. They ask because they don't yet understand the difference between a temptation and a test, so let's first look at some examples of temptations to help us know the difference.

Guys, if a woman walks by in a string bikini, is this a test from God to see if you can maintain pure thoughts, or to see how well your eyesight functions, or anything like that? No. This is the devil tempting you to sin.

Gals, if a guy walks by shirtless, showing his tanned, rippled abs and huge pecs, is this a test from God to see if you can keep your mind focused on the Lord or on your husband? No. This is the devil tempting you to sin.

If someone has been delivered from alcohol, will God send a buddy to their house with a six-pack to see how they're doing? No. This is the devil tempting them to sin.

You may be laughing as you think about these examples, but a lot of people struggle with not knowing the difference and not understanding a temptation is never a test.

A temptation is the enemy trying to steal from you. John 10:10 says it's the thief (devil) who comes to steal, kill, and destroy, not God. God doesn't steal our health, our money, and He doesn't send trouble our way. God sent Jesus to give His children abundant life (John 10:10), so anything that is not abundant life is not from God.

Let's look at some more examples.

Let's say a man, who used to steal when he was a kid, is standing in front of an ATM when, suddenly, it begins to spit out thousands of dollars. This money is not his, so is that God testing him? No. This is the devil tempting him to sin.

What if an armored car came down the street and dropped $10,000. Is that a test from God to see what you will do? No. God does not set you up for failure. This is the devil tempting you to sin.

Temptation is never a test from God. So, how does God test us? He gives us open book tests regarding His Word. In other words, God will check to see if we're being obedient to His Word and following the leadings and promptings of the Holy Ghost.

Let's look at some examples of God testing us.

God asks you to do something, like help in the church or visit a neighbor. The test is, will you obey, and do it?

God asks you to give additional money above your tithe to either the church, a worthy cause, or to someone personally. The test is, will you obey, and do it?

God reminds you to be a good steward of what you have. The test is, will you handle what you have been given in a godly way to meet all your expenses?

That's how God tests us. He tests our obedience because when we obey, He is able to give us even more.

Temptation is the devil wanting to get us into sin, to put us on a road to destruction and off the road of blessing. James 1 told us that the devil is the one who comes to tempt us, and he's not playing around. The devil wants you to mess up and get you into as much trouble as possible. The devil is out to ruin your life; but for those who are born again, we can avoid this because we have His Word on it.

So, when sin comes to tempt us, we don't have to wonder, "Where is this coming from?" Instead, we'll know and confidently say, "That's the work of the devil trying to get me out of the will of God and pull me away from my heavenly Father and from my family. That's the devil trying to ruin my life! No way, devil! Back off!"

The devil doesn't come against us in a red suit with a tail, horns and carrying a pitchfork, so how does the devil come? The devil comes with sin, sickness, confusion, and with every other evil work, but here's the good news...

1 John 3:8 (NKJV) ...**For this purpose the Son of God was manifested, that He might destroy the works of the devil.**

You've got to clearly know that the temptation to sin is the work of the devil, and as a born-again believer, there's always a way out, so you don't have to give in to temptation and commit sin.

It's also important to know that the temptation is not the sin. Temptation to sin first comes as a thought to disobey God and His Word, but in and of itself, the thought is not sin. The sin comes when a person acts upon the thought. So, don't act upon thoughts of temptation; cut them off before they escalate.

Jesus Himself was tempted. Hebrews 2:18 says, "For in that he himself hath suffered being tempted, he is able to succour them that are tempted." The word "succour" means to run to the cry of, to assist and relieve those who are tempted. In 2 Peter 2:9 (NKJV) it says, "The Lord knows how to deliver the godly out of temptations…" Who are the godly? Those who are born again. So, if you find yourself tempted, you have help available. God has made a way out of that temptation, and He will deliver you out of them all if you'll follow Him.

The bottom line is this, a test from God is meant to prove you, and a temptation from the devil is meant to move you.

YOUR PART OF THE EQUATION

We've established that the devil is responsible for introducing temptation and sin in the Garden of Eden, but there's more to this story. James explained that there is another element in the sin equation. James said that temptation comes when we are drawn away by our own lust and then, when lust is conceived, it produces sin (James 1:14-15). That means the devil isn't the sum total of the sin problem; we're the other half. The devil may dangle temptation in front of you, but you are still the one who chooses whether you will give in to sin or turn it down. And remember, the power of the Holy Spirit that is working in you, will enable you to turn it down. The Bible will arm you with insight concerning your enemy and will give you all the equipment you need to defeat both the temptation and the devil.

God's Word says,

- **We are more than conquerors (Romans 8:37).**

- **We can do all things through Jesus Christ who strengthens us (Philippians 4:13).**

For this to happen, it is our job to understand the sin process and how it works, so we can walk in the freedom from sin that Jesus won for us.

THE PROCESS OF SIN

The first thing we need to understand about this process is that sin doesn't just happen out of the blue one day. A person might feel like it came that way and even shocked that they gave in and sinned, but the truth is that the act of sin was a process that developed over time.

SIN PROCESS:

- **One wrong thought that led to more wrong thoughts then...**

- **One bad choice after another then...**

- **The desire to sin overpowered the person and they acted on it.**

Sin is the result of giving in to the temptation. Temptation comes to everybody. Every man, woman, and child must endure temptation. If we don't deal with temptation when it first raises its ugly head, when it's small, it's likely to grow beyond our ability to control it.

Notice, again, what God's Word says.

> **James 1:14-15**
>
> **14 But every man is tempted, when he is drawn away of his own lust, and enticed.**
>
> **15 Then when lust hath conceived, it bringeth forth sin: and sin, when it is finished, bringeth forth death.**

This is the devil's formula: Temptation + lust = sin conceived. The word "conceive" means to become pregnant with, to take into one's mind, to cause to begin, to form and imagine in one's own mind.

Do you see the pattern here? The devil will dangle a well-chosen carrot of sin in front of a person to entice them. If that person takes hold by considering it, thinking on it, imagining it, playing with the possibility of it in their mind, they will become pregnant with it; and once it has fully formed, it won't be long before they act on it.

Some time back, as I was studying on this and reading James 1:14-15, the word "conceive" seemed to jump off the page, and it gave me real insight. This word "conceive" highlighted an important point to me: It takes two to tango.

The process of sin is similar to the process of creating a baby. When a man and a woman come together to conceive a child, it takes both the sperm and the egg. If the sperm and the egg don't come together, there will be no child. In the same way, the process of sin also requires two components to come together: temptation and lust. So, it comes down to this. We can't control what the devil does or when he comes, or stop sin from producing death, but we can control the lusts of our flesh because without its participation, sin will not be conceived. Instead, it will be stopped cold in its tracks.

Sin always begins with a single thought and then, continues to grow as it's fed with more thoughts and imaginations, followed by poor choices and then, ending up with wrong actions. It's important for you to understand that the devil is after your mind and body because that's where he can do his dirty work to influence you. If he can dominate your mind and your body, your spirit, on its own, won't be able to rise up and shut down the enemy.

Let's put a stop to that right now by exposing his tactics and strategies because if we know how he operates, we can refuse to cooperate with him and be empowered to "go and sin no more."

To understand more about how the enemy works, let's remember that we are a three-part being. We are a spirit, we live in a body (a suit of flesh), and we have a soul (mind, will and emotions). If you're born again, the Spirit of God lives in you, so when it comes to the devil, you're large and in charge, as long as you follow God and obey His Word.

The devil has no authority over our born-again spirit where God dwells. Our part is to walk in the freedom and authority God has given us. When we do, every sin that we have been dealing with will begin to drop off because we are no longer ignorant of the devil's devices and schemes. This is how we break free from sin.

STRATEGY LEADING TO SIN

Ecclesiastes 1:9 says that there's nothing new under the sun, which means the devil has been using the same old tricks since the beginning of time. The devil doesn't have any new tricks, just new people to trick. In fact, the same way the devil tempted Eve's flesh in the garden, is the same way he comes to tempt you and me.

Genesis 1:26 tells us that Adam and Eve were made in the likeness and image of God and were totally alive unto God. Before they fell into sin, they were perfect because God had made them perfect. So, how could someone perfect sin? Because God had given them a will of their own, and with that free will, they chose to disobey God and give in to the temptation the devil had brought to them.

If you're thinking, "What chance do I have if Adam and Eve, who were perfect, couldn't withstand temptation?" Let's look in the Bible for the answer to that question.

In the Garden of Eden, God had created the perfect setting. He made a beautiful and lush garden. We can look at the Earth today and see that God never does anything halfway. God said that everything He had made was good. I'm sure the skies were shimmering with light, the water was crystal clear, and the fruit was bountiful and tasty. Life was perfect for Adam and Eve. They lived in a paradise that they could enjoy as God regularly fellowshipped with them.

God had put them in charge and told them to guard and protect the garden. They had dominion over the fish of the sea, every fowl of the air, every beast on the ground and everything that creeps. God only gave them one thing not to do and that was not to eat from one tree. Then, the devil showed up to tempt Eve. In 2 Corinthians 11:3 it says, "…the serpent beguiled Eve through his subtilty…"

Think about this. Adam and Eve already had dominion over the serpent (devil) because they had been given authority over everything that creeps on the ground, but the enemy still showed up to tempt Eve's resolve with his trickery.

Genesis 3:1-15 tells us about the encounter Eve had with her enemy and ours. As we look at this unfortunate first encounter with sin, remember that the devil is using this same strategy today. These verses reveal his strategies and tactics for all mankind to see. We learn that the devil is subtle, he's a liar, and a deceiver who uses his skills to entice us with sin. Remember that Jesus called the devil the "father of lies" (John 8:44); so that means if the devil tells you that something is good, and we know he is a liar, we know that means it's not good.

We also learn that the devil likes to challenge the Word of God. That's the trick he pulled on Eve.

> **Genesis 3:1 (AMPC)** **Now the serpent was more subtle and crafty than any living creature of the field which the Lord God had made. And he [Satan] said to the woman, Can it really be that God has said, You shall not eat from every tree of the garden?**

Think about what the enemy did here and how he uses the same technique today. The enemy's first shot was trying to get Eve off of what God had said. The devil wanted her to question and disagree with the Word of God.

Hasn't the devil tried the same with you by saying…

- **Did God really say…?**
- **Would it really be so bad if you…?**
- **Would it really hurt for you to do it just this once? Who will know?**

What a liar he is! Who would know?! God would know, and, eventually, everyone else would know.

This is exactly what the devil did to Eve because he wanted to pull her away from what God had said and get her out of obedience; he questioned her to see what she knew about the trees in the garden. The devil knows the Word of God, so when the woman said, "…We may eat of the fruit of the trees of the garden: But of the fruit of the tree which is in the midst of the garden, God hath said, 'Ye shall not eat of it, neither shall ye touch it, lest ye die.'" (Genesis 3:2-3), immediately the devil challenged Eve's knowledge of that Word. He said, "You won't die!" That was actually half true, and the devil is good at half-truths. The whole truth was that by eating the fruit, Adam and Eve would not physically die, but they would spiritually die because they would be separated from God.

The devil's next trick was to put a first-class spin on sin, and Eve wasn't able to pass it up. The devil told Eve that God was holding back on them. The enemy was definitely working hard to push all her buttons; and was very slick about convincing her that God wasn't giving them everything they needed to be all they could be.

In Genesis 3:5 (NLT), the devil said to Eve, "God knows that your eyes will be opened as soon as you eat it, and you will be like God, knowing both good and evil." Can you believe it? The devil was telling Eve that she and Adam had not yet "arrived," and it was God's fault that they were not as "large and in charge" as they could or should be. Through deception and lies, he convinced her they would be as gods if they would eat the forbidden fruit.

The most interesting thing to me is, in reality, Adam and Eve were already the "gods" of this world because God had given them charge and authority over the whole Earth. Doesn't this sound familiar? Isn't this tactic so like the devil? When he entices you with sin, he always tries to convince you that you're missing out on something; but usually, it's something you already have or have access to because the Word of God tells us that all the promises of God are yes and amen and belong to us (2 Corinthians 1:20). God is not withholding any good thing from those who walk uprightly (Psalm 84:11), which means God is not withholding anything from a born-again believer. Everything He has is yours. And if He doesn't have it, He will make it for you. The only thing God cannot do is lie. God has bound Himself to keep His Word (Numbers 23:19).

So, back to Eve. Sure enough, her flesh began to "rare up" and cause problems. In the following verse, the whole process of temptation leading to sin is revealed.

> **Genesis 3:6** And when the woman saw that the tree was good for food, and it was pleasant to the eyes, and a tree to be desired to make one wise, she took of the fruit thereof, and did eat, and gave also unto her husband with her; and he did eat.

What we have here is the devil's foremost strategy in a nutshell. The devil targeted three things in Eve:

1. **The lust of the flesh.**
2. **The lust of the eyes.**
3. **The pride of life.**

We see these three strategies used over and over again in the Word of God and in our life to get us to fall into sin, so I want to go into more detail concerning each one of them.

THREE CATEGORIES OF TEMPTATION

The Holy Spirit, through the Apostle John, warns us about these three types of temptation in 1 John, which are the same ones the devil used against Eve resulting in the fall of mankind.

The devil targeted Eve, and Jesus, too, with these same three temptations. Think about it. The devil went after the "big dogs" in the Bible using these tactics, so you can be sure he'll use them on you and me!

Let's look at what 1 John 2 has to say.

1 John 2:15-16

¹⁵ Love not the world, neither the things that are in the world. If any man love the world, the love of the Father is not in him.

¹⁶ For all that is in the world, the lust of the flesh, and the lust of the eyes, and the pride of life, is not of the Father, but is of the world.

LUST OF THE FLESH

First is the **lust of the flesh**, which deals with the appetites of the flesh, our five senses and bodily cravings. In Eve's case, it was the appeal of the fruit being good for food that had her mouth watering. She, literally, had to have it at any cost. Does your flesh ever tell you that you have to have something? What are the appetites the devil tries to stir up in you until it drives you so crazy that you've just got to have it? We each need to identify our weaknesses, so we can shore up our resolve concerning them.

Adam and Eve were perfectly created in the likeness and image of God, and there was no sin or flaw in them. The problem was that there was a serpent in the Garden of Eden, a mouthy serpent, who understood they had a free will and getting a child of God to entertain lust would open the door to sin.

LUST OF THE EYES

Next is the **lust of the eyes**. The food was pleasant to Eve's eyes, which is a big problem because the eyes are the window to our soul. The devil will always bring temptations before your eyes by bringing you pictures of your past and even imaginations of what could have been. And, unfortunately, there are times when we cannot help what our eyes see because the devil will make sure that things pass before us. That's why we must keep our eyes focused on God's Word.

In other words, Eve craved something she was not supposed to have, that was bad for her, and would eventually destroy her, but she kept looking at it anyway, which allowed that lust in her to grow. I'm sure you've noticed that your flesh works that way too, always wanting what it shouldn't have and finding it difficult to walk away from it.

In the garden, there was an abundance of food to choose from; but naturally, Eve wanted the one thing God told them not to eat. Why? It was pleasant to the eyes (Genesis 3:6), and the lust of her eyes had taken hold and she wanted it. The eyes love to look at things they should not look at, and the devil loves to tempt us with things to see. If the devil can get us to look at things we shouldn't be looking at and keep us looking, then he can gain access to our soul realm where sin is ignited.

This is true for all of us, both men and women. Too often people think that the lust of the eyes is just a male problem, but that's not true. It's a human problem, and we all need to be careful about what we gaze (steadily look) at. That's why the Lord tells us to meditate on the Word, day and night, and keep it before our eyes because what we see is important. And when you think about it, we can lust after just about anything we see, whether it's something big like a new BMW or as small as a piece of coconut cream pie. It doesn't matter what we're lusting after, lust is wrong. It's not godly, but it is deadly.

In case you haven't noticed, the devil likes to play the "sex" card on a pretty regular basis by tempting men and women with attractive members of the opposite sex. In teaching the men of our church, my wife, Rhonda, who pastors alongside me, often says, "Maybe you couldn't help the first look, but you sure can with the second, third and fourth look." Unfortunately, what tends to happen is looks are turned into stares, which is what can lead us right into sin. There's so much wisdom in my wife's statement. In fact, if King David had understood this principle of turning away after the first look, he never would have gotten into a sinful relationship with Bathsheba (2 Samuel 11). I'm not just talking about sexual sins here.

These three temptations are pathways the devil uses with every temptation to sin.

THE PRIDE OF LIFE

The last one is the **pride of life**. Eve saw that the tree would make her wise. In fact, the devil told her that she would be like God. The pride of life tries to get us to elevate ourselves above others and to do it in our own strength. The enemy wants us to make our life all about us.

As a pastor, I see this happen all the time. I've watched the devil destroy people by convincing them that life is all about them, their wants, needs, and desires. The bottom line is the pride of life is the devil getting you to think about you!

Notice how the devil's temptation strategy on Eve is something he knows about. Why wouldn't he. It was his original sin. The devil thought he would elevate himself above God, and we all know how that turned out. God kicked him out of Heaven. The devil wants every one of us to adopt that same prideful attitude that says, "I don't need God; I can do it on my own." Eve fell into that trap and obeyed her flesh, and it cost her, it cost Adam, and it cost all of humanity.

Rhonda and I often tell a story from our early years of marriage that's funny to us now. We were newly married and having a little spat, when Rhonda said to me, "Adam, be careful what you let in the garden." She said that because I had let some strife get into our home. We don't normally deal with strife but back then, we were just learning a lot of things about being married. After she said that, I looked at her and said, "Well, Eve, if a snake gets by me, just don't talk to it." This would have been good advice for Adam and Eve and is definitely good advice for us today. Men, don't let snakes in your garden; and women, if a snake slips in, don't talk to it!

Adam and Eve did not do that. God had given them authority and dominion over the garden and everything on the Earth and told Adam to till the garden and watch over and protect it. So, the first problem we see wasn't when Eve ate the fruit. It was Adam letting his guard down, so the snake was able to get in the garden. Adam wasn't being diligent, or maybe he thought one snake wasn't a problem, but he was wrong. It was a big problem!

If you're thinking, "Well, I'm created in the likeness and image of God, so I'm sure I will never fall for any of those temptations," all I can say is, "Ouch," because that statement is prideful, and that kind of arrogance can get you in big trouble. We cannot afford to think that what happened to Eve could never happen to us. It's one thing to be sure of who you are in Christ, but it's another thing altogether to think you cannot be tempted or snared by sin. The minute you think that way, you're opening the door to trouble because God has already warned us, in His Word, that the devil will come at us through the lust of our flesh, the lust of our eyes, and the pride of life; so, at some point, we will all be faced with the desire of, "I want it, and I want it now."

God wants us blessed. He wants us to have nice things. He wants to meet the desires of our heart, but it's another thing altogether for us to lust after things. Matthew 6:33 says, "But seek ye first the kingdom of God, and his righteousness; and all these things shall be added," so let's let God do the adding.

JESUS BEATS TEMPTATION

Over the years, as a pastor, I've watched people begin to walk in the blessings of God but then, be unable to continue in their walk. Why? Because they didn't have enough Word in their hearts, so the lusts of their flesh began to take over. Just as it says in the parable of the sower (Mark 4), the lusts of the flesh choke out the Word to where the person no longer serves God. So, these three categories of temptation are serious, and we need to avoid them like the plague they are.

When you think about it, Eve showed us exactly how to fail when temptation comes because when she was tempted, she gave in and sinned. On the flipside, Jesus showed us how to succeed because when He was tempted, He spoke the Word and did not sin. Where Eve fell, Jesus stood and won over temptation. That tells me that although we can learn from Eve's mistakes, we need to make Jesus our example. We need to follow His lead and take a closer look at how He handled temptation and won.

So, now that we've outlined some of the devil's playbook when it comes to him enticing us to sin, the good news is that God has given us His playbook too. The devil obviously has strategies he uses to get us off track, but God has shown us what they are and has given us His strategies to win.

In Luke 4:1-14, we see the three temptations that the devil used on Jesus. Luke 4 says that after Jesus returned from Jordan, the Spirit led Him into the wilderness where He was tempted by the devil for 40 days. So, immediately, at what we call the temptation of Christ, the devil pulled out his playbook and hit Jesus with his best moves. The first play he used was the lust of the flesh. The devil knew Jesus was tired and hungry, so he started talking about food because he wanted Jesus thinking about loaves of bread. The devil started by saying, "…If thou be the Son of God, command this stone that it be made bread" (Verse 3). Was it even possible for Jesus to turn a stone into bread?" I'm sure Jesus could have done it; otherwise, it would not have been a legitimate temptation. After all, Jesus did turn water into wine.

So, how did Jesus resist the temptation? Jesus looked the devil square in the face and boldly said, "It is written, that man shall not live by bread alone, but by every Word of God" (Luke 4:4). So, how did Jesus defeat the devil? With the Word. Jesus spoke the Word, using the exact scripture that pertained to His situation. What do you think that says about how we should handle temptation? We, too, are to speak the Word. That's definitely one strategy we all need to put in our "Overcoming Temptation" playbook.

The next call from the devil's playbook was taking Jesus to a high mountain and showing him all the kingdoms of the world. The devil told Jesus he would give them all to Him if He would bow down and worship him. How interesting it is that the devil often dangles in front of people what seems to be the end of their goals.

The devil was offering Jesus a short cut to one of the very things Jesus came to this Earth to do, which was to take back the authority Adam had surrendered to the devil. It certainly would have been easier on Jesus' flesh to bypass the crucifixion, but the end result would have been the continued bondage of mankind to Satan and sin. This tells me that the easy way out is not always the right way.

So, how did Jesus handle this temptation? He basically told the devil, "No way," by saying, "Get thee behind me, Satan: for it is written, thou shalt worship the Lord thy God, and him only shalt thou serve" (Luke 4:8). Jesus was telling the devil that worshipping him was not going to happen. Once again, Jesus defeated the devil with the spoken Word that had to do with His situation.

Finally, the devil made his last call by bringing Jesus to Jerusalem, where he set Him on the pinnacle of the temple. The devil's goal, in this instance, was to trick Jesus into questioning who He was. Keep in mind, the devil used this same lie on Eve, and it worked, but this strategy wasn't going to work on Jesus because He knew who He was and did not need to prove Himself to the devil. The devil said to Jesus, "If you're really the son of God, throw yourself down. The angels will protect you." Can you imagine the devil throwing scripture back at Jesus like that? As shocking as that is, we shouldn't be surprised because he does the same thing to you and me. The devil knows the Word of God well enough to misquote and twist it for his purpose, so keep that in mind the next time he starts quoting the Bible to you. Jesus put the father of lies in his place and answered right back saying, "…It is said, thou shalt not tempt the Lord thy God" (Luke 4:12). With that, the devil had no choice but to leave Jesus alone for a time and go find someone who didn't know the Word as well. Bottom line: Speaking the Word, specifically pertaining to your situation, will get you out of temptation every time.

In Luke 4:14 it says, "Jesus returned in the power of the Spirit into Galilee; and there went out a fame of him through all the region round about." Refuse to give in to temptations, and you, too, will become stronger in the power of the Spirit every time you withstand the enemy.

DRAWN AWAY BY LUST

We must understand that as born-again Christians, our citizenship is in Heaven, and we should act like it. Even though we live on this Earth, we are foreigners and aliens down here. We are citizens of Heaven and should be living a godly lifestyle. In 1 Peter 2:11 it says, "Dearly beloved, I beseech you as strangers and pilgrims, abstain from fleshly lusts, which war against the soul."

As visitors on this planet, God expects us to refrain from carnal lusts that draw us into the strategic warfare the devil has designed for us. Remember, Eve obeyed her flesh, and it cost her everything. The devil would like nothing better than for all of humanity, especially those who are born of God, to obey the impulses of their flesh, so don't let that happen to you. Instead, let God's Word and His Spirit arm you with the supernatural equipment you need to overcome anything the devil brings your way.

Chapter Two Questions

1. What are some examples of temptation described in the Bible, and how do they relate to my own experiences and struggles?

2. Reflecting on past experiences, what are some common triggers or situations that lead us into temptation?

3. Who is the tempter? How is sin conceived? What is the sin process?

4. **What is the difference between a temptation and a test?**

5. **What is the devil's three foremost strategies?**

6. **How Did Jesus resist temptation, and how do we do the same?**

Chapter
Two
Confessions

＊ Because I have been raised to sit in heavenly places with Christ Jesus, the devil is under my feet. (Ephesians 2:6, Ephesians 1:22)

＊ Because I am not ignorant of the devil's devices, I will win against the enemy every time by speaking the Word of God to that situation. (2 Corinthians 2:11, 14)

＊ I am more than a conqueror in Christ Jesus. (Romans 8:37)

＊ I can do all things through Jesus Christ who strengthens me. (Philippians 4:13)

＊ God always causes me to triumph in Christ. (2 Corinthians 2:14)

chapter 3:
my flesh!
my flesh!

Years ago, I would jokingly say that someone should really make a list of sins, so there would be a universal awareness of exactly what God considers sin. Then, I learned that when it comes to the works of the flesh, the Bible already has a list in Galatians 5.

Someone might think, "Why would I want to read about a bunch of sins when I'm trying to stop sinning?" The answer is that we must thoroughly understand what sin is and what causes us to sin, so we can get out and stay free from it. For us to win over sin, we need to take the blinders off, turn on the lights, and look sin square in the face with the Word of God.

TURNING ON THE LIGHTS

I was so filled with compassion for people I was counseling that I asked the Lord in prayer one day, "Why do some folks struggle to get victory over sin, even though Jesus set them free;

and why do some people keep going around the same mountain, getting stuck in bad habits and wrong behaviors in their lives?" This is what He spoke to my heart, "Anytime a person repeatedly and consistently has the same issues, whether it be sin, insecurity, sickness, or whatever it is, the person sits in darkness in that area.

Even if you're born again, Spirit filled, and walk in the light of God's Word in other areas, if you struggle with sin on a consistent basis or cannot seem to break free from sin's control in a particular area, it's because in that area you sit in darkness (lack understanding). So, what gets rid of darkness? Light! Once you shine the light of God's Word on your situation, you're on your way out of the prison house because what has bound you will begin to fall off.

The devil does not want God's light to shine. As the god of this world, he blinds the eyes of unbelievers to keep them in darkness, so they cannot be saved (2 Corinthians 4:4). The way to turn on the lights is to receive Jesus as your Lord and Savior. Colossians 1:13 says that at the moment a person receives Jesus, they are translated out of the kingdom of darkness into the kingdom of light.

If you're thinking, "I'm already a Christian and have been translated into the kingdom of light, so how could I ever be in the dark again about anything?" The answer is that if you lack revelation of God's Word in any area of your life, you lack God's light and, therefore, sit in darkness in that area. What will the light of God's Word do? It will show you the truth.

John 8:31-32 (NLT)
31 ...remain faithful to my teachings
32 And you will know the truth, and the truth will set you free."

So, if you don't know the truth, how can it set you free? It can't. That's how the devil keeps people blinded.

The good news is, Jesus knows exactly how to turn the lights on for both believers and unbelievers.

Matthew 4:16 The people which sat in darkness saw great light; and to them which sat in the region and shadow of death light is sprung up.

Habits, addictions, and behavior patterns of sin have a nasty way of making people feel like helpless victims. I've dealt with people in these situations who have told me that it's a constant struggle, and it makes their life not worth living; but life is worth living because Jesus didn't just bring us to the light, He is the light!

Whether the darkness of sin has trapped someone from a young age or just showed up yesterday, it makes no difference. God said He will deliver you out of your troubles. God wants you to have exceedingly, abundantly above all you could ever ask or think in this life (Ephesians 3:20). He wants you to live a life that's full and complete. And even though trouble does come because you live on this Earth, God has made a way for you to be victorious so nothing can bind you, and you don't have to sit in darkness anymore.

> **Isaiah 42:6-7 (NKJV)**
>
> ⁶ I, the Lord, have called You in righteousness, And will hold Your hand; I will keep You and give You as a covenant to the people. As a light to the Gentiles."
>
> ⁷To open blind eyes, To bring out prisoners from the prison, Those who sit in darkness from the prison house.

Verse 7 tells us that the purpose of this light is to open blind eyes and set people free. Let's look at more scriptures about the light.

> **Ephesians 1:18 (AMPC)** By having the eyes of your heart flooded with light, so that you can know and understand the hope to which He has called you, and how rich is His glorious inheritance in the saints (His set-apart ones)."

> **Psalm 119:130 (NKJV)** The entrance of Your words gives light; It gives understanding to the simple.

That's what you're doing right now as you read this book, you're turning the lights on!

If there's a habit or a pattern that you need to change, get real with God, and say, "All right, Lord, you set me free over 2,000 years ago, so I'm done hanging around the prison house.

I no longer want to be in bondage to sin."

Most people want to get out of sin, but they just don't know how, so let's start right now. Pray this out loud, "Lord, take the blinders off my eyes and flood me with light. Shine Your light on me!"

I can't promise you that the devil will never bother you again, but I can promise you that God has all the answers; and if you'll stick with Him, He will deliver you out of whatever trouble you're in because Jesus already paid the price for your freedom on the cross and wants to help you walk in the freedom He has provided for you.

DEFEATING SIN

We've seen that by shining the light of God's Word on sin, the way out comes into focus. So, let's shine a spotlight on the temptations and enticements that come to us all regarding the works (lusts) of the flesh that are listed in Galatians 5. As we look at each one, the light of God's Word will begin to shine even brighter to show us how we can defeat every work of the flesh.

Most people are surprised to see exactly what each work of the flesh includes, and how someone can so easily fall blindly into its trap. In fact, when a person sees a list of the works of the flesh, most think, "They don't have anything to do with me. I don't have a problem with things like witchcraft, emulations, or seditions, so I'm good." Really, are you so sure? Let's keep reading and see because once you know what they are, many of them will hit most of us right where we live. The truth is, each one of us can take an inventory and discover that we've all dealt with one or more of these works of the flesh at one time or another.

Galatians 5:19-21

¹⁹ Now the works of the flesh are manifest, which are these; Adultery, fornication, uncleanness, lasciviousness,

²⁰ Idolatry, witchcraft, hatred, variance, emulations, wrath, strife, seditions, heresies,

> **21 Envyings, murders, drunkenness, revellings, and such like: of the which I tell you before, as I have also told you in time past, that they which do such things shall not inherit the kingdom of God.**

Verse 21 says that those who do such things shall not inherit the kingdom of God. This is not saying they won't go to Heaven. I believe this is talking about those who are doing such things will not being able to walk in the blessings of God while living here on the Earth. I know a lot of saved people who are going to Heaven that are not fully walking in the promises of God. Why? Because it's difficult to walk in God's blessings on a regular basis when someone is walking in the flesh and yielding to the works of the devil.

In the next chapter, we will look at the works of the flesh in detail to see exactly what each one is.

Chapter
Three
Questions

1. What does it take to break free from sin's control in a particular area in your life?

2. Why are Christians still in sin's control in certain areas?

3. Why do some people repeatedly and consistently fall into the same things?

4. How can we overcome the works of the flesh?

5. How do we get rid of the darkness? What can we pray to open our spiritual eyes to the truth?

Chapter
Three
Confessions

✳ **Because I continue in Your Word, I know the truth and it sets me free. (John 8:31-32)**

✳ **The Lord has made me righteous. He is holding my hand and is keeping me. He has opened my eyes and brought me out of prison. (Isaiah 42:6-7)**

✳ **The entrance of God's Word gives me light and understanding. (Psalm 119:130)**

✳ **God's Word floods me with light so I can know the hope He has called me to and how rich His glorious inheritance is to me. (Ephesians 1:18)**

✳ **I no longer sit in darkness because I have seen a great light. God's light has sprung up in me and removes all darkness and any shadow of death for me. (Matthew 4:16)**

chapter 4: works of the flesh

ADULTERY

In the original Greek, there was one word, "porneia" (Strong's G4202), for both adultery and fornication. It was the translators who separated the two for clarity. The Greek word "porneia" means to act the harlot. If you don't already know, it is where we get the word "pornography." Most of us realize that adultery occurs when there is sex or an inappropriate relationship that involves a married person and someone other than their spouse, but as we mentioned earlier, the act of adultery doesn't just happen out of the blue one day without warning. Adultery first begins as a thought that eventually becomes an action. No matter what it may seem like to the person, adultery simmers underneath the surface until it boils over the top. It's attitudes and thoughts that keep popping up until they grow bigger and bigger and are conceived into action.

Adultery starts when the devil brings the thought to your mind that your spouse doesn't appreciate you. Then, he will point out all the ways you are dissatisfied at home and all the things you're missing out on. He will lie and tell you that marriage doesn't need to be a lifetime commitment with one person. Then, the devil will see to it that just the right person comes across your path to provide maximum temptation; and believe me when I say, the devil knows exactly how to bring it.

So, how do we resist this work of the flesh? First, and foremost, we do what 1 Thessalonians 5:22 says, "Abstain from all appearance of evil." That may sound simple, but it's profound; and it's also really good advice. If you want to stay away from adultery, don't put yourself in a compromising situation.

The bottom line is this. If a situation looks wrong, it probably is wrong, even if it doesn't look wrong to the world. If your Master and Lord says it's wrong, then it's wrong. Does it seem wrong in your spirit? If so, that's the Holy Spirit giving you that uneasy feeling in your spirit to warn you; and if you will heed that warning and back away, you can save yourself a world of heartache and trouble. What else does the Word say?

> **Romans 6:13** Neither yield ye your members as instruments of unrighteousness unto sin: but yield yourselves unto God, as those that are alive from the dead, and your members as instruments of righteousness unto God.

What does it look like when you yield your members as instruments of unrighteousness? It's being in the wrong place with the wrong people. It's looking and wondering, and even fantasizing about the wrong people and sharing intimately with the wrong people. That is exactly what yielding your members to unrighteousness looks like. This is before the act of adultery occurs; and if you remain on that course, you'll likely end up in adultery.

God tells us to yield our members to righteousness, which means that everything we do in relationships, even the small things, should be proper and pleasing to Him.

FORNICATION

This work of the flesh is anyone having a sexual relationship outside of marriage. As mentioned before, the root word in the Greek is the same word used for adultery, which is "porneia," and it means to act the harlot.

I know the world sneers and laughs at this one, but the Word plainly teaches that God has reserved sex for marriage only. The Bible says that when a man and a woman unite in intercourse, they become one. It's an important act designed to create a permanent bond that links the man and woman together, spirit, soul, and body.

We can see now why people in our society are so confused about this one. Many freely share themselves in a way that God reserved for marriage, and then wonder how and why they ended up in such a mess.

Fornication doesn't just happen out of the blue any more than adultery does. The sin of fornication is a process; and just like adultery, it begins with thoughts that eventually become actions.

UNCLEANNESS

The word in the Greek is "akatharsia" (Strong's G167), which means impurity (the quality) physically or morally. The Life Application New Testament Commentary defines uncleanness as "moral uncleanness". The reference says, "Perhaps no sexual act has taken place, but the person exhibits a crudeness or insensitivity in sexual matters that offends others." Uncleanness begins with vulgar or unclean thoughts that the devil brings to our mind. Most people don't understand that every thought they think is not their own. The devil is very good at bringing all kinds of lewd and unclean thoughts, imaginings, doubt, fear, panic, and the list goes on. Anything that leads to destruction or temptation, the devil will drag before your mind. Why? The devil is after control of your thought life because he knows that unclean and vulgar thoughts will eventually produce unclean and vulgar actions leading to sin. So, to keep your actions in check, you must control your mind by choosing what you think on.

Maybe you've noticed that the devil likes to bring you images and memories from your life of sin before you were born again. It's like he's walking around with a photo album to embarrass and harass you every chance he gets. Unfortunately, many people don't do anything to get rid of these rogue thoughts when they first begin firing at their mind, and that's what gets them into trouble. Don't ignore bad thoughts, arrest them, and replace them with good thoughts, godly thoughts. Stop wrong thoughts before they become wrong actions. Controlling your thought life is vital if you want to walk with God and overcome sin.

When a thought, picture, or imagination comes to your mind that is lewd or unclean, or just plain unwanted, do what 2 Corinthians 10:4-5 says, "Cast it down." You do that by opening your mouth and boldly saying, "I am a new creature in Christ Jesus, and I refuse that thought in Jesus' name!" You can take harassing thoughts captive every time they come by speaking God's Word, which we'll talk more about in Chapter 13.

LASCIVIOUSNESS

This work of the flesh in the Greek is "aselgeia" (Strong's G766), which means "extreme indulgence, excessive overeating, and wild, out-of-control living." According to Vine's Expository Dictionary, it "Denotes excess, licentiousness, absence of restraint, indecency, wantonness." The Life Application New Testament Commentary says, "The person has no sense of shame or restraint." In other words, the flesh does not like to be disciplined at all, but to let our flesh eat excessively or live a wild, out of control life is not godly living, and it will open us up to sin. I didn't say this. God's Word says this.

It says in 1 Corinthians 9:25, "And every man that striveth for the mastery is temperate in all things…" Being "temperate in all things," which is a fruit of the Spirit, is key to bringing the body in line. How do we do it? We must, on purpose, diligently pursue a lifestyle of moderation, whether it's food or whatever it might be. Bottom line is, we should not be excessive in any area.

We also need to do what Romans 13:14 (NKJV) teaches, "Put on the Lord Jesus Christ, and make no provision for the flesh, to fulfill its lusts." When we clothe ourselves with Jesus by keeping our eyes on Him and the Word, there will be no room for lasciviousness.

IDOLATRY

We are to avoid idolatry. If you're thinking, "I do not have any idols sitting around my house, so let's move on to the next one." Not so fast. The word idolatry comes from the Greek word "eidololatres" (Strong's G1496), and according to The Life Application New Testament Commentary, it refers to a person who "Creates substitutes for God and then treats them as if they were God," so the act of idolatry is not just bowing down to a statue. It could be anything or anyone who comes before our relationship with God, which includes any excessive attachment or extreme reverence for anything or anyone above God.

When we adore something or someone more than God, that's a problem. This definition could single out so many things in our lives such as:

- **Focusing more on career and leaving no time to pray or read the Word.**

- **Preferring to sleep in rather than go to church.**

- **Always playing or watching sports and leaving no time to serve at church.**

- **Following friends in what they say rather than doing what God's Word says.**

This list is endless, but we can all tell when we have elevated something or someone before God.

As a pastor, for over 30 years, I've seen believers put people, careers, houses, sports, hobbies, possessions, and many other things above God. Most people won't admit they do this, but it shows by their actions. Don't elevate anything or anyone above God in your life by giving it more attention and importance.

Thank God, we have the Bible that tells us how we can stay free from idolatry.

> **1 Corinthians 10:14 (AMPC)** Therefore, my dearly beloved, shun (keep clear away from, avoid by flight if need be) any sort of idolatry (of loving or venerating anything more than God).

Do you love and honor anything or anyone more than God? Maybe you've been living in idolatry and didn't even know it. Now that you do know, you can put an end to any idolatry in your life with God's Word and His compassionate nature that will show you what you need to change.

There's nothing wrong with putting your all into a career and working hard to succeed, but if your career comes before your relationship with the Lord, that's trouble. The Lord is not against your success. Quite the opposite. God wants you to succeed as long as it's done in the proper order, which means God must always be first place in your life.

WITCHCRAFT

The interesting thing about this work of the flesh is that most Christians are sure this sin does not apply to them because this is just talking about Ouija boards, or going to a fortune teller, or calling a psychic, right? That is definitely part of it, but it includes more than that. Let's look at what the word witchcraft really means.

The Greek word is "pharmakeia" (Strong's G5331). This is the root word from which we get the word pharmacy. The Vine's Expository Dictionary says, "Witchcraft is the use of medicine, drugs, spells, poisonings and even sorcery." In other words, witchcraft is the flesh attempting to medicate itself to escape from things. In our society, and even in the church, many people medicate their flesh by abusing legal and illegal drugs or alcohol, while others medicate with food.

Why is this work of the flesh so prevalent in the world today? I believe it's because people are hurting, and they don't like their lives, but I'm so glad God has the cure for this.

> **Luke 4:18 (NKJV)** **The Spirit of the LORD is upon Me, Because He has anointed Me To preach the gospel to the poor; He has sent Me to heal the brokenhearted, to proclaim liberty to the captives And recovery of sight to the blind, To set at liberty those who are oppressed.**

Broken hearts are not an uncommon thing because life can deliver some really hard knocks to all of us, but thank God, Jesus came to heal the brokenhearted. If we will let Jesus heal our hurts, we will not need to medicate. The Lord wants us to turn to Him instead of turning to substances. There's just no reason to turn our flesh over to these abuses when we have a Savior able and ready to heal every hurt.

HATRED

This work of the flesh comes from the Greek word "echthra" (Strong's G2189), and it means exactly what it says: to hate. According to Vine's Expository Dictionary, it is used, especially, to describe "Malicious and unjustifiable feelings toward others, whether toward the innocent or by mutual animosity." People who yield to hatred hold grudges and harbor deep resentments with roots of bitterness. How do we get rid of this work of hatred? The

Bible, once again, gives us the answer.

> **1 John 2:5-6 (NKJV)**
>
> **⁵ But whoever keeps His word, truly the love of God is perfected in him. By this we know that we are in Him.**
>
> **⁶ He who says he abides in Him ought himself also to walk just as He walked.**

We must combat hatred with the Word of God. First, we must obey God's Word that tells us to love others. Second, we must let the love of God be perfected, which means mature in us. Third, we must learn to abide in Him and live vitally united with Him, so His ways, His thoughts, and His Word become ours. And finally, we must walk on this Earth as He walked. Jesus never hated anyone, and we should imitate Him and walk in love (a fruit of the Spirit) with others.

As we look at these works of the flesh, we can already see that they have everything to do with you and me, and how they can affect our everyday lives. Maybe there's one you battle with more, or less than others, but we all have opportunities to deal with them continually in life, so let's keep going.

VARIANCE

This work of the flesh comes from the Greek word "eris" (Strong's G2054), which means "Of uncertain affinity; quarrel, i.e. (by implication) wrangling." The Life Application New Testament Commentary says it like this: "Quarreling, competition, rivalry, bitter conflict, the seeds and the natural fruit of hatred." A person involved in variance is a person who is quarrelsome. They are contentious and like to cause controversy. This person feels they always have to be right. I think this starts when a person mistakenly believes that being wrong is a weakness, which is certainly an opinion many in our society promote. Consequently, the person who gives in to variance will exaggerate, make excuses, and even lie to protect their position.

How do we escape this work of the flesh? By reading, studying and absorbing God's Word, so we won't act this way. We'll look at scriptures on this topic more specifically in the chapters to come but let me say that although our old nature may have given way to variance, our new, born-again nature is able to refuse variance and its chaotic ways. We don't have to be right all the time. In fact, it's good to admit when we're wrong.

If we will purpose to renew our mind every day, variance won't be able to lodge itself in our thinking. I guarantee that getting rid of variance in our lives will make a big difference in our marriage, our families, and our friendships.

If you're thinking, "It's so much work to get out of sin; how can I really do it and stay free?" The truth is, you need help; and you have all the help you need in the Holy Spirit. He's your helper, and He's on call 24/7 to help you get out of sin and stay free from it, so let's keep going.

EMULATIONS

This word in the Greek is "zelos" (Strong's G2205). Vine's Expository Dictionary defines it as "To be jealous, to burn with jealousy." This person is not only jealous, but also moves with malice to get what they envy.

This person desiring to be superior to others creates a rivalry, and, subsequently, will often put other people down to get what they want. While this description is true before a person gets born again, it should not be true after.

The way the Spirit of God dealt with me on how to overcome the works of the flesh was to get so full of God that it would push out carnal things. We don't need to focus on what's wrong; we need to focus on God's Word that will fix what's wrong. Let God's Word drive out what's wrong. We all have many opportunities to pass up sin and keep our bodies under control, and it's just a whole lot easier to do when we've got wall-to-wall God on the inside of us.

I'm sure we've all displayed emulations in our life, but our mission is to overcome this work of the flesh, and that's done by walking in the love of God. If you're thinking, "I sure wish I had that God kind of love," the good news is that if you're born again, you do. Romans 5:5 (NKJV) says "...the love of God has been poured out in our hearts by the Holy Spirit who was given to us," so whether you feel like showing love or not has nothing to do with it. If you're born again, God's love is in you because God said he put it in there. What you must realize is that we're not talking about a feeling, we're talking about making a choice. You must choose to walk in love; and when you do, the love of God, will shut down emulations.

After all, God wants us to rejoice with others and not compete with them. Jealousy, agitation, and irritation are ugly, so we need to put God's love to work in our lives instead. We can all walk in love by following the guidelines in 1 Corinthians 13, which we will discuss more when we talk about the fruit of the Spirit.

When we walk in this God kind of love, we will not give in to emulations or any other work of the flesh. When we walk in God's love, we will never fail because His love never fails!

You might be wondering about now, "How much more could possibly be wrong with my flesh?" The truth is, before we were born again, there wasn't anything right with our flesh. Our flesh inherited its makeup from fallen man and this world's system. That's why our flesh has trouble living sin free, but thank God for His Word that helps us live a life pleasing to the Lord. I believe every born-again person wants to please God because it's in our new DNA.

WRATH

This work of the flesh should be no mystery at all. It is the Greek word "thumos" (Strong's G2372), which describes a person in constant anger. The Life Application New Testament Commentary definition says, "Outburst of anger, selfish anger. The plural form conveys the meaning of continual and uncontrolled behavior."

We've all encountered a wrathful person, someone who could blow up at any moment in any situation. And frankly, no one wants to be around such a volatile, walking, talking human explosive who is capable of causing widespread destruction. No one likes to be with a person like this because it's impossible to know what they will say or do next. Wrathful people are explosives ready to blow and disasters waiting to happen. You know the people I'm talking about. That person in your dinner group that if the food comes out wrong or the waiter does something they don't like, they're like a volcano waiting to erupt.

I used to work retail and whenever I saw a group of ladies together and then, one would start to approach the counter while the others hung back, I knew it was on because this volcano, this tornado was coming and ready to erupt. The other ladies hung back because they were embarrassed about how this lady was going to act, but not enough of a friend to tell her that she was walking in the flesh and to quit it. We shouldn't be acting like that, especially if we're born again.

Let's not make excuses for our flesh. Let's not try to justify when we act out in anger saying it's because we think the person has it coming. Nobody has it coming. That's just an excuse we make so we can get angry and tell someone off. It doesn't matter who it is or what has happened, as a Christian, we are not to act like that.

Maybe you've heard someone say, "I have red hair and that's why I have a bad temper," or "I'm Irish, and that's why I get worked up so easily." Bless those who have red hair and are Irish because they have taken a bad rap from our society. We must stop that kind of talk because it's carnal; and now that we are born again, we have the power of the Holy Spirit living on the inside of us to overcome a bad temper, so the color of our hair or ethnic background doesn't really matter because we have been given the authority to rule over our flesh. Don't ever buy into the lie that you cannot help it because God said you can.

So, what should you do if you happen to be one of these hotheads? How can you change your "thumos" to a stable demeanor? How can you go from explosive to smooth and calm? The Bible has the answer. In fact, the chapters that follow will outline many helps for every work of the flesh, but first, let's focus on the picture James gives us of a cool, calm, and collected Christian.

James 1:19-20 (NKJV)

19 So then, my beloved brethren, let every man be swift to hear, slow to speak, slow to wrath.

20 for the wrath of man does not produce the righteousness of God.

These instructions in James, although simple, will really get the job done.

1. **Be a good listener.**
2. **Don't rush to talk.**
3. **Don't get mad quickly.**

BE A GOOD LISTENER.

This makes a lot of sense because then, we can really understand what people are saying to us. In fact, have you ever been in a heated discussion with someone who didn't hear a word you were saying because they were too busy "loading their guns," with what they were going to say next? So, instead of trying to understand what you were saying, they were collecting bullets to fire at you during their next round. We all know how it feels when a person isn't listening because they are getting ready to blast and blow you out of the water. It might sound funny when we think on it, but it wasn't funny at the time, and it's definitely not right. It's fleshly, and as Christians, we cannot allow ourselves to behave that way.

DON'T RUSH TO TALK.

Being slow to speak can be a real challenge for some people. Have you ever noticed that just because you can say something, doesn't mean you should? I've heard people say, "Well, I'm the kind of person who just has to speak my mind," or "I've just got to get this off my chest!" or "I'm going to give that person a piece of my mind!" My response is, "No, please don't."

Let me throw in a little marriage counseling by saying if more people would put their hands over their mouths and use their ears more, we'd have happier couples. Our ears are not just hooks on the side of our head for hanging earrings, they are for hearing and to listen to others. The right words spoken can disarm anger by bringing peace to a situation, but the wrong words spoken can inflame it. Maybe, somewhere in the world, there are a few virtuous married couples who seldom argue; but for the rest of us, we are still learning that speaking the wrong words in anger is like throwing gasoline on a fire, and instant combustion is the result. If we will choose to do things God's way, which includes being slow to speak, we could keep from having so many charred remains.

James 1:22 points out the importance of being a doer of the Word. It says, "But be doers of the word, and not hearers only, deceiving yourselves." So, it's not enough just to go to church and hear the Word. If you want to live sin free, you must put God's Word into practice in your life every day. If you don't, the Bible says you are deceived.

When people are deceived about the works of their flesh, they think they cannot help sinning, but that's a lie! We can control our flesh. We can subdue it. We can crucify it. We can change, and God will help us.

James 1:26 (NKJV) also deals with being slow to speak by saying, "If anyone among you thinks he is religious, and does not bridle his tongue but deceives his own heart, this one's religion is useless." Does this mean we're supposed to buy some expensive contraption to lock down our tongue? Of course not. It's as simple as the instruction I got from my Mamaw who said, "Just keep your mouth shut." She used to say, as I'm sure many of us have heard, "If you don't have anything good to say, just don't say anything at all," so keeping our mouth shut can actually be a godly and spiritual thing to do.

DON'T GET MAD QUICKLY.

We must be slow about getting mad. If you will not immediately jump to anger but will walk in love and listen, you can avoid this anger coming forth.

I'm not telling you to be a doormat, but I am saying to keep quiet when someone wrongs you or cheats you. I'm not telling you that you can't be straightforward and speak up, but I am saying, "no wrath allowed."

STRIFE

The word strife in the original Greek is "eritheia" (Strong's G2052), and it means contention, conflict, discord. Avoiding strife is a huge challenge for many of us; and, honestly, there are very few Christians who don't deal with strife on a regular basis. It's a constant and dangerous enemy, but with God's help, we can avoid it. The real issue with strife is that a person's main concern is getting whatever they want at any cost. People who operate in this work of the flesh will say anything and make whatever sacrifice needed to achieve their desired end while blinded to the injuries they inflict on others along the way.

The Bible warns us in James 3:16, "Where envying and strife is, there is confusion and every evil work." One thing I've learned about God, is that He doesn't exaggerate. So, when God says where strife exists, there is every evil work, He means it. Strife is an open invitation for the devil to come into your life and wreak havoc. This is serious, and we need to especially be on guard for this one. We must crucify any fleshly lusts that try to lead us into strife because the price tag for strife is way too high.

As a pastor, I take extra precaution when it comes to strife in our church. I tell every new member that my wife and I will love them through anything, backsliding, sin, divorce, or whatever it is, but if they cause strife in the church, I will ask them to leave. Since strife opens the door to every evil work, it's no wonder why the power of God is not operating in many of our churches today like it should. Let me encourage you to determine there will be no strife, not for you, not in your family, not in your workplace, not in your church, or anywhere else in your life.

Believe me when I say, the devil will throw opportunities at you to get you in strife because Mark 4:15 says that when you receive God's Word, the enemy immediately comes to steal the Word sown. So, don't be surprised if strife tries to come, even as you're reading this book. It's inevitable because the devil is wanting to steal this Word that you are now putting in your heart, so don't let him.

I remember when Rhonda and I first got married. It seemed like every time we were driving to our church service, we found ourselves arguing. It didn't take us long to figure out that the devil was trying to get us out of unity, so we wouldn't be able to minister in the service. Maybe you have a little one fussing in the back seat on your way to church, or you want to go to a certain restaurant, but your child wants to go to McDonalds, so they throw a fit. It's hard to hold on to your joy when things like that happen, but you must hold on to it anyway.

The devil is working hard to get you into strife, so he can bring every evil work your way. For one thing, strife will bring your faith to a screeching halt, and your profession (confession) of faith won't override strife. You can confess and pray all you want, but if you're in strife, your faith won't work. Confession won't work for a husband who is screaming at his wife morning, noon, and night. You may know someone like that, and everywhere they go, strife goes with them. They cause strife at work, at church, and definitely at home. So, how can this husband, and the rest of us, stay away from strife?

Galatians 5:25 **If we live in the Spirit, let us also walk in the Spirit.**

We'll talk more about walking in the spirit in Chapter 7 but for now, let me say, we must choose to avoid strife at every turn to save ourselves from a whole lot of trouble.

SEDITIONS

The Greek word for seditions is "dichostsis" (Strong's G1370), which means dissension. This person causes division and insurrections. That sounds pretty ominous doesn't it, so this one certainly can't apply to us, right? Just hold on. We're not done. To put it more simply, this person loves drama. They like stirring up commotion and keeping things in an uproar. Does that hit closer to home?

It's interesting to me that the word insurrection is included in this definition because that is talking about someone who revolts against the established authority. Think about that. When you and I rebel against authority, it's considered a form of sedition. Even if you do not personally participate in the rebellious act, to incite others to do so is considered sedition. How do we do that? It could be as simple as talking to others formally or informally to rebel, or posting words that incite others. This makes rebellion sound like it includes a lot more folks, doesn't it? The truth is, we can all fall into this one if we're not careful.

In my years of ministry, I've watched this work of the flesh operate in many people. I've learned that if sedition isn't eradicated the moment it surfaces, it will blow up and really hurt the people involved and those around them. That's why the devil loves it when we yield in this way to our flesh because that's his playground.

A person yielding to sedition also defies those in authority over them, including pastors, leaders, parents, bosses, and so on. Doesn't that sound like a trademark of the devil? The one who defied God's authority and got kicked out of Heaven! Let's make sure we don't take the same route he did by defying God's authority. Let's determine to never let the enemy use us to defy those who have been placed in authority over us. Let our reputation be one of loyalty.

HERESIES

This definition totally surprised me. I thought heresies had to do with wrong doctrines, but it actually has more to do with how we think about ourselves. We get the word heresy from the Greek word "hairesis" (Strong's G139). The Life Application New Testament Commentary defines it as, "The feeling that everyone is wrong except those in your own little group; dissension created among people because of divisions." Thus, describes the tendency to look for allies in conflict. The almost spontaneous generation of cliques demonstrates this characteristic of sinful human desires."

Bottom line is that heresies amount to us thinking we are better than others. It's like high school all over again when we had that clique mentality. And when you think about it, the clique mentality was bad enough in high school, so we sure don't want it in the body of Christ or in the local church.

We know that it's human nature for birds of a feather to flock together; but the flipside of that is, hanging with the wrong people, although their thinking is similar, can get us into trouble because 1 Corinthians 15:33 clearly tells us, "Bad company corrupts good morals." James also tells us to beware of treating people differently.

> **James 2:9 (AMPC)** If you show servile regard (prejudice, favoritism) for people, you commit sin and are rebuked and convicted by the Laws as violators and offenders.

We are to love our neighbors as ourselves according to the law of love. So, that means it would be wrong to judge our neighbors by how they look, dress, talk or any other external factor. The Bible tells us to treat others like we want to be treated, without partiality. When we do, we will avoid heresy.

ENVYINGS

This word in the Greek is "phthonos" (Strong's G5355). The definition in Vine's Expository Dictionary says, "Envy is the feeling of displeasure produced by witnessing or hearing of the advantage or prosperity of others." Envy is when a person so deeply resents another's blessing that they attempt to take it.

An example would be if someone pulled up in a brand new, bright red sports car and you folded your arms thinking, "Well now, look at that. Isn't that special. I'm a tither. Where's mine?" This is an attitude that needs adjusting because the Bible says we are to rejoice with those who rejoice.

If this applies to you, maybe you need to bless the person who has been blessed. Maybe the best way to bring this attitude in check is to give the new car owner some money to help them make their car payment or offer to wash or detail their new car. I say this because sometimes it's necessary to get radical to bring your flesh under. If you're thinking, "I'm not doing that," or "If they have enough money to buy that car, they can pay to get their own car cleaned," that's definitely a case of envy running wild.

This same attitude also happens in the workplace because our attitudes go to work with us. It could be that a co-worker got a promotion that you wanted and thought you deserved. So, instead of being kind, gracious and supportive of this person, you envy them thinking, "They didn't deserve that position. I should have gotten it." Even if you did deserve it, as a Christian, you are not supposed to be looking to the world's system to obtain your blessings or promotions. If you're thinking, "Maybe I'll just tell the boss what I know about that person," that won't do any good. In fact, it could make things worse. When someone acts like this, it tells me that they're trusting in man's ways and not God's ways to receive what they desire.

The Bible tells us more about envy.

> **James 3:14 (AMPC)** **But if you have bitter jealousy (envy) and contention (rivalry, selfish ambition) in your hearts, do not pride yourselves on it and thus be in defiance of and false to the truth.**

You can see that envy and jealousy bring us in defiance to the truth of God's Word, so how do we deal with envy?

> **James 4:2 (AMPC)** **You are jealous and covet [what others have] and your desires go unfulfilled; [so] you become murderers. [To hate is to murder as far as your hearts are concerned]. You burn with envy and anger and are not able to obtain [the gratification, the contentment, and the happiness that you seek], so you fight and war. <u>You do not have, because you do not ask</u>.**

The answer to envy is to get in faith and ask God for whatever it is you desire and then, receive the blessing for yourself. God is not a respecter of persons according to their need or desire; He is a respecter of faith. As you and I learn to ask God in faith, we will never have to be envious or jealous again because we will have our own.

MURDERS

"Murders" was not listed in the original Greek text as a work of the flesh. It was added by the translators. So, for the intent of this book, I will not be including it. The Bible does say, "Whoever hates his brother is a murderer, and you know that no murderer has eternal life abiding in him," (1 John 3:15), and I will leave it at that.

DRUNKENNESS

This work of the flesh comes from the Greek word "methe" (Strong's G3178), and it means "habitual intoxication".

Why even start participating in this one when it could potentially lead to your destruction? My advice is, "Just say no!" Those who choose to habitually drink definitely need the fruit of joy in their life rather than drinking to achieve a false joy that getting drunk can bring.

REVELLINGS

The last work of the flesh is revellings, which comes from the Greek word "komoi" (Strong's G2970). It means "A carousal (as if letting loose)." This is someone who always needs to be entertained, who likes to party. This is someone who needs to continually keep occupied, so they don't have to face what is wrong in their life. This person lacks peace, which is a fruit of the Spirit we will discuss in more detail in Chapter 9.

This reminds me of when I was backslidden and away from God years ago. I couldn't be in a room without some noise. I had to have the television on or the radio blaring; something had to be going on around me all the time.

This is a person who is always moving; they cannot sit still because they haven't brought this work of the flesh under control. Usually, these folks avoid the quiet because they don't want to deal with any personal issue or hurt. If someone can't sit still, there's something in their soul that needs healing, and the best way to deal with it is to let Jesus minister to their soul.

Too often, people who cannot stand to be alone, or sit quietly, have an ache on the inside that cannot be fixed by humanity, a doctor, or anything else. These people keep busy so they won't have to deal with themselves, but Luke 4 says that Jesus came to heal the brokenhearted, so I'm telling you that Jesus can heal you if you have this restlessness on the inside of you.

Jesus healed me. In 1986, when I was working as an accountant in Indianapolis, my sister, Robin, dragged me to church. I came back to the Lord and got filled with the Holy Spirit. That's when my life suddenly and dramatically changed. It was only a short time after that, I would catch myself reading my Bible in a room with no noise at all. Before that time, there was no way I would have sat still or been quiet long enough to do that. I had to have something going on all the time because I couldn't stand the silence until God touched my life with overwhelming peace; and, for me, there's no price tag that can measure its value.

Maybe you know someone like this, who is always moving, always on the go, always craving noise. That person may need something on the inside fixed, and I'm telling you that Jesus is the only One who can do the fixing.

So, attention you workaholics! Let God bless and prosper you instead of spending 120 hours a week at your job or business. It's one thing to be busy, but to drive yourself to extremes tells me there's something in you that God needs to fix.

God doesn't want that for any of His children. God doesn't want your flesh to dominate you or drive you to sin, or even drive you overboard in doing good. God doesn't want your flesh driving you at all, so refuse to give in to your flesh. Refuse to allow anything to come between you and God, which also means between you and your church, your Bible reading, your prayer life, or your serving.

We must allow the Holy Spirit to dominate our lives, which means giving the spiritual arena first place in our lives. When we do, our flesh will be put under, and we will walk in life and peace. The reason many people cannot sit still and enjoy peace and fellowship with God is because of a soulish problem that needs to be put under, but by concentrating on the things of the spirit, it will put our souls at peace.

We've turned the lights on and broken down each work of the flesh. So, now that we know what each one is, we can clearly see that they do, indeed, pertain to us, and that we all deal with them on a regular basis.

OVERVIEW OF THE WORKS OF THE FLESH:

ADULTERY
Sex with someone not your spouse
"porneia" (G4202)

FORNICATION
Sex outside of marriage
"porneia" (G4202)

UNCLEANNESS
Immoral, impure, vulgar/lewd actions
"akatharsia" (G166)

LASCIVIOUSNESS
Extreme indulgence; excessive overeating and wild,
out of control living
"aselgeia" (G766)

IDOLATRY
To elevate and give more attention to anyone or
anything above God
"eidololatres" (G1496)

WITCHCRAFT
Sorcery, magic, medicating to numb oneself in
order to escape
"pharmakeia" (G5331)

HATRED
Malicious, intense feelings of hate toward someone
"ecthra" (G2189)

VARIANCE
Quarrelsome, controversial, always has to be right
"eris" (G2054)

EMULATIONS
Burn with jealousy; needing to feel superior to
others
"zelos" (G2205)

WRATH
Constant anger; enraged; explosive
"thumos" (G2372)

STRIFE	*Heated and bitter disagreement, causes conflict to get what they want* *"eritheia" (G2052)*
SEDITIONS	*Division, disagreement, insurrections; defies authority; loves drama* *"dichostsis" (G1370)*
HERESIES	*Cliques, thinking they know better than others in what should be* *"hairesis" (G139)*
ENVYINGS	*Deeply resenting what someone has and wanting it* *"phthonos" (G5355)*
DRUNKENNESS	*Habitual intoxication; overconsumption* *"methe" (G3178)*
REVELLINGS	*Always needing noise or something going on; can't sit still* *"komoi" (G2970)*

This list will help you take a personal inventory and identify those works of the flesh you need to deal with.

For anyone who says, "I've tried and tried to get certain behaviors under control, but it hasn't worked," I would say it's probably because you are trying to do it on your own. The good news is, you have God and His Word to help you, so believe that He is helping you and keep reading because in the next chapter, we will talk about God's escape theology for getting you out of any sin that you are in.

Chapter
Four
Questions

1. By giving our past failures and shortcomings to God we allow Him to heal our broken hearts so we can be completely free. What are some things that you have been holding onto that you would like to give to God today so He can be the healer of your broken heart?

2. What does it mean to yield our body to unrighteousness? What does it mean to yield our body to righteousness?

3. As you were reading this chapter and the Holy Spirit was ministering, was there a work of the flesh He challenged you on? Which ones and why?

4. Some of these works of the flesh are actually norms in the world, what can you do in order to make sure that you don't fall back into the worlds habits but continue to live by the Spirit?

5. How do we put on, clothe ourselves with the Lord Jesus Christ?

Chapter
Four
Confessions

✴   I will abstain from all appearances of evil.
(1 Thessalonians 5:22)

✴   I will not yield my body to wrongdoing but will yield
my body to righteousness for the glory of God.
(Romans 6:13)

✴   I will cast down imaginations and every high thing that
exalts itself against the Word of God.
(2 Corinthians 10:5)

✴   I have the love of God because it has been poured
out in my heart by the Holy Spirit. (Romans 5:5)

✴   I will be swift to hear, slow to speak and slow to get
angry because I am a doer of God's Word.
(James 1:19, 22)

chapter 5: escape theology

People often ask if it's really possible to escape temptation and sin, and I enjoy telling them that it's absolutely possible, no doubt about it. In fact, let me share an entire escape theology that's found in the Bible. There's no question in my mind that God wants us to escape temptation every time it comes and that's why He gives us an escape route.

The Bible has a lot to say about escaping temptation, so let's begin with 1 Corinthians 10:13, a scripture that many use and abuse or at the very least, misquote. Maybe you've even heard someone say, "God will never give you more than you can bear," but that's only part of the scripture. It's important that we quote the entire scripture, so we can really understand what the Lord is telling us.

> **1 Corinthians 10:13 (NKJV)** No temptation has overtaken you except such as is common to man; but God is faithful, who will not allow you to be tempted beyond what you are able, but with the temptation will also make the way of escape, that you may be able to bear it.

Those who say, "God will never give you more than you can bear," have taken out of context the phrase, "God...will not allow you to be tempted beyond what you are able." Because they haven't thoroughly studied this verse, they focus on this portion of scripture and have come to the wrong conclusion. They mistakenly believe that God is the One handing out the suffering and implying He will only give a person as much suffering as they can bear.

Some people even take this scripture to mean that toward the end of a temptation or trial, God will eventually rescue them after they've taken all they can handle. Would God do that? Is that what the Bible says? Is that what you and I are to take away from this scripture? No. Let's read this verse in the Amplified Classic to better understand its meaning.

> **1 Corinthians 10:13 (AMPC)** For no temptation (no trial regarded as enticing to sin), [no matter how it comes or where it leads] has overtaken you and laid hold on you that is not common to man [that is, no temptation or trial has come to you that is beyond human resistance and that is not adjusted and adapted and belonging to human experience, and such as man can bear]. But God is faithful [to His Word and to His compassionate nature], and He [can be trusted] not to let you be tempted and tried and assayed beyond your ability and strength of resistance and power to endure, but with the temptation He will [always] also provide the way out (the means of escape to a landing place), that you may be capable and strong and powerful to bear up under it patiently.

This scripture lays out exactly how we can live a sin-free life. First, it says that temptation is common to man, which means it comes to all of us. None of us will ever arrive at a place where we are no longer tempted. If you're looking for that place, you'll have to wait until you get to Heaven because as long as you live in a body, and there's a devil on the Earth, you will face temptation.

Next, this scripture makes it clear that temptation is not beyond human resistance. That means it doesn't matter what temptation it is or how and when it comes, you can resist it. Let me say that again. You can resist it!

I've had people come to me, with tears in their eyes, and say, "I cannot get out of this sin. It's too hard. God must have made me this way. This must be my cross to bear." No. That's not true, and it's not Bible. No sin has ever been given to you by God as your "cross to bear" because sin always leads to death, and God is never the author of death. This is a major lie that the devil uses to convince people that they can't stop or resist sin. Even religion will tell people, "You just need to learn to live with it;" but God said you can resist and walk free from it, so in no way are we supposed to put up with any sin in our life. That's why God sent Jesus to pay for the sins of all, so that whoever would believe in Him would be free.

The last insight I want to point out in this verse is that God is faithful. God never lies; He can be fully trusted with your life and your deliverance from sin. But for you to receive anything from God, it begins with you believing God's Word, and that He keeps His Word. You must put your trust in Him so He can bring His Word to pass in your life. In order to live a life free from sin, fear, and failure, you must recognize that God is not your problem, He is your only answer, and you can count on Him because He will never disappoint you.

Notice again what the last phrase of 1 Corinthians 10:13 (AMPC) says, "…God is faithful [to His word and to His compassionate nature], and He [can be trusted] not to let you be tempted and tried and assayed beyond your ability and strength of resistance and power to endure…" God is promising His faithfulness to you, and you have His Word on it. Then, the very next phrase in this verse contains the Bible's great escape clause…

> **1 Corinthians 10:13 (AMPC)** …with the temptation He will [always] also provide the way out (the means of escape to a landing place), that you may be capable and strong and powerful to bear up under it patiently.

Think about that for a minute. God's Word says that you have the ability, the strength of resistance, and the power to endure any temptation the devil brings until you come out on top. This scripture is talking to you. So, when you're tempted by something, no matter what it is, the Bible says you can bear it, you can endure it, and you can get free from it. God, Himself, said you can deal with it, overcome it, and rise above it. You can win every time!

It's unfortunate that many people automatically assume that 1 Corinthians 10:13 is saying we're just stuck with that temptation and will have to live with it and endure it forever, carrying it around like a badge. Again, no way!

Does this scripture say to just bear the temptation? No. It says, "That you may be capable and strong and powerful to bear up under it patiently on your way out of it." Notice, the fruit of patience is required because you may find yourself dealing with certain temptations more than once. But no matter how many times a temptation tries to mess with you, if you will keep applying God's Word, and walk in the spirit, you will be able to resist it and get the victory over it.

Patience has turned into somewhat of a bad word in our society. It seems most folks don't want to be patient anymore. If it's not fast, like drive-thru, they don't want anything to do with it, but let's be honest. Sometimes we must keep after things for a while in order to achieve the victory. What choice do we have? It all comes down to this. We either learn to resist the temptation to sin by walking in the spirit, or we yield to the temptation and fall into sin where, ultimately, we will take home a paycheck of death.

Resistance is never futile. It will always work in the kingdom of God, so plan to escape every temptation that comes your way by patiently using God's Word as your escape route. When you do, you will always land in a safe place. Keep after the temptation by resisting it no matter what it is or how many times it comes. Determine that sin, and, consequently, the death that sin brings is not an option for you because you're not going to give in to it.

You can do it!

- **Resist temptation.**
- **Escape from it.**
- **Go and sin no more.**
- **Live a sin free life!**

THE GREAT ESCAPE

The Bible provides a clear road map of how to escape the temptation to sin. In fact, Hebrews 2:3 (NKJV) tells us, "How shall we escape if we neglect so great a salvation…". The truth is, we won't escape if we neglect our salvation, but we will escape if we attend to our salvation, so let's take a closer look at how to attend to our salvation.

The word "salvation" means being born again, but it also means so much more than that. In fact, salvation in the Greek (Strong's G4991), means "deliverance, safety, preservation, healing, and soundness". In other words, salvation includes all the blessings that God bestowed on mankind through Jesus' redemption for us on the cross. This makes it clear that we cannot neglect our salvation and still be empowered to resist sin because salvation is what established our relationship and blood covenant with God. To resist sin, we must first and foremost receive Jesus Christ as our Lord and Savior. Receiving Jesus is the most important decision you will ever make, and it's just the beginning. It's the first step through the door to a whole new life; and your new Christian walk is just that, a walk with many more steps to take in God.

So, before we continue, let me give you another invitation. If you're not born again, I encourage you to turn to Page 263 and give your life to Jesus. It is the first step in turning your back on sin and escaping the corruption that sin brings.

If you are already born again, let me challenge you to dig in even further to understand the full extent of the freedom that's already been provided to you.

DIVINE NATURE

As we attend to our salvation, we can fully partake of the divine nature of God Himself and receive His promises that have the power to free us from sin and death.

2 Peter 1:3-4 (NKJV)

³ As His divine power has given to us all things that pertain to life and godliness, through the knowledge of Him who called us by glory and virtue,

> ⁴ **by which have been given to us exceedingly great and precious promises, that through these you may be partakers of the divine nature, having escaped the corruption that is in the world through lust.**

By partaking of His divine nature, we can receive these exceedingly great and precious promises that will enable us to escape the corruption that is in the world.

So, what does it mean to partake? Well, on occasion, I like to partake of coconut cream pie. I see it, and I seize it. I put it in my mouth, and I happily partake (eat it). If I partake of coconut cream pie too often, it will begin to show on me. It's not hard to tell what people partake of on a regular basis because it always shows. That's why God says if we partake of His Word regularly, His divine nature will show on us. Can it get any better than that? Peter is saying that if we delve into God's Word, we will get so full of God Himself that His divine nature will show on us and be obvious and evident for all to see.

Let's think about that. If you need more of His divine nature to show up on the outside of you, then you need to spend more time partaking of God's Word and His Spirit on the inside. So, what will this new nature do when it shows up on you? The answer is found in the last part of 2 Peter 1:4, which basically says that it will enable and empower you to escape the corruption that tries to come through the lusts of the flesh.

What does the lusts of our flesh produce? Sin. What does sin produce? Death. And what does partaking of His divine nature produce? Life, which means we can live free from sin. Glory to God! God has given every born-again believer personal access to His divine nature; and by regularly partaking of His nature and precious promises, we can literally escape the corruption of sin. It's knowing who we are in Christ and understanding that with this new, divine nature on the inside of us, we can resist every temptation.

It's so important that every Christian understand what's been given to them and who they are in Jesus so they can partake of this amazing, supernatural equipment that is part of their new nature. The more we learn about our new nature and walk in it, the more enabled we will be to rule and reign over our flesh.

BRAND NEW YOU

Biblically speaking, there are only two races (families) on the Earth. You're either in God's family or in the devil's family. Those are your only choices; and once you choose, your father has been decided for you. If you're born again, God is your Father, and you have God's nature, His Spirit, on the inside of you. If you are not born again and have not accepted Jesus as your Lord and Savior, you have the nature, or spirit, of this fallen world, and your father is the father of lies, the devil. In other words, until we are born again and become a new creation, alive unto God, we are by nature sinners. Our nature, before receiving Jesus Christ, craved sin; it yielded freely to the lusts of our flesh without thought or hesitation, and this nature was in full agreement with our flesh.

As we discussed earlier, every human being is a three-part creation.

- **You are a spirit, and it's that part of you that will never die. Your spirit is the real you and will spend eternity either in Heaven or Hell.**

- **The second part of you is your soul realm, which is your mind, your will, and your emotions. This realm is where decisions are made, and emotions are felt.**

- **The third part of you is your body, your flesh, the house you live in. Someday, when you die, your body will return to dust.**

For those who are born again, your spirit was reborn, and you received a new nature.

> **2 Corinthians 5:17 (NKJV)** Therefore, if anyone is in Christ, he is a new creation; old things have passed away; behold, all things have become new.

The real you, your spirit, is now a new creation, someone who has never existed before, created with the nature of God. It is like you were put back to the way God had originally designed you to be before man fell.

Before we were born again, our conduct was the result of our fallen nature and our flesh cooperating with it, so we really had no choice but to live in sin. This makes it a lot easier to understand why sinners are so busy sinning. It is their legacy, their heritage, their very nature because that's what sinners do, they sin.

PIGS DO WHAT PIGS DO

This reminds me of a simple, yet profound, lesson I learned growing up on our farm, and that is, you can put a dress on a pig, but a pig is still just a pig. Turn that pig loose, dress and all, and it will still wallow in the mud if it can find any. Why? That's what pigs do. It's their nature.

In the same way, the nature of someone not born again is to sin. We can dress them in religion, laws, rules, and regulations, and anything else we can think of, but sooner or later, they are going to sin. Why? Because it's their nature and no matter what name you put on them, until they're born again, their nature is that of a sinner.

> **Ephesians 2:3** **Among whom also we all had our conversation in times past in the lusts of our flesh, fulfilling the desires of the flesh and of the mind; and were by nature the children of wrath, even as others.**

Based on this scripture, we could say it this way, "Our sinful behavior was a manifestation of our nature. Because we were not born of God, we were controlled by our sinful nature and in line for God's wrath."

Let's look at another scripture.

> **1 Peter 2:11 (AMPC)** **Beloved, I implore you as aliens and strangers and exiles [in this world] to abstain from the sensual urges (the evil desires, the passions of the flesh, your lower nature) that wage war against the soul.**

You can see the sensual urges come from what this verse calls our lower nature, which has not been born of the Spirit of God. The only way to get rid of this lower, sensual nature is to trade it in for a new nature by getting born again.

It's futile to try to clean up the old nature before you come to God. That's like trying to put a dress on a pig, and we already know that doesn't work, and it will never work. Instead, we must come to God and allow Him to remove our old nature and give us a new one. Let's look at 2 Corinthians 5:17 in the Modern English Translation.

> **2 Corinthians 5:17 (Modern English Translation)** Therefore, if a man is in Christ he becomes a new person altogether – the past is finished and gone, everything has become fresh and new.

This says, for those who are in Christ, the old person is gone, done away with forever. The old person, whose nature was to sin, has died, so you need to tell it, "Goodbye; so long, and don't let the door hit you on the way out!" You are now a new creation, a brand-new you. It is an ultimate new beginning. You have now been made righteous (2 Corinthians 5:21) with a new nature created in God's likeness and image, which means you have the power within you to live free from sin.

It's plain to see from God's Word that only born-again people can consistently live a lifestyle free from sin. The only way to really be able to say "No," to sin continually is to receive this new reborn nature and then, learn how it works so you can walk in it.

Sadly, there are a lot of born-again people who still struggle with sin. They don't want to sin, but they still do. They try to overcome sin, but they fail. They wring their hands and shed buckets of tears, but they still give in to sin. They try to fight the devil, but they always come up short. They hurt loved ones, and damage relationships; they just can't seem to help it. They dislike themselves and feel powerless; but God has the solution for this. God says in His Word that you can break free, stay free, and live free from sin.

God is all about your freedom, and it all begins by understanding who you are in Christ Jesus. When you were born again, something very radical happened to you. There was a funeral and a resurrection at the same time. The old you died and a new you was resurrected, so don't try to go back and live like you did before.

Unfortunately, that's exactly what a lot of born-again Christians do because they lack understanding. They now have this new nature, but they choose to continue to live like the devil, as if they never received a new nature at all. Some even end up burying the new man because they've never learned about walking in their new nature. They will say, "I'm just a sinner saved by grace," which sounds very religious and humble, but that's not who they are anymore. It's a phrase inspired by the devil through the traditions of men to keep Christians bound to their old nature. Now that they are born again, they are no longer a sinner because they've been made new by His amazing grace, which means they can get out of sin, out of the mud. Don't stay in that place of thinking you're still a sinner, or a reformed sinner, or any kind of sinner. Get away from that wrong thinking. The Spirit of God has changed you into a saint, a born-again child of God, who is no longer given to sin, so walk in the new you and let it dominate your life!

NEW CLOTHES

It's time for us to walk and talk differently like the new creations we are. We all know it's easy to do that when we're in church. There, we can say "Amen" with a smile and a nod, but how do we walk the walk and talk the talk 24/7? We have to put on our new clothes by walking in our new nature.

Your new nature is the doorway to your freedom; but even then, you must still choose to walk in the freedom that your new nature provides. Ephesians tells us to put on this new nature.

> **Ephesians 4:22-24 (NKJV)**
>
> **22 That you put off, concerning your former conduct, the old man which grows corrupt according to the deceitful lusts,**
>
> **23 and be renewed in the spirit of your mind,**
>
> **24 and that you put on the new man which was created according to God, in true righteousness and holiness.**

We must put on our new nature just like a person puts on a sweater or a jacket. We are to clothe ourselves with the Lord Jesus by putting on His ways, His words, His actions, and His manner of living. When we are clothed with His presence, live by His Word, and walk in the spirit, we will have no room for any wrong desires and the lusts of our flesh will not stand a chance.

Let's look at how The Amplified Classic clarifies these verses even more.

Ephesians 4:22-24 (AMPC)

22 Strip yourselves of your former nature [put off and discard your old unrenewed self] which characterized your previous manner of life and becomes corrupt through lusts and desires that spring from delusion;

23 And be constantly renewed in the spirit of your mind [having a fresh mental and spiritual attitude],

24 And put on the new nature (the regenerate self) created in God's image, [Godlike] in true righteousness and holiness.

The Apostle Paul, inspired by the Holy Spirit, instructed believers to take off something, which is the old you. It tells you to get rid of the old you that existed before and tolerated deceitful lusts before you were born again. Paul said you are to strip off your former nature. I like these descriptive words in the Amplified Classic because it gives me a mental picture of tossing something away, getting rid of it, discarding it.

Verse 24 says you are to get dressed in your new clothes, in your new nature; that is, in God's image. Did you notice that you are the one who must dress yourself in your new clothes? In other words, they won't just drop on you automatically.

So, how do you put on your new nature? How would you put on a coat? You do it on purpose. You don't accidentally put on your coat; you have to choose to put it on, so it will cover and protect you from the weather. Likewise, you must put on your new nature which is your covering and protection from sin.

Colossians encourages us with these words.

Colossians 3:9-10 (AMPC)

9 Do not lie to one another, for you have stripped off the old (unregenerate) self with its evil practices,

10 And have clothed yourselves with the new [spiritual self], which is [ever in the process of being] renewed and remolded into [fuller and more perfect knowledge upon] knowledge after the image (the likeness) of Him Who created it.

What do we do with this formerly, sinful, lustful, deceptive, delusional self? We take it off and get rid of it, like an old tire! You don't need to repair it because your spirit has been made new. There is no need for us to try and cover the old person with the new. Instead, we should take off the old and throw it away. Don't save it. Get rid of it. Trash it. Burn it. Then, right after you take off those filthy rags, put on your new robe of righteousness that's guaranteed to be a perfect fit. Wearing your new clothes in the spirit will position you to speak up and say, "Sin? No! I don't want to, and I don't have to."

You don't even have to go shopping for these new clothes. No browsing store aisles and waiting in line to purchase them. These clothes of righteousness were delivered to you by the Holy Spirit when you were born again.

Notice the instructions we are given.

> **Romans 13:14 (AMPC)** But clothe yourself with the Lord Jesus Christ (the Messiah), and make no provision for [indulging] the flesh [put a stop to thinking about the evil cravings of your physical nature] to [gratify its] desires (lusts).

I personally like new clothes, and I like to buy them; and apparently God likes new clothes too because He tells us in His Word to put on the new. Notice, He never tells us to put the new over the old.

Remember, your spirit, your inner man of the heart, was born again, but your flesh did not get born again, so those lustful cravings of the flesh are still there. The same sort of things that tried to get hold of you and tempt you before you were saved still want to grab hold of you now. That's why you must cooperate with the new nature you received when you became a child of God. You must now partake of this divine nature that is on the inside of you by stripping off sin and putting on righteousness. Then, and only then, will you be able to go and sin no more.

We've looked at Ephesians 2:3, which explained man's sinful nature of wanting to sin and follow after lusts, but let's pinpoint the source of that nature. Where did it come from? As we discussed, when Adam and Eve sinned and committed high treason (Genesis 2-3), they fell from grace and could no longer partake of God's nature. Their sin separated them from God, so they could no longer fellowship with Him. But I'm so glad God had a plan to restore mankind back to Himself. God sent Jesus to pay the price for man's sin, and through His death, burial, and resurrection, we can now be restored to God. Jesus has provided salvation for all; His work is finished. It's now up to us to choose to receive the forgiveness He purchased for us. It's not automatic, but it's available to all.

Someone might say, "If Adam and Eve sinned with God's divine nature inside them, what hope do I have? Do you really think I can succeed where they failed?" You bet I do. For one thing, you have a choice just like they did. And even though Adam and Eve made the wrong choice, that doesn't mean you have to crash and burn too.

God has given you His personal manual, the Bible, to help you succeed in this life. If you are born again, you have precious promises to help you partake of this new divine nature and put on your new clothes. You also have the Spirit of God leading and guiding you to victory.

So, take out the trash and dispose of the garbage in your life; then, put on your supernatural self created in God's image. Dump the trash and bring in the treasure. How often must you do this? Every day the trash of this world tries to push out your treasure, so every day you must decide what stays and what goes. You must refuse to let the old person dominate you. You must use God's Word to put on the new person every chance you get because it's this new person who will help you live free from sin.

Colossians 3 tells us exactly how the new person will look.

Colossians 3:10, 12-14 (NKJV)

10 ...Put on the new man who is renewed in knowledge according to the image of Him who created him,

12 Therefore, as the elect of God, holy and beloved, put on tender mercies, kindness, humility, meekness, longsuffering;

13 bearing with one another, and forgiving one another, if anyone has a complaint against another; even as Christ forgave you, so you also must do.

14 But above all these things put on love, which is the bond of perfection.

We have to take off the old to put on the new; never try to put the new over the old. If you were to put new clothes on over your stinky gym or greasy work clothes, would you be clothed properly? No; the filth and grime of the old clothes would contaminate the new clean clothes, and you wouldn't want to put up with the stink that would come through. In the same way, once you have become a new creation, you are ready to discard the old and put on the new man.

Again, how do you put these spiritual clothes on? The key words in Colossians 3:10 are "knowledge" and "image." Where do we find God's knowledge? In the Word of God. Where do we get the correct image of ourselves? In the mirror. What is the mirror? James 1:23 compares the Word of God to a mirror, a supernatural mirror that reflects who you are in Christ. Take a good, long look in the mirror of God's Word and see if the correct reflection is staring back at you.

We are given a new nature when we are born again and then, the Word of God will show us exactly what we should look like. We've been made righteous and holy, so it's not what we're trying to become but understanding who we really are; and in this perfect law of liberty, in this mirror, we will not see a sinner because we have been changed and recreated in the image of God. We put on this new nature, like we would a shirt or a coat. Only in the realm of the Spirit can we dress ourselves by what we believe in our heart and say with our mouth.

The Bible is clear. You and I have been given a new nature, God's very own nature, and He is now asking us to dress accordingly. We're supposed to clothe ourselves in this new nature because God wants us to know that we are more than simply forgiven. God wants us walking, talking, and dressing like the children of God we are.

> **Colossians 3:9-10 (MSG)**
>
> [9] **...You're done with that old life. It's like a filthy set of ill-fitting clothes you've stripped off and put in the fire.**
>
> [10] **Now you're dress in a new wardrobe. Every item of your new way of life is custom-made by the Creator, with his label on it. All the old fashions are now obsolete.**

Walk in your new clothes!

DEAD MEN WALKING

After we've changed clothes, Colossians 3 tells us where to direct our attention.

> ## Colossians 3:1-3 (NKJV)
>
> **¹If then you were raised with Christ, seek those things which are above, where Christ is, sitting at the right hand of God.**
>
> **² Set your mind on things above, not on things on the earth.**
>
> **³ For you died, and your life is hidden with Christ in God.**

We are to seek those things which are above and set our affections on Him, so that we are pleasing to Him in all our ways. We are to run every life decision by the Word of God and through Him in prayer instead of making all the decisions ourselves and then asking God to bless it. Our heart and its desires must be turned toward God and not the things of this Earth. The things of this Earth are no longer our priority because God is now first place in our lives.

This is the big one. We must consider ourselves dead to our old nature because dead men don't sin. Someone might say, "Wait! Do you mean dead, like really dead?" No. I mean that the old you is dead, and the new and improved you now lives a life hidden with Christ in God. Your old dreams and desires are dead, and you've now picked up God's dreams and desires for your life, which are bigger and better in every way than anything you could dream up for yourself.

See the old you as being dead. Put up a tombstone and take flowers to the gravesite if you have to, but then, don't go back and don't look back. There's nothing to go back to anyway. The old man is dead and the divine, full-of-God new nature in you is ready to live free from sin. The next move is up to you. You're the boss of your flesh.

Chapter
Five
Questions

1. Take a moment to consider your new identity in Christ. List traits from your new identity in Christ that would help you walk in your freedom.

2. You are responsible for clothing yourself in your new nature, what are some ways you can start clothing yourself in this new nature?

3. What in your life could be distracting you from your walk with Christ? Do you keep your affections on things above?

4. Why is patience important in saying no to temptation?

5. How much do you partake daily in the Word? How can you improve or increase your intake of the Word?

Chapter
Five
Confessions

✻   **No matter what temptation comes, God is faithful and has made a way of escape for me.** (1 Corinthians 10:13)

✻   **God has given me everything that pertains to life and godliness, and it is mine as I grow in the knowledge of Him.** (2 Peter 1:3)

✻   **God has given me exceedingly great and precious promises, and I receive them as I walk in my new, divine nature.**
(2 Peter 1:4)

✻   **Because I am born again, I am a new creation in Christ Jesus and old things have passed away.**
(2 Corinthians 5:17)

✻   **I will clothe myself with the Lord Jesus Christ and make no provision for the lusts of my flesh.**
(Romans 13:14)

chapter 6: you're the boss

Sin is a three-part equation that includes the devil, the temptation, and you. Although the devil is the one who lines up tempting scenarios for you along the way, it's still up to you to choose. You get to call the shots but to make the right choices, you must become the boss of your flesh, or it will have its own way.

When temptation comes, you can't just say, "The devil made me do it!" like Flip Wilson used to say. He was a comic in the 1970's who would jokingly blame the devil whenever he got in trouble or did something wrong. It sounds funny, but that's exactly what people still try to say today. The truth is the devil isn't strong enough to make you do anything. Although the devil is happy to suggest various sins to you because he wants to get you out of the will of God, the choice is still yours. The enemy will do his best to keep his part of John 10:10, which is to steal, kill, and destroy because he wants to destroy your life. One of his favorite weapons he uses to talk Christians into giving into the temptation and falling into sin is deception, but you can choose not to participate.

The devil is not playing. If he can destroy your family, he will. If he can destroy your body, he will. The devil attacks us because that's just who he is, but we don't have to give him any open doors of access into our lives. We need to keep all doors closed to him.

Even though the devil will do his best to ruin your life, he cannot pull it off without your help. Jesus defeated the devil, so his only weapon is to tempt and persuade you to sin through lies and deception. Sin is a choice, so just don't choose it.

Let's face it. Our flesh craves things that can cause us a heap of trouble if we give in to them. The flesh wants to get even with people and have its revenge. The flesh wants to gossip, cheat, overeat, lie, and be lazy. The flesh wants to get away with a whole lot of stuff. That's why we need to understand how our flesh operates, so we can refuse to let it run the show. We must crucify our flesh and show it who's boss, and God will help us do that. He is available, 24/7, and is waiting for us to come to Him for help.

CRAVINGS OF THE FLESH

As long as you live in a body on this Earth, it will crave things that can get you in trouble. In fact, through the years, I've watched new Christians leave themselves wide open for trouble in this area because they just didn't understand this fact.

As a pastor, I've had new believers say to me, "I thought I was saved. I got filled with the Holy Ghost, and yet, I still want to sin. I just don't understand why I want to do the same things I used to do before I was born again." And so many times, they really believe they're trapped by these lusts and desires, but that's a lie! Remember what Jesus told the woman caught in adultery? He said "I don't condemn you. Now, go and sin no more."

Jesus is saying the same thing to us today, "I don't condemn you for your past failures and mistakes, but I want you to learn how to live in victory, so you won't sin anymore." There isn't anyone who can lift up their hands and say, "I've made it through my whole Christian life without sinning?" That's why every Christian needs 1 John 1:9.

1 John 1:9 **If we confess our sins, he is faithful and just to forgive us our sins, and to cleanse us from all unrighteousness.**

This scripture wouldn't be necessary if Christians didn't sin, but it is necessary because we all can mess up. We have all been tempted and have fallen into sin; but thank God, we have an advocate with the Father who paid the price for our sins by shedding His blood to wash them away.

HOW YOUR BODY OPERATES

Let's look at Ephesians 2:3 again, which tells us how to control the flesh. This letter is one of the epistles, which means it was written to the church at Ephesus as well as to Christians today.

> **Ephesians 2:3 (AMPC)** **Among these we as well as you once lived and conducted ourselves in the passions of our flesh [our behavior governed by our corrupt and sensual nature], obeying the impulses of the flesh and the thoughts of the mind [our cravings dictated by our senses and our dark imaginings]. We were then by nature children of [God's] wrath and heirs of [His] indignation, like the rest of mankind.**

This scripture shows us once again that no Christian is beyond sin or temptation. If you don't think your flesh has impulses, you're just kidding yourself, and that could be the reason you are having trouble conquering sin in your life. To overcome temptation and sin, you cannot live in denial. Temptation and sin must be faced head on.

The devil will spend all day long trying to get you to give in to these sinful impulses. Why? So, he can get you into sin. Why? Because the devil wants you to feel condemned. Why? So, you will throw up your hands in disgust and give up. This is the devil's plan, and he is a master at getting it done; but we no longer have to fall prey to this. In 1 Peter 4:2 (AMPC) it says, "...no longer spend the rest of his natural life living by [his] human appetites and desires, but [he lives] for what God wills." That's good news! God says we no longer have to spend the rest of our life giving in to our fleshly desires. The more we learn about being free from human appetites and desires, the freer we will become and the sweeter our walk with God will be.

So many people get frustrated because they seem to commit the same sins over and over again, until they finally give up and say, "I cannot serve God." That's when the devil wins, and the person loses. We can't give up. If the Lord were standing right in front of you, and He's actually closer than that because He lives in every born-again believer, He would say, "Neither do I condemn you. Go and sin no more." It's the "go and sin no more" part that trips a lot of people up.

God doesn't want you getting tripped up by sin and living in guilt, but only you can decide whether you will live in victory over sin. Living a life of sin will cause a person to have a sad, defeated, and carnal walk. This includes Christians filled with the Holy Spirit, who choose to follow after their human appetites rather than to reign over them. A carnal Christian is simply one who has let their supernatural help lie dormant.

Is that really a normal happening for Christians? Yes, and it happens way too often. That's the problem. Paul wrote to the Corinthians and said they were carnal Christians "mere (unchanged) men" (1 Corinthians 3:3 AMPC). In other words, Paul was telling them they had chosen to live as mere men, by the dictates of their flesh, instead of living the supernaturally empowered life God intended. What a miserable life. And even worse, they had chosen a dead-end road, one that leads to death because Romans 8:6 says to be carnally minded is death. Sin always results in a paycheck of death. Sin doesn't necessarily produce physical death, but it will produce death just the same. Sin in a marriage can cause the death of a marriage. Cheating or stealing at work can cause the death of a job. Lying about a friend or spreading gossip can cause the death of a friendship. And the list goes on.

That's why Peter said, by the Holy Spirit, that we should not spend the rest of our natural lives living by our human appetites. Today, we would say, "Don't live by your flesh; let your spirit man dominate." If you live by the dictates of your body and soul, your attitude will be "Whatever feels good, do it; whatever seems right, try it." It's letting your body and soul go wild (lasciviousness).

Sometimes, Christians will say, "Oh, I could never go wild and sin like that," but, without realizing it, they turn their body loose all the time. If their body wants to be late for work, they just hit the snooze button, or if their body wants to stay home, they call in sick thinking, "That's all right. I've got sick days left, so I'll just use one." Yielding to your flesh like this will open the door to your flesh wanting more. You've got to keep your body under control, or it will put you under.

If you think you could never do that, but then say, "I've got to have my morning coffee, so I don't tear into everybody I meet." Really? That's turning your flesh loose! You've let coffee have dominion over you. Think about it. We all have issues where our flesh wants something, and it's up to us to put our flesh down when we know we shouldn't have it.

I will say this. Because you're reading this book, I know you don't want to yield to your flesh. You don't want the devil to win. You want to keep your flesh in line. So, the first step is to admit you have human appetites that need to be put under and controlled because you can't fix a problem you won't admit to having. We all have cravings of the flesh we have to put down. There are no exceptions, so we may as well admit it to ourselves.

When we let our body do whatever it wants and say whatever it wants, the door to trouble is wide open. If you say, "But I just have to say what's on my mind," actually, no, you don't. If you're always saying what's on your mind, you're yielding to your flesh because no one's thoughts are always holy, pure, peaceable, lovely, kind, gentle and long-suffering, so you shouldn't speak every thought you have. Instead, you may need to find your delete button and hit it more often.

If what's on your mind doesn't agree with God's Word, you shouldn't keep thinking on it, and you definitely shouldn't say it. Galatians 5:16 (NKJV) says, "...Walk in the Spirit, and you shall not fulfill the lust of the flesh." If you don't walk in the spirit, what happens? You will give way to the lusts of your flesh and fulfill its appetites morning, noon, and night.

The Bible gives us some good advice in 1 John.

> **1 John 3:6 (AMPC)** No one who abides in Him [who lives and remains in communion with and in obedience to Him – deliberately, knowingly, and habitually] commits [practices] sin. No one who [habitually] sins has either seen or knows Him [recognized, perceived, or understood Him].

This scripture makes it clear. No one who deliberately, knowingly, and habitually practices sin really knows God because those who do, don't want to live in sin.

Galatians 5:19-21 lists the works of the flesh, but let's look at the last part of Verse 21 to nail this down even more.

> **Galatians 5:21** ...that they which do such things [sin] shall not inherit the kingdom of God.

The phrase "do such things" comes from the Greek word "prasso" (Strong's G4238), which means "to practice, to perform repeatedly or habitually as a way of life". This means, this verse can be literally translated as,

> **"Those who put these things into practice in their lives and do these things routinely as a manner of lifestyle, shall not enter the kingdom of God." (Rick Renner, Sparkling Gems)**

There's a big difference between committing sin in a single instance and practicing sin as a lifestyle. One instance of sin can be the result of a poor choice, impulsive behavior, or losing control in the moment; but practicing sin is willful, deliberate, and premeditated. The Bible is saying that we may occasionally miss the mark and sin, and that 1 John 1:9 is our solution, but there's no excuse for living in sin day in and day out.

Let's look at another scripture which I like to call the "maintenance scripture" for Christians because it will keep us in right standing with God.

> **1 John 1:8-10**
>
> **8 If we say that we have no sin, we deceive ourselves, and the truth is not in us.**
>
> **9 If we confess our sins, he is faithful and just to forgive us our sins, and to cleanse us from all unrighteousness.**
>
> **10 If we say that we have not sinned, we make him a liar, and his word is not in us.**

Notice that both Verses 8 and 10 make it clear that even as Christians, we still sin. How do I know that? Because the epistle of 1 John was written to Christians.

> **1 John 2:1** My little children, these things write I unto you, that ye sin not. And if any man sin, we have an advocate with the Father, Jesus Christ the righteous.

This letter is talking to Christians because it starts with, "My little children;" and it tells us that it is the will of God that His children don't sin, but if they do sin, there's help available. If a child of God sins, they have an advocate in Jesus, who will be their lawyer.

So, does that mean it's okay to sin 101 times a day because we can confess our sins 101 times and be forgiven and then, do it all over again the next day because we have 1 John 1:9? No. This scripture is not a license for someone to intentionally sin. Now, for those who are truly struggling with a particular sin and are repentant, they can confess and be forgiven as many times as needed. Although God is full of infinite mercy and forgiveness, He expects us to take control of our flesh and put an end to the practice of sin.

TAKING CONTROL

Let's look at a scripture that will help us face the problem of the flesh head on and take control.

Romans 6:12 **Let not sin therefore reign in your mortal body, that ye should obey it in the lusts thereof.**

This verse tells us that sin doesn't have to reign in our bodies because we no longer have to obey our fleshly lusts. It doesn't say that we don't lust or to just ignore this lust. To ignore the fact that our flesh has unholy desires is very dangerous. The main point of this scripture is to tell us that we don't have to allow sin to rule and reign in our bodies now that we are born again.

As we've discussed in previous chapters, our spirit was reborn at the new birth, but our body and our mind were not. So, even though we were born again, and our sinful nature was replaced with a divine nature, our soul was not. Our soul must be cleaned up and retrained to live a new and different way. For a lot of people, that means having a "Come to Jesus meeting" to get their will lined up with His. Jesus Himself went to the Garden of Gethsemane and told the Father, "Not my will but Yours be done." If Jesus had to commit His will to the Father, we, too, need to commit ours on a regular basis. And as we renew our mind to the will of God, our will and emotions will come in line with the Word of God and keep our flesh under control.

Let me remind you of a scripture we've looked at because it really helped start me along this entire journey of ruling over my flesh. Galatians 5:16 (NKJV) says, "…Walk in the Spirit, and you shall not fulfill the lust of the flesh." This is saying if you walk in the spirit and become more aware of spiritual things than natural things, you will not fulfill the desires of your flesh. Make no mistake about it, your flesh has desires, and most of them are not godly. If you don't walk in the spirit, that means you will walk by the dictates of your flesh; and it's those fleshly cravings that will lead you right back into the sin and misery that had you bound in the first place.

So, what do you need to do with your flesh? Kill it! Of course, I don't mean that you literally kill your flesh, but you kill it metaphorically. In other words, subdue it, control it, rule over it, and be the boss of it. If you don't boss your flesh, it will boss you. If you don't kill your flesh, it will end up killing you. Remember, the paycheck of sin is ultimately death.

The sum total of how to handle your flesh is found in one word: No! Just say no. If you want to live free from sin and its effects, you'll have to tell your flesh, "No," and you'll have to tell it, "No," on a regular basis.

Colossians 3:5 (AMPC) says, "So kill (deaden, deprive of power) the evil lurking in your members..." When we say "kill*,*" we're talking about depriving our flesh of the right to rule and reign in our lives. Crucifying the flesh sounds painful, and it can be, but it sure beats the penalty of death that results from sin.

If someone asks, "Wasn't Jesus crucified so I wouldn't have to be?" The answer is "Yes," Jesus was crucified to pay the penalty for your sin, but you still need to discipline your flesh and keep your body under. Even the great Apostle Paul had to deal with his flesh. Let's look at how he got the job done.

1 Corinthians 9:27 (NKJV) **But I discipline my body and bring it into subjection lest, when I have preached to others, I myself should become disqualified.**

Let's see how The Amplified Classic translates this verse, "But [like a boxer] I buffet my body [handle it roughly, discipline it by hardships] and subdue it..."

If you're thinking, "I thought you said this was going to be easy?" It is easy because you don't have to discipline and control your flesh on your own. You've got help! And if you say, "I just cannot control my flesh. I've tried, and I don't have enough willpower to do it," I'm not talking about you ruling over your body with willpower. I'm talking about you ruling over your body with God power. I'm talking about walking in the spirit as you're led by the Spirit of God, so you can walk in the power of His Word and His Spirit that will put you over in this life. If you ask, "Shouldn't there be some kind of a line at church where the pastor prays for us and then, our bodies will just want to do right after that?" I wish it was that easy, but it isn't. In 1 Thessalonians 4:4 it says, "Every one of you should know how to possess his vessel [body] in sanctification and honour." Since the Bible is telling us we should know how to possess our vessel, that means we can, so let's do it!

THE PANGS OF SACRIFICE

Practically speaking, how do we possess our vessels (bodies)? How do we take control? The Bible tells us to present our bodies as a living sacrifice.

> **Romans 12:1** **I beseech you therefore, brethren, by the mercies of God, that ye present your bodies a living sacrifice, holy, acceptable unto God, which is your reasonable service.**

We are to bring our body, like a sacrificial lamb, as an offering before the Lord, and give it to Him for His use, His honor, and His glory.

To just let our flesh do whatever it wants will set us up for failure. If we let sin rule in our bodies, we will obey its lusts. So, what do we do? We must refuse to let sin rule. We must pick up our flesh and haul it to the altar and lay it down. We must present our flesh as a living sacrifice and tell our flesh that it won't be having its way anymore. We must tell our body that a new day has dawned and our regenerated, reborn, redeemed, blood-bought spirit is calling the shots from here on out. Then, we must choose to walk on in the spirit. My wife says that the only problem with a living sacrifice is that it's always trying to get off the altar and walk away. That's why you have to put your flesh on the altar and keep it there.

We are to yield our body as an instrument of righteousness.

> **Romans 6:12-13**
>
> **12 Let not sin therefore reign in your mortal body, that ye should obey it in the lusts thereof.**

> **13 Neither yield ye your members as instruments of unrighteousness unto sin: but yield yourselves unto God, as those that are alive from the dead, and your members as instruments of righteousness unto God.**

Offering our bodies as a living sacrifice is our reasonable service because our bodies are now the temple of the Holy Spirit. When we have a revelation that we are the temple of the Holy Ghost (1 Corinthians 3:16; 6:19) and understand that our bodies carry the presence of God, we will keep our temples holy. In 2 Corinthians 4:7, it says we have a treasure in our earthen vessels, that we are carriers of the glory of God.

Let me give you a number of reasons why you should keep your flesh under and a list of ways to do it. Let's first see what the Apostle Peter had to say.

> **1 Peter 4:1-2 (AMPC)**
>
> **1So, since Christ suffered in the flesh for us, for you, arm yourselves with the same thought and purpose [patiently to suffer rather than fail to please God]. For whoever has suffered in the flesh [having the mind of Christ] is done with [intentional] sin [has stopped pleasing himself and the world, and pleases God],**
>
> **2 So that he can no longer spend the rest of his natural life living by [his] human appetites and desires, but [he lives] for what God wills.**

This scripture brings to light two important points to help us keep our bodies under. It says that some suffering may be required to stop sin and that we must no longer live to please ourselves.

The New Living Translation says:

> **1 Peter 4:1-2**
>
> **1So then, since Christ suffered physical pain, you must arm yourselves with the same attitude he had, and be ready to suffer, too. For if you have suffered physically for Christ, you have finished with sin.**

> **² You won't spend the rest of your lives chasing your own desires, but you will be anxious to do the will of God.**

Does this mean we should fly ourselves to Golgotha, erect a cross, and suffer as Jesus did on the cross? Of course not, but it does mean that you will have to tell your flesh "No" from time to time and suffer the pangs that come with denying your flesh something it wants.

Let's look at yet another modern-day translation of this verse from The Message.

> **1 Peter 4:1-2 (MSG)**
>
> **¹Since Jesus went through everything you're going through and more, learn to think like him. Think of your sufferings as a weaning from that old sinful habit of always expecting to get your own way.**
>
> **²Then you'll be able to live out your days free to pursue what God wants instead of being tyrannized by what you want.**

Do you see the heart change needed to drive sin far away from you? To get victory over sin, first and foremost, you must put what God wants ahead of what you want. If it's painful, then think of your "sufferings" as a weaning from the old sinful habit of always expecting to get your own way. Then, arm yourself with the same attitude that Jesus had; and in doing so, you will see that it is no longer be about pleasing yourself.

The truth is that the will of God opposes our flesh today and will oppose our flesh tomorrow and forever. It will oppose the flesh in big things and in small things; but by doing the will of God, the by-product will be that our flesh will be trained to walk in line with God's Word.

How do you train your flesh? Usually, it means going against what feels good to your body. For instance, the Bible says, "Forsake not the assembly of yourselves together" (Hebrews 10:25). So, that means when it's time to go to church, you go whether you feel like it or not. Your flesh may say, "I don't want to," or "I'm busy," or "I'm tired;" but you tell your flesh, "You're going anyway because that's where a Christian belongs!" Then, when you get to church and it's time to praise and worship God, your flesh may say, "But what if I don't want to sing? What if I don't like the songs? What if the drums are too loud? What if I don't want to stand?" You tell your flesh, "You're doing it anyway! I'm here to worship God, and that's what we're going to do!"

Here's a good one. What are you going to do when it's offering time, and you're to obey the Lord by giving your tithe (10 percent of your income, Malachi 3), but you don't want to? You give it anyway. Why? Because you are training your flesh to obey the Word of God by putting His will above your wants and desires, so that sin will not have dominion in your flesh.

If you will regularly tell your flesh what to do in the smaller things, your flesh will know who is boss when it comes to the bigger things. Don't wait until your flesh is under crisis to try and put it under because it's a lot harder then and sometimes impossible to do. You must keep your flesh under all the time.

The devil will look for any lusts of the flesh you have, and when he finds them, he will tempt them; but if you continually keep your flesh under, when the devil comes, he will find nothing to work with in your life.

Another way to keep our flesh under is through reverence. Consider this scripture.

> **2 Corinthians 7:1** **Having therefore these promises, dearly beloved, let us cleanse ourselves from all filthiness of the flesh and spirit, perfecting holiness in the fear of God.**

Don't let the word "holiness" scare you. Being holy isn't acting all spooky or weird; it's just living like Jesus did when He was on this earth. We could also say that reverencing God is having a reverential fear of God. Does that mean we're supposed to be afraid of God? Of course not. Fear of God is having an awesome respect for Him, for who He is, and what He has done. When we reverence God, it will help us cleanse ourselves from the filth of the flesh. As we exalt God to first place in our lives, things of the flesh will fall by the wayside.

THE WAR IN THE SOUL

Let's look at a scripture that talks about the war that lust creates in our soul.

> **1 Peter 2:11** **Dearly beloved, I beseech you as strangers and pilgrims, abstain from fleshly lusts, which war against the soul."**

I want to quote a passage from *Sparkling Gems from the Greek,* written by one of my favorite authors, Rick Renner. In this passage, he amplifies the meaning of 1 Peter 2:11,

> **"Dearly beloved, I sincerely beg and warn you to live as if you are travelers here in this world. Never forget that this is not your real residence and that you must not become too attached to the environment around you. I urge you to refrain from any carnal, low-level desires that try to engulf you and thus drag you into a very long, protracted, strategic and aggressive war in your mind, will, and emotions."**

Today, we face more temptation to our eyes and ears than ever before. It's everywhere: television, movies, print, media, Internet, billboards, and signs everywhere we go. We're continually confronted with words, pictures, and messages that, in times past, no one could have imagined would be posted in public forums. The devil is doing this because he knows that temptation enters your heart through your eyes and ears and chokes out God's Word, so he wants to expose you to as much as possible.

Now, I'm not going to preach you a sermon, and tell you to throw out your television or never read another magazine. I'm not saying disconnect your Internet, but I am saying that you've got to understand how the enemy works; he's out to tantalize your flesh in any way he can. And we all know that our flesh wants what it wants and sometimes what it wants isn't holy. I'm not just talking about sexual sins. Most Christians may not be sinning by committing adultery or fornicating, but are you making crude remarks, hating others, excessively overeating, losing your temper, stirring up trouble, jealous of others, and so on? These are all sins, too, and works of the flesh.

We all understand that our flesh lusts for things. God understands that, too, and His solution is pretty simple. His Word tells us to get our flesh under control and show it who is boss. And we do that by learning and obeying the Word of God, walking in the spirit, and following the leadings of the Holy Ghost.

Chapter
Six
Questions

1. What is the three-part equation of sin?

2. What are some ways you have had to decide to live in victory over sin?

3. What is a carnal Christian?

4. **Sin always produces death. What kind of death can it produce and can you think of any death it has produced in your life?**

5. **Instead of willpower, how do we rule over our body?**

6. **How do we take control over our bodies (vessel)?**

Chapter
Six
Confessions

✻   I will not allow my flesh to dominate me in any area of my life; and because I walk in the spirit, I will not fulfill the lusts of my flesh. (Galatians 5:16)

✻   I will walk in a way that is holy and honorable and present my body as a living sacrifice to God every day. (1 Thessalonians 4:4, Romans 12:1)

✻   I shall discipline my body and bring it into subjection, so I can be a witness to others.
(1 Corinthians 9:27)

✻   I will not let sin reign in my body; I will not obey the lusts of my flesh. (Romans 6:12)

✻   Because I am a temporary resident of the Earth, I will abstain from fleshly desires that war against my soul.
(1 Peter 2:11)

chapter 7: walking in the spirit

The Bible tells us in Galatians 5 that if we walk in the spirit, we will not fulfill the lusts of the flesh. That means that every step we take in the spirit is another step away from sin which is our answer to winning over sin. Does walking in the spirit mean we should walk around all woo-woo, with our head stuck in the clouds? No. It simply means living a life that's pleasing to our Lord. Galatians 5:16 in the Amplified puts it this way.

> **Galatians 5:16 (AMPC)** But I say walk and live [habitually] in the [Holy] Spirit [responsive to and controlled and guided by the Spirit]; then you will certainly not gratify the cravings and desires of the flesh (of human nature without God).

The Apostle John gives us more insight when he said he was, "In the spirit on the Lord's Day" (Revelation 1:10). Does that mean John found a new location somewhere? No. John wasn't talking about a geographical location; he was talking about a spiritual position.

If you were to ask 100 people what being "in the spirit" means, you would probably get 100 different answers. Being in the spirit doesn't mean having an out-of-body experience or speaking in thee's and thou's. Now, there are some who say they are in the spirit when in reality they have become part of the granola club of nuts, fruits, and flakes and actually do act all woo-woo. This is not how you do it. I believe the best explanation of being in the spirit is that you are more aware of spiritual things than you are natural things. It's living your life by the Word of God and the leadings of the Holy Spirit. It's walking in the light of God's Word which makes you better, not weird. It's making God's Word your final authority.

Walking in the spirit should not be something out of the ordinary for a believer; it's what we are supposed to do all the time. Galatians 5:16 refers to it as a daily experience of living out of our spirit and being responsive to the Holy Spirit, so He can guide and direct us in all the affairs of our life. In fact, just a few verses down, Galatians 5:25 (NLT) says, "Since we are living by the Spirit, let us follow the Spirit's leading in every part of our lives." This means that when the Holy Spirit urges us to do something, we should quickly obey. If the Holy Spirit prompts us to make changes in certain areas, we should change. If He prompts us to go somewhere or do something, we should do it. If He prompts us to not do something, then we should not do it. If He prompts us to pray for someone, call someone, or minister to someone, we should do it. When we read our Bible and something jumps off the page at us, we should respond by putting what it says to work in our lives. Living in the spirit means we're not just hearers of the Word of God, but we actually do it.

Unfortunately, for some people, letting the Holy Spirit control their lives just seems to be a promise they make to God in church when the music is playing, and the minister asks everyone to confess this out loud together. Then, Monday morning comes and what happens? What do they do at work when the Spirit of God deals with them not to accept an invitation to meet up with their colleagues at the bar, or to not join in talking trash about the boss? What happens when they're at home and are tempted to give their spouse a piece of their mind? Will they follow the leadings of the Spirit of God then? These are moments in our life where the "rubber-meets-the-road," and our choices will reveal whether or not we are living guided by the Spirit of God. It's His job to guide us into all truth, and we need to let Him do His job.

Consider this. Have you ever gone on a tour with a knowledgeable guide? A good guide will lead you to the best places to give you the most out of your tour. A good guide will also know how to help you avoid the pitfalls and traps that could disappoint and ruin your experience. In the same way, the Holy Spirit is your own personal tour guide through life; He knows how to help you remain in the high places and stay out of trouble.

> **Galatians 5:25 (AMPC)** If we live by the [Holy] Spirit, let us also walk by the Spirit. [If by the Holy Spirit we have our life in God, let us go forward walking in line, our conduct controlled by the Spirit].

When our conduct is controlled by the Spirit, that means we have yielded ourselves and our body to Him. That's what we're supposed to do because 1 Corinthians 6:19 does say that our body is the temple (home) of the Holy Spirit.

Think about that. The Holy Spirit cannot help you with your flesh if He does not live in you. That's why you can never overcome sin on your own, apart from the new birth. Anyone who says, "I think I can handle this sin thing when it comes to the Ten Commandments." Really? I don't think so. God gave us the "Big Ten" to show us we needed a Savior. And those of us who have received Jesus Christ as Lord and Savior know how important it is to be controlled, guided, and empowered by the Holy Spirit through life.

WHAT IT'S NOT

Sometimes, in order to understand something better, we need to consider what it's not. So, although we've talked about what walking in the spirit is, let's talk about what it is not, or what it looks like to be controlled by your flesh.

> **Romans 8:5 (AMPC)** For those who are according to the flesh and are controlled by its unholy desires set their minds on and pursue those things which gratify the flesh, but those who are according to the Spirit and are controlled by the desires of the Spirit set their minds on and seek those things which gratify the [Holy] Spirit.

Someone who is flesh driven is not controlled by the Holy Spirit. Why is this important?

Because, as we said earlier, the devil is looking for any lust in us he can use to tempt us to give birth to sin. And the devil knows that the more we think about fleshly things and gravitate toward them, the more ammunition we're giving him to fire our way.

To be controlled by the flesh means we let our flesh have its way whenever it wants. The thing is, everyone has unholy desires; and that includes your minister, Saint Sally, your grandma (oh, yes, she does) and the worst sinner you've ever met. The only difference is what each person does when unholy desires come. Do they give into them or not.

Some people, either on purpose or just by hanging around God for a long time, have learned how to put down their flesh and to let God dominate in their lives. They have learned to pass up marvelous opportunities to sin. They have renewed their mind, so they no longer gratify their flesh, but those who are flesh-ruled, do whatever they want whenever they want. Their motto is, "If it feels good, do it." They live by momentary pleasures and give no thought to the fact that the devil is standing by waiting for their lust to conceive sin and produce a paycheck of death.

In Romans 8, we get a Holy Spirit lesson on the difference between walking in the flesh and walking in the spirit.

> **Romans 8:13 (NKJV)** For if you live according the flesh you will die; but if by the Spirit you put to death the deeds of the body, you will live.

This scripture tells us the difference: death or life. It draws a clear line for us and is key to our breaking free and staying free from sin. If we really want to win over sin, we must understand that the only way to do it is to walk in the spirit.

Remember the phrase that the devil used on Eve (Chapter 2)? God had warned Adam and Eve not to eat of a certain fruit or they would die; but when the devil was tempting Eve, he said, "Oh, you won't actually die." What a liar! Death came to all mankind because Eve believed that lie, and the devil is still saying the same thing to you and me today. When he's trying to talk you into sinning, he'll say, "You don't really think that just this one time will hurt, do you? Who's going to find out? What harm could it cause to try it just this once?" Don't believe him! He's such a liar just like he was back in the Garden of Eden. Sin will always cause death in your life; it may not be physical death, but make no mistake about it, death in some form will occur.

If something has to die, let it be the deeds of the flesh, and the Holy Spirit will help you.

> **Romans 8:13 (AMPC)** **For if you live according to [the dictates of] the flesh, you will surely die. But if through the power of the [Holy] Spirit you are [habitually] putting to death (making extinct, deadening) the [evil] deeds prompted by the body, you shall [really and genuinely] live forever.**

The desires of your flesh need to die, and once that happens, you can really start living. The devil may have just whispered to you, "There goes all your fun," but that's just another lie! If you think death is fun, I warn you now, you will regret it. I know from experience that nothing can measure up to the life God gives. It's full, rich, and over-the-top wonderful!

Once you've walked in the spirit, you'll want to walk there all day long, every day. "Why would I want to do that?" someone might ask. The answer is simple. On this Earth you're limited by the knowledge and help that is available in this world, but if you walk in the spirit, you walk with all of Heaven at your disposal.

Let me quote another passage from Rick Renner's book, *Sparkling Gems from the Greek*, which talks about walking in the spirit as our lifestyle. Here he conveys the meaning of Galatians 5:16,

> **"Make the path of the Spirit the place where you habitually live and walk. Become so comfortable on this spiritual path that you learn to leisurely and peacefully stroll along in that realm. Living your life in this Spirit realm is the best way to guarantee that you will not allow the yearnings of your flesh to creep out and fulfill themselves."**

WAYS TO WALK IN THE SPIRIT

If you're thinking, "Walking in the spirit sounds amazing, but how do I do it?" It starts by simply reading and speaking the Word of God and connecting with His presence. John 6:63 quotes Jesus saying, "…the words I speak unto you, they are Spirit, and they are life." When you and I speak His Word, it puts us in the realm of the Spirit because His Word is spirit, and it is life!

Another way we can get into the spirit is to worship God. John 4:24 says, "God is a spirit; and they that worship him must worship him in spirit and in truth." This scripture tells us that we must worship God with truth, which is His Word, and we must come to the Father by His Spirit. This is how we enter the realm of the Spirit.

If someone says, "The only time I worship is when I sing at church," that is not enough, and it just shouldn't be that way. You can worship anytime, with or without music, in your home, your car, at school, at work, or wherever you are. God has called you to be a worshipper, and you can magnify and worship God loudly or by quietly lifting your voice and speaking just above a whisper, "God, You're so good" or "God, You're so faithful." Both are worshipping Him. Worship connects you with the Spirit of God, and you become more aware of God than the natural things that surround you. This is what brings God on the scene on your behalf and changes your environment.

God offers us many ways to get in the spirit. Another important way is by being full of the Holy Spirit. The Bible tells us that when a person is born again, they receive the Spirit of God on the inside. Acts 2 talks about receiving the baptism of the Holy Spirit, which is an additional baptism of the Spirit with the evidence of speaking in other tongues. Acts 1:8 (NKJV) says, "But you shall receive power when the Holy Spirit has come upon you…" This word "power" in the Greek is "dunamis" (Strong's G1411), and it's where we get our word dynamite and dynamo. In other words, the infilling of the Spirit is power; and this power is for service and for living. No Christian should be without it. Acts 2:4 tells us that the initial evidence of this experience, subsequent to salvation, is the evidence of speaking in other tongues. As a pastor, I strongly recommend that every Christian ask for this Holy Spirit baptism. It's the gateway to more of God in your life and will give you the boldness to rise above sin.

I've counseled many people and will often say to them, "Try praying in tongues when you're tempted to sin. It will stop you in your tracks." Can you imagine committing adultery while praying in tongues, or singing, "How Great Is Our God" while practicing sin? Of course not, and that's the point. The more you are in the spirit, the less you will yield to your flesh. Being in the spirit will stop you from yielding to temptation and practicing and living in sin. You will be free from sin and begin to experience life instead of death, and you will be a person full of joy and victory.

Let's look at walking in the spirit from one more perspective. If all we speak about are natural things or how we feel about things, we have locked ourselves into the natural, physical flesh realm, and the more stuck in the flesh realm we are, the easier it is for us to yield to our flesh. Then, unfortunately, most people already know the rest of the story. That's when the devil comes and tempts the flesh with an assortment of lusts and sin is usually the end result. But if we will continue to walk in the spirit, we can resist temptation and be free from sin, so we can live the good life God planned for us.

FRUIT TELLS THE STORY

"How can I know if I'm walking in the spirit?" someone might ask. That's easy. Your fruit tells the story. Galatians 5:19-21 tells us that if we walk by our flesh, we will manifest the works of the flesh, which starts with adultery and ends with revellings; but if we walk in the spirit, we will manifest the fruit of the Spirit listed in Verses 22 and 23, which are love, joy, peace, long-suffering, gentleness, goodness, faith (faithfulness), meekness, and temperance. So, by our actions, it's easy to tell which realm we are walking in.

God wants us all to walk in the spirit, so it's not just for certain people to do at church. It is something we all can do anywhere, anytime, and where we walk will determine what our life will produce. Each of us will either produce the fruit of the Spirit or the works of the flesh. It's not up to God; it's up to you and me. In Chapters 8-11, we will talk in more detail about this fruit.

Does being filled with the spirit make you perfect? Of course not. In fact, sometimes, people will ask crazy questions like, "I heard that a Spirit-filled preacher stole $100,000 from his church, so was he in the spirit when he did that?" Obviously not! He certainly wasn't full of the Holy Spirit that day. Just because someone spoke in tongues yesterday, doesn't mean this person is immune from yielding to the devil. Can you prove that? I can.

Remember when Peter said, "You're the Lord. You're the Christ. You're the son of the living God." Jesus was pleased with him because he spoke truth that was supernaturally revealed to him. But shortly after that, when Jesus talked about being crucified on the cross, Peter said "Not so!" Jesus turned right around in the same breath and rebuked Peter, saying, "Get behind me Satan!" Peter went from being in the spirit to being in the flesh (Matthew 16). Can people flip on a dime like that? Yes. Peter did.

If you're married, have children, work, drive in traffic, or have pressure of any kind, which includes everyone, you know how easy it is to be in the spirit one moment and then, in the flesh the next. We can be driving on the highway praising the Lord but then, when someone cuts in front of us, here comes our flesh. Whiplash! So, who determines whether you walk in the spirit or walk in the flesh? Do circumstances? Do the people around you? No. Only you determine where you walk.

We need to realize that just because a person has spoken in tongues doesn't mean they can't ever mess up; just because a person is Spirit-filled or has received the baptism of the Holy Spirit does not mean that they are always walking in the fullness of the Spirit. Ephesians 5:18 says "And be not drunk with wine, wherein is excess; but be filled with the Spirit." The Greek word for "filled", "pleroo" (Strong's G4137), actually means "be being filled" or "continually being filled." Bottom line, even people who get filled must continually get refilled in order to stay filled.

Let me put it this way. Christians who walk in the spirit do pray in other tongues, but not all Christians who pray in other tongues yield to the Holy Spirit and walk in the spirit. Speaking in tongues will help you walk in the spirit, but you still have to do the walking. When we walk in the spirit, it is the gateway to so much more. Walking in the spirit also means crucifying the flesh and walking by the Word, which requires diligence and discipline.

For those who saw the movie, "The Passion of the Christ," you saw a graphic crucifixion, with lots of blood and gore. You witnessed the suffering, pain, and anguish Jesus' body endured as He paid the price for our salvation. This salvation, paid in full, is available to all who will believe and receive what Jesus has provided. But to walk in its fullness, we are instructed to crucify our flesh and offer our body as a living sacrifice to God (Romans 12:1).

Am I saying you're supposed to hang on a cross and be crucified? Of course not, but you must kill off sinful desires, lusts, and appetites, and sometimes, that's painful. If that sounds hard, it's really not when you walk in the spirit. I heard a preacher say it this way, "Dead men don't sin." Can a dead man talk back? Can a dead man get angry? Can a dead man get worked up and agitated in traffic? No. Why not? Because a dead body can't respond in the flesh because it's dead. That's the whole point of being a living sacrifice; your body is dead to sin.

So, put your flesh under and keep it under by putting your flesh on the altar and keeping it there. If it squirms off the altar for a day, what do you do? Repent and put it right back on the altar. And yes, we can all mess up, but that's why we have 1 John 1:9, so we can be forgiven and begin again.

If you still think it's too hard, all I can say is, don't be a sissy Christian. Get back on that altar and let's do this, so we can please God and give Him the glory and honor He deserves. He's made a way for us out of darkness into light, so let's stay in the light. With His help, you can do it; with His help, you can do anything!

SOW TO THE SPIRIT

All day long, every single day, you are confronted with choices as to whether you will walk in the spirit or in the flesh. Galatians 6 says that with every choice you make, you are either sowing to the spirit or to the flesh.

> **Galatians 6:7-8 (NKJV)**
>
> **7 Do not be deceived, God is not mocked; for whatever a man sows, that he will also reap.**
>
> **8 For he who sows to his flesh will of the flesh reap corruption, but he who sows to the Spirit will of the Spirit reap everlasting life.**

What is sowing to the flesh? It is allowing your flesh to do what it wants. What is sowing to the spirit? It is following after the Word and the Spirit of God. What's the difference? Sowing to the flesh reaps death, but sowing to the spirit reaps life.

Let me give you a practical example. Maybe you want to have the last word in an argument but instead, you kill that temptation by putting your hand over your mouth. What just happened? You chose to sow to the spirit by aligning your speech with what God's Word says about love and forgiveness. Sometimes, walking in love can simply be keeping your mouth shut. That may not sound spiritual, but it can be a very spiritual thing to do.

Most of the time, sexual sins are the first to come to our mind on the topic of sin, but there are many ways to "flesh out." What about excessively overeating? Nobody likes to talk about this one, even though it's one of the biggest health problems in America today. The point is, we must get every lust we have under control because if we don't, we will open ourselves up to destruction in every area of our life by creating a wide-open door for the devil. So, the next time you're staring down at a coconut cream pie with meringue piled a mile high and want to overindulge, what will you do? Will you sow to the flesh or to the spirit? The choice is yours.

Let's look at some other examples of temptations to sin.

- **What if you're married but an attractive co-worker invites you to lunch?**

- **What if you're in charge of the office petty cash box, and you think temporarily borrowing $20 wouldn't be a big deal?**

- **What if someone undeserving is promoted over you?**

- **What if you feel like giving someone a piece of your mind?**

What will you do in each of these situations and all the other situations you face daily? Will you sow to the flesh or to the spirit?

Ephesians tells about the good life God has for us.

> **Ephesians 2:10 (AMPC)** **For we are God's [own] handiwork (His workmanship), recreated in Christ Jesus [born anew] that we may do those good works which God predestined (planned beforehand) for us [taking paths which He prepared ahead of time], that we should walk in them [living the good life which He prearranged and made ready for us to live].**

So, if we want to walk in the "good life" God has planned for us, we must do the good works that God has predestined for us, which requires that we walk in the spirit and in the fruit of the Spirit, so we can reign over the works of our flesh.

Chapter Seven Questions

1. What is a good definition of walking in the spirit?

2. We as Christians should be walking in the spirit daily. List some examples of what that may look like.

3. What does it mean to be controlled by the flesh or flesh-ruled?

4. How can you tell if someone is walking in the spirit or in the flesh?

5. Is praying in tongues the will of God? And why is it important in overcoming sin?

Chapter Seven Confessions

* My body is the temple of the Holy Spirit who lives in me. I am not my own. I belong to God. (1 Corinthians 6:19)

* Your Word is spirit, and it is life, so I will read and speak Your Word to stay connected to You. (John 6:63)

* I am God's workmanship, created in Christ Jesus, and I shall walk in the good works He has ordained for me. (Ephesians 2:10)

* I will walk and live in the spirit. I will be responsive, controlled and guided by Him, so I will not gratify the cravings of my flesh. (Galatians 5:16)

* Jesus is the vine, and I am the branch, so I will stay vitally connected to the vine. (John 15:5)

chapter 8: fruit over flesh

We looked at the works of the flesh in Chapter 4 and how important it is to walk in the spirit in our last chapter. In this chapter, we will focus on how walking in the fruit of the Spirit will enable us to rule and reign over our flesh.

Some years ago, the Lord began to talk to me about how walking in the fruit of the Spirit will take care of all the works of the flesh, and I want to share with you what the Lord has taught me.

Our flesh has lusts that we must flee from.

> **2 Timothy 2:22** Flee also youthful lusts: but follow righteousness, faith, charity, peace, with them that call on the Lord out of a pure heart.

Lusts from our youth can rise up in us no matter how old we get. This scripture says we are to "Follow righteousness, faith, charity (love), and peace," so we won't give in to these lusts.

When we received salvation, we were made righteous (in right standing with God), so He expects us to walk uprightly. That's why He has put in our born-again spirit, the fruit of the Spirit which is found in Galatians.

Galatians 5:22-23

22 But the fruit of the Spirit is love, joy, peace, longsuffering, gentleness, goodness, faith [faithfulness],

23 Meekness, temperance: against such there is no law.

When we walk in these nine fruits, they will displace all the works of the flesh (adultery, fornication, uncleanness, lasciviousness, idolatry, witchcraft, hatred, variance, emulations, wrath, strife, seditions, heresies, envyings, murders, drunkenness, and revellings that we talked about in Chapter 4.

Walking in the fruit of the Spirit doesn't happen overnight. It's a process. Someone who consistently walks there had to work at it and get with God to figure out their part, especially if walking in a certain fruit wasn't part of their natural make-up. Walking in this fruit isn't automatic. We must choose to walk in the fruit on purpose and continually to receive all of its benefits. Have any of us fully arrived? No, but we're all growing as we continue to walk in the fruit every day.

There are nine fruits in all, and when we don't walk in them, we are letting our flesh dominate us and have its way. When our flesh rules and reigns, it will produce the works of the flesh that will lead us into sin.

Why do the works of the flesh still rise up after we are born again? Because when we got born again, our body did not. Only our spirit was recreated. Our body remained the same, so the works of our flesh will still try to rise up; and if we don't stop them by walking in the fruit, our flesh will dominate.

We are all confronted with these works of the flesh, and which ones we deal with differ for each of us, but no matter which ones you deal with, growing in the fruit of the Spirit is your answer. It is the cure that will keep your flesh under and put an end to walking in the flesh.

Those who continually walk in the fruit of the Spirit and allow this fruit to grow in them, can actually get to a place where it feels like they don't have a flesh to contend with at all because the fruit is keeping their body under. That's a place we should all strive to get to.

How do we grow this fruit that we have been given? The Bible likens a believer to a tree planted by the river.

Psalms 1:1-3

¹Blessed is the man that walketh not in the counsel of the ungodly, nor standeth in the way of sinners, nor sitteth in the seat of the scornful.

² But his delight is in the law of the Lord; and in his law doth he meditate day and night.

³ And he shall be like a tree planted by the rivers of water, that bringeth forth his fruit in his season; his leaf also shall not wither; and whatsoever he doeth shall prosper.

To be a strong tree bearing fruit, we are to find our delight in the Word of God and continually meditate on it. It also says we should not receive counsel from the ungodly, stand with sinners, or sit with those who are scornful. We can help them, but we can't walk closely with them. If we do, we may find ourselves falling into the same sin they are in.

1 Corinthians 15:33 (NKJV) Do not be deceived: "Evil company corrupts good habits."

It is so important who we keep company with, and who we listen to, especially staying away from those who mock and don't value the things of God. Psalm 1:1-3 in the Message Bible puts it in everyday language to help us better understand.

Psalms 1:1-3 (MSG)

¹ How well God must like you - you don't hang out at Sin Saloon, you don't slink along Dead-End Road, you don't go to Smart-Mouth College.

> **² Instead you thrill to God's Word, you chew on Scripture day and night.**
>
> **³ You're a tree replanted in Eden, bearing fresh fruit every month, Never dropping a leaf, always in blossom.**

That says it plain. Who we walk with will affect our tree. It is up to us to protect our tree, so the fruit of the Spirit can grow in us for our sake and for the sake of everybody around us.

HOW TO WATER OUR TREE

We water it with the Word of God. We must read, study, meditate, and speak the Word. It's what will keep us planted by the river of living water, which is the power of the Holy Ghost. We should go to a good Bible teaching church, so our roots can grow deep as we hear the anointed Word taught.

The problem with a lot of Christians today is they're always transplanting themselves, going from church to church, so they never develop strong roots. If I had some plants in my front yard, and every week I moved them to another location, they would never be able to take root, and without roots they will not grow, and may even die. The same is true of a believer. God expects us to stay firmly planted in the Word and where He has put us, so whenever we experience a drought in any part our life, we can receive the water of the Word that will help us remain strong, so we can continue to produce much fruit.

PRODUCING FRUIT

How much fruit we produce is up to us. How much love, joy, peace, longsuffering, gentleness, goodness, faithfulness, meekness, and temperance we have is our choice, our responsibility. We are to watch over the "tree" of our heart and walk in this fruit we have been given so it will grow. We should all want to be a strong tree bearing much fruit. Growing in this fruit will help us mature in the things of God and will benefit those we come in contact with because they can partake of the fruit we display to help them be encouraged in their day and in their journey. And, in the hour we live in, we all need to have this fruit coming out of us. Every believer ought to be as "fruity" as possible, in a good way, by walking in these nine fruits every day.

Keeping our flesh under isn't something that just happens by saying, "I've got to quit doing this, so I'm just going to stop." We've all said that and us wanting to quit is good, but we already know we need to quit, and still, we keep doing it. Why? Because we've allowed our flesh to become so powerful and more in charge than our spirit, so we aren't able to stop.

RULING AND REIGNING OVER OUR FLESH

We begin taking control of our flesh by watering ourselves every day with the Word to renew our mind. Everything that comes to us goes through our mind, so the best way to continually walk in the fruit of our born-again spirit is to renew it with what the Word of God says. When our mind agrees with the Word, we can then know what the good, acceptable, and perfect will of God is (Romans 12:2), and our mind will no longer oppose our spirit. When our mind agrees with our spirit man, it's a lot easier to operate in the fruit of the Spirit on a continual basis.

The fruit that has been deposited in us is part of our born-again DNA, so it's something every believer can access, put on, and walk in. When we walk in this fruit, we are partaking of the character and nature of God because these nine fruits are His character and nature.

WHAT FRUIT IS NOT

The fruit of the Spirit is not part of the gifts, manifestations of the Holy Spirit, which are listed in 1 Corinthians 12 (word of wisdom, word of knowledge, faith, healings, miracles, prophecy, discerning of spirits, tongues [public], and interpretation of tongues).

Most Christians are more impressed and focused on the gifts because when they are in operation, they are more spectacular. I like it too when these gifts manifest, but we can't control when they will be in operation because it's as the Spirit wills. No one can walk in the gifts of the Spirit all the time like they can with the fruit of the Spirit. These gifts are for the benefit of the body of Christ while the fruit of the Spirit is for us to grow up. We can only cooperate in the gifts when the Holy Spirit puts them on us.

The gifts of the Spirit are like the tree we have at Christmas. I remember the first tree my wife decorated after we got married. The tree wasn't alive anymore because the roots had been cut off, but it still smelled nice, and we put the trunk in water to keep it looking fresh. My wife decorated it with lights, garland, and ornaments, and put an angel on top. It was beautiful, but the tree had nothing to do with it. The tree didn't grow that way. It manifested into a beautiful, sparkling tree only because my wife put all those things on it. It's the same with the manifestations (gifts) of the Spirit. The Holy Ghost puts the gift on the person who will yield and have the faith to operate in that particular manifestation of the Spirit. This doesn't mean this person is more mature or has grown in the fruit of the Spirit. It just means they're good at yielding.

I love to flow in the Holy Ghost. Whatever He wants to do, I'm ready; but my running around the sanctuary, or dancing in the spirit, or laying hands on someone, or giving a tongue and interpretation, or singing in the spirit has nothing to do with how much fruit I walk in. Again, it's about how good I am at yielding and obeying the Holy Spirit. I know a lot of good yielders who operate in the gifts, but they are not very good fruit walkers. That's why when someone is operating in these gifts, we're all, "Wow," but then, when the service is over, these people can disappoint us when they don't act very loving. What happened? They yielded to the Spirit and flowed in the gifts which was amazing; but then, when the power of God was no longer manifested, they reverted back to their own Christian walk and displayed very little fruit because they hadn't spent time tending to their fruit so they could walk in it toward others.

Yielding to the Spirit is great, and we should all do that when the gifts are in operation, but the fruit of the Spirit is something we can choose to walk in all the time and the fruit will cause us to receive the blessings of God and live a victorious life.

Some people refer to the fruit of the Spirit as the fruit of the Holy Spirit, but that's not totally accurate. Yes, the Holy Spirit has placed the seed of this fruit within our born-again spirit, but because the fruit is now within us and not something the Holy Spirit puts on us, it's up to us to walk in it so it will grow in us.

I'm so glad we don't have to choose between the fruit of the Spirit and the gifts of the Spirit (1 Corinthians 12), but if I had to choose, I would choose the fruit because I would rather see good fruit continually coming forth from me than to operate in the gifts occasionally. It's the fruit that will change my life and cause me to mature in the things of God. But thank God we don't have to choose because we can have both. We can all be a strong tree with much fruit growing in us, and we can also have some lights like my wife used on the Christmas tree (gifts of the Holy Spirit).

DO NOT NEGLECT THE FRUIT

Why is it important to God that we don't neglect the fruit of the Spirit that is in us?

It seems to me, He is positioning us for more, for the greater. I believe it is very difficult, if not impossible, for God to bless us, fully and completely, when we are being led by our flesh (body) and soul (mind, will, and emotions) and allowing them to do whatever they want. When we are flesh ruled, we can only receive from the flesh arena; but when we walk in the fruit of the Spirit, we are operating in the heavenly arena and can receive all that God has for us.

How do we know if we are walking in the flesh or in the fruit? We can tell by what is produced.

- **Walking in the Flesh: Being angry, mean, uncaring, full of hate, acting in a way that is ungodly or walking in any other work of the flesh.**

- **Walking in the Spirit: Being joyful, peaceable, gentle, showing care, acting in a way that prefers others or walking in any other fruit of the Spirit.**

It's just that simple. Can we have moments when we go back and forth? Absolutely, but since we know better, we can stop ourselves when we are walking in the flesh, ask God to forgive us (1 John 1:9), and then, get right back to walking in the fruit of the Spirit. We can quickly jerk ourselves back by speaking the Word or praying in tongues; and if it involves a husband and wife, instead of staying irritated with each other, they can grab hands and start praying in the Holy Ghost together. We must do whatever it takes to stay in the spirit and walk in the fruit of the Spirit, so we can be led by our spirit. Otherwise, our actions will become fleshly and carnal, like it was in the Corinthians Church. They had so many manifestations of the Holy Ghost happening and could talk in tongues more than anybody, but they were so fleshly in how they acted that the Apostle Paul addressed them as mere men (1 Corinthians 3:1-3).

I find it hard to understand, knowing all that God has provided, why anyone would want to see how worldly and carnal they can become before they go to Heaven rather than choosing right now to walk in His Word and in the fruit of the Spirit, which is what will bring His blessings to us every day.

It is the will of God for all of us to produce all nine of these fruits on a very regular basis. When we walk in the fruit, and serve and obey the Lord, He will perfect everything that concerns us (Psalm 138:8). He will intervene in our personal life and help us. He will keep us and our family safe, and He will lead and guide us.

It starts with knowing who you are in Christ.

- **You are the righteousness of God in Christ Jesus.**
- **You are holy and sanctified by the blood of Jesus.**
- **You are loved by God.**
- **You are a son and daughter of the Most High God.**

There are many more in the Bible. Look them up!

Knowing your born-again identity will cause you to want to walk in the fruit that is on the inside of you; and as that fruit grows, it will push out all the lusts of your flesh because you are doing it from your position in Christ, from the inside out, instead of trying to do it in your own strength.

If you never walk in this fruit, it will remain dormant in you and do you no good. You must choose to walk in the fruit of the Spirit; and when you do, you will walk in victory!

FRUIT WILL CRUCIFY OUR FLESH

The fruit of the Spirit will crucify the flesh.

The fruit of the Spirit is listed right after the works of the flesh (Galatians 5) to show us that by walking in the fruit, we can rule and reign over our flesh. Verse 23 says, "Against such there is no law," and Verse 24 says, "They that are Christ's have crucified the flesh."

Crucify! Yes, and we do that by keeping our flesh under, so it cannot rule and reign over us. The flesh doesn't want to be crucified. It wants to have its way, but God has given us everything we need to keep our flesh under, so we can walk uprightly. And it's not a hard thing to do because when we choose to walk in the fruit of the Spirit, it will do the crucifying.

When your flesh rises up, just get more Word in you concerning that area because the more

Word you have, the more insight and revelation you will be given, and the more purposely you will be able to walk in the fruit of the Spirit.

Through the years, I've watched people try to crucify their flesh by willpower instead of walking in God power to grow their fruit. Our willpower is no match against the temptations the devil brings. Trying to do it by willpower is very difficult and, most of the time, impossible or unsustainable. I believe those who try doing it in their own ability are the ones who seem to deal with the same bad habits and problems over and over again.

Choosing to walk out this Christian life in your own strength comes from the traditions of men and the law that never was enough. If the Mosaic law could have done it, it would still be in place today; but all it did was show us we couldn't do it on our own, that we needed a savior, a redeemer, a nature change; and thank God when we were born again, that's exactly what we got. So, now we can walk from the inside out by walking in the fruit of the Spirit. When we do, we will see the victory every time. We were never meant to crucify our flesh on our own. That's why we were given the fruit of the Spirit. Each fruit is there to help us crucify one or more works of the flesh, so keep walking in the fruit and then, as your fruit grows, watch those lusts you've been dealing with in your flesh for so long begin to drop off.

HOW BRIGHT IS YOUR LIGHT

Those who are born again are new creations in Christ Jesus.

This means we are no longer to follow after the world. We should not be acting, talking, or walking like them because that is no longer who we are. We are now children of the light, so the more light of God's Word we have, the more we will worship in spirit and truth, the more we will pray, the more we will serve, the more we will think on godly things, the more fruit of the Spirit we will have, and the more we will experience victory and freedom in our life and be a light that will shine to others.

Ask yourself, "When someone runs, bumps, or collides into me, what do they get from me?" What they should get coming out of you, first and foremost, is faith followed by the fruit of the Spirit. That is what should be coming out of every believer when they get squeezed. I like to say it this way. When you squeeze an orange, you get orange juice. When you squeeze a grape, you get grape juice. And when you squeeze a believer, you should get faith and the fruit of the Spirit (love, joy, peace, longsuffering, gentleness, goodness, faith [faithfulness], meekness, and temperance). That's what walking in the light of the Word and being a doer of it will do.

ONLY YOU CONTROL YOURSELF

We can't control others, not those in the body of Christ, not our spouse, not our grown children, not our friends, nor people we meet; but we can control how we walk.

It's interesting to me that some people think it's their job to control others by being their fruit inspector, but I don't see that job description in the Bible. Yes, we are to admonish one another (Romans 15:14), but that word "admonish" means to warn, counsel, and exhort, and that's only to those you have a close relationship with. No one has the ministry of correction. Fruit inspectors tend to inspect others for what is lacking in their own life. Those who judge others as inferior tend to do it to make themselves feel superior, but what it actually shows is that they are not walking in love and most likely have a problem loving themselves. Don't inspect or judge others. Instead, inspect and judge yourself, so you won't be judged (1 Corinthians 11:31).

Only you can walk uprightly. Ephesians tells us more about how to walk and how not to walk.

Ephesians 5:1-10

¹Be ye therefore followers of God, as dear children;

² And walk in love, as Christ also hath loved us, and hath given himself for us an offering and a sacrifice to God for a sweetsmelling savour.

³ But fornication, and all uncleanness, or covetousness, let it not be once named among you, as becometh saints;

⁴ Neither filthiness, nor foolish talking, nor jesting, which are not convenient: but rather giving of thanks.

⁵ For this ye know, that no whoremonger, nor unclean person, nor covetous man, who is an idolater, hath any inheritance in the kingdom of Christ and of God.

> **⁶ Let no man deceive you with vain words: for because of these things cometh the wrath of God upon the children of disobedience.**
>
> **⁷ Be not ye therefore partakers with them.**
>
> **⁸ For ye were sometimes darkness, but now are ye light in the Lord: walk as children of light:**
>
> **⁹ (For the fruit of the Spirit is in all goodness and righteousness and truth;)**
>
> **¹⁰ Proving what is acceptable unto the Lord.**

Galatians 5:21 says that those who walk ungodly will not "inherit the kingdom of God."

> **Galatians 5:21** **Envyings, murders, drunkenness, revellings, and such like: of the which I tell you before, as I have also told you in time past, that they which do such things shall not inherit the kingdom of God."**

This is not talking about being born again and going to Heaven. This is talking about walking in His kingdom while we are here on the earth. To inherit His kingdom and receive His blessings while on the earth, requires faith and obedience. It's very hard for a person to receive anything from God when they are walking as a mere, carnal Christian controlled by their flesh.

Paul said, "At one time, we were some of these" (Titus 3:3), but now that we are born again, we should no longer be like them. We need to stay kingdom minded which includes walking in the fruit of the Spirit. We can all walk in this fruit because it is in our born-again spirit. It is not something we do when we feel like it. It's a choice, so we must choose to walk in it all the time. If you haven't been walking in this fruit, you can start today. And as you continually walk in it, this fruit will continue to grow bigger in you.

Keeping your body under is a lot easier and doable when you walk in the fruit, renew your mind with the Word of God, and do the Word. We need to bear this fruit more than ever, and God, through His Word and the leadings of the Holy Spirit, will teach us how to grow and walk in each fruit. It doesn't matter how long you've been walking with God, there will always be things in your flesh and situations to deal with, but when you do it God's way and walk in the fruit, you won't get frustrated.

It's never too late in your Christian walk to begin growing your fruit. The Bible gives us a reminder of this in the parable about the fig tree.

Luke 13:6-9

6 He spake also this parable; A certain man had a fig tree planted in his vineyard; and he came and sought fruit thereon, and found none.

7 Then said he unto the dresser of his vineyard, Behold, these three years I come seeking fruit on this fig tree, and find none: cut it down; why cumbereth it the ground?

8 And he answering said unto him, Lord, let it alone this year also, till I shall dig about it, and dung it:

9 And if it bear fruit, well: and if not, then after that thou shalt cut it down.

This fruit tree, planted in a vineyard, had never produced any figs (fruit), so the owner ordered it to be cut down. The worker asked the owner to give the tree one more chance to produce figs, to let him watch over it and help it grow by digging around the plant and fertilizing it. This parable shows the mercy and goodness of God because the owner gave this plant another chance.

There are times when we all need another chance. This is a good prayer to say for someone who is not doing what they should, and it's also good to pray for ourselves. God said that when no fruit is produced, He will cut it off (John 15:2), so you can ask the Lord for another chance for that person or yourself, like the worker did with the fig tree. When you ask with all our heart and really mean it, the mercy of God will be there for you; but then, it's up to you to start fertilizing and grow in the things of God. If you pray that for someone else, you can also put some fertilizer on them by speaking and encouraging them with the Word of God.

You can do it! You can walk in the fruit! Don't ever say, "There's no way I'm ever going to be able to produce this fruit." Instead, be like that fig tree and get the fertilizer out, which is the Word of God; then, ask the Lord to help you, and start walking in the fruit one day at a time, or one hour at a time, or one minute at a time if that's what it takes. If you still don't see any fruit being produced in your life, ask God, "Why am I not producing that fruit?" and then listen for His answer.

For example, if someone is having a hard time being faithful (on time, fulfilling what they say they will do), they can pray, "Lord, you're faithful and you live in me; teach me to be faithful like you, and if there's something I need to change, I ask you, Holy Ghost, to show me because I want to be faithful." This is a good place to begin. God will help us when we ask and then, things will change when we do what He shows us to do.

We all have certain tendencies and learned behaviors that come from our family and environment, but it's still just our flesh and fallen nature acting out. The cure for that is to learn about the fruit and let God help us walk in it. Someone who is not mature in a particular fruit, doesn't always mean they're refusing to walk in it. It could be this person stays so busy that they haven't taken the time to learn about that fruit and what is needed to grow it. God is ready to help them, but this person must come to Him and ask, so God can show them how to better walk in that fruit.

It's important to begin walking in this fruit so it will push out the things in your flesh that you have been dealing with. And if you're already walking in the fruit, it's important to continue to walk in it and let it grow. This is something we all have to work on continually. John 15:5 says, "He's the vine, we're the branches," so let God help you. Psalm 33:11 says, "His counsel and Word will stand forever," so we need to stay connected to Him to receive the help we need to bear much fruit.

OVERVIEW OF WHICH FRUITS WILL TAKE CARE OF WHAT WORKS OF THE FLESH

LOVE   *Adultery, Fornication, Hatred, Emulations, Strife*

JOY   *Witchcraft, Wrath, Drunkenness*

PEACE   *Lasciviousness, Strife, Envyings, Revellings*

LONGSUFFERING   *Hatred, Wrath, Seditions*

GENTLENESS   *Variance, Emulations, Heresies*

GOODNESS   *Adultery, Uncleanness, Strife, Heresies*

FAITH (FAITHFULNESS)   *Adultery, Idolatry, Seditions*

MEEKNESS   *Lasciviousness, Hatred, Variance, Wrath, Strife*

TEMPERANCE   *Uncleanness, Lasciviousness, Witchcraft*

In the next three chapters, we will look at each fruit of the Spirit and the works of the flesh it will stop. Each work of the flesh can be overcome by one or more of these fruits in operation. By walking in this fruit, it will keep all the works of the flesh under.

Chapter
Eight
Questions

1. Can you name the nine fruits of the Spirit?

2. What must we do to become strong trees that bear fruit? How do we water our tree?

3. God is pleased with trees that produce fruit. What are some things you can do in your life to ensure that more fruit is being produced?

4. What is the difference between the gifts of the Spirit and the fruits of the Spirit?

5. How can we know if we are walking in the flesh or the fruits of the Spirit?

6. When someone bumps into you, what should come out of you?

Chapter
Eight
Confessions

✳   **I will flee from all lusts and keep my heart pure.
(2 Timothy 2:22)**

✳   **I will not walk in the counsel of the ungodly, I will not
get advice from sinners, and I will not sit in the seat of
the scornful; but I will delight in the Lord, meditate on
His Word, and be like a tree planted by the rivers of
living water. (Psalm 1:1-3)**

✳   **I will not be deceived by hanging with those who
practice evil because evil will cause corruption in me.
(1 Corinthians 15:33)**

✳   **The Lord will perfect all that concerns me.
(Psalm 138:8)**

✳   **I will be a follower of God and His Word because I am
His child. (Ephesians 5:1)**

chapter 9: fruit of the spirit
love, joy, peace

FRUIT OF LOVE

Love, which in the Greek is "agape" (Strong's G26), is the first fruit listed in Galatians 5:22. It is the God kind of love. It is the highest and best love. It is caring for and seeking the highest good for another person without motive or expecting gain. Ephesians 4:1-2 (NASB) says we are to walk in a manner worthy of the calling with which we have been called, with all humility and gentleness, with patience, showing tolerance for one another in love.

I don't think it's a coincidence that love is the first of the fruit of the Spirit mentioned in Galatians 5:22. What was written down in the Bible by holy men of old, as they were moved by the Spirit of God, was how God wanted it to be. I believe love is listed first because it is the biggest. 1 Corinthians 13:13 says that of faith, hope, and love, the greatest of these is love. God knew we would need love as our foundation. Love is where all the fruits begin.

Love is the greatest commandment. We are to love the Lord, our God, with all our heart, soul, and mind, and we are to love our neighbor as we love ourselves (Matthew 22:37-39). Who is our neighbor? Everybody, whether they're born again or not.

How can we know when we are walking in agape love? 1 Corinthians 13 answers that question and gives us God's roadmap to follow.

> **1 Corinthians 13:4-8 (AMPC)**
>
> 4 Love endures long and is patient and kind; love never is envious nor boils over with jealousy, is not boastful or vainglorious, does not display itself haughtily.
>
> 5 It is not conceited (arrogant and inflated with pride); it is not rude (unmannerly) and does not act unbecomingly. Love (God's love in us) does not insist on its own rights or its own way, for it is not self-seeking; it is not touchy or fretful or resentful; it takes no account of the evil done to it [it pays no attention to a suffered wrong].
>
> 6 It does not rejoice at injustice and unrighteousness, but rejoices when right and truth prevail.
>
> 7 Love bears up under anything and everything that comes, is ever ready to believe the best of every person, its hopes are fadeless under all circumstances, and it endures everything [without weakening].
>
> 8 Love never fails [never fades out or becomes obsolete or comes to an end].

Many call this the "Love Chapter" because it gives a clear definition of exactly what agape love is and what it is not.

- Love endures long. How long? Longer than you think.

- Love is patient and kind. It shows care and understanding.

- Love is never envious or jealous. It rejoices with those who have been blessed.

- Love does not boast or seek glory, nor is it haughty or conceited. It's not about telling everybody how great we are, but how great our God is.

- Love is not rude. It's being polite and nice to others. Those justifying their wrong behavior by saying it's just part of their personality or culture are just making excuses so they can act out. A believer who says, "I've just got to speak my mind," needs to learn to keep their mind quiet because there is no excuse for being rude.

- Love does not act unbecomingly. It's imitating Jesus and not acting out.

- Love is not self-seeking, insisting on its own rights or its own way. It prefers others.

- Love is not touchy, fretful, or resentful. It does not make it all about us.

- Love does not keep track of wrongs done. It doesn't hold unforgiveness or meditate on the wrong done to it, hoping the other person gets theirs. We are to forgive and let it go just like God has forgiven us (Ephesians 4:32).

- Love does not rejoice at injustice but rejoices when right and truth prevail. It's not being happy when someone gets what's coming to them because, thank God, I'm sure glad I didn't get what was coming to me.

- Love is ever ready to believe the best of every person. It doesn't believe the worst.

- Love bears all. It goes the extra mile with others and even further.

- Love never gives up. It never let's go.

- Love believes the best of others. It looks for the good in everybody.

- Love never fails. It always works when we walk in it and don't stop.

If we will walk in love as our foundation, it will push away the works of the flesh.

Every believer can walk in love because this agape love in us is not a feeling. It's a choice. We can choose to prefer others. The more we choose to walk in love, the more love we will have.

Another way we can walk in love is by serving one another.

Galatians 5:13-14

13 For, brethren, ye have been called unto liberty; only use not liberty for an occasion to the flesh, but by love serve one another.

14 For all the law is fulfilled in one word, even in this; Thou shalt love thy neighbour as thyself.

There are so many opportunities for a person to serve others, both in their local church and in their community. Step out in love and find your place to serve.

We all have the love of God in us.

Romans 5:5 **... God's love has been poured out in our hearts through the Holy Spirit Who has been given to us.**

God's love has been given to every born-again believer but walking in it is up to us. We all have to learn and grow in our love walk by choosing to love others every day. I know a lot of Christians who don't walk in love. Some just refuse to while others don't know how because they don't have enough Word in them.

Christians who don't walk in love give the body of Christ a bad name and that is why so many people call us hypocrites. We must demonstrate our love to everybody, so they too will see how much God loves them. Again, it is a growth process. Those who walk in love started out by preferring others and following the guidelines in 1 Corinthians 13; then, as they obeyed the Word and followed the leadings of the Holy Spirit, their love got bigger and bigger. This is how all the fruits in a believer's life grow; and the more they grow, the more we can walk in them on a consistent basis.

1 John 4:16 **And we have known and believed the love that God hath to us. God is love; and he that dwelleth in love dwelleth in God, and God in him.**

This says that God is love and to dwell in Him, we must dwell in love. So, if we're not walking in love, we're not really dwelling in God. Amos 3:3 says, "How can two walk together unless they agree?" That's why God has put His love in us, so we can walk with Him. His love is in you and is for you, and it should be coming out of you to others because it's the love, compassion, and goodness of God that brings people to repentance (Romans 2:4).

Why do some people have trouble showing love?

I've found that many who struggle with loving others don't really love themselves. The reason some people can be so mean and find fault with everybody else is because they're always finding fault with themselves. Some husbands can't love their wife like Christ loves the church because they have something in their soul that they need to let God heal before they can love their wife and family as they should.

Not loving ourselves isn't just a woman problem, it's a human problem. For us to love ourselves so we can love others, we have to see ourselves in Christ because in Him we are complete; we are accepted.

Colossians 2:10 **And ye are complete in him, which is the head of all principality and power:**

Ephesians 1:6 **We are accepted in the beloved [Jesus].**

Let's look at Galatians 5:14-15 in the Amplified Classic.

Galatians 5:14-15 (AMPC)

14 For the whole Law [concerning human relationships] is complied with in the one precept, You shall love your neighbor as [you do] yourself.

> **15 But if you bite and devour one another [in partisan strife], be careful that you [and your whole fellowship] are not consumed by one another.**

This says we are not to use the freedom God has given us as an excuse to bite and devour others, and we certainly see a lot of that happening today. When we participate in this kind of behavior, we're not walking in love.

The devil knows if he can get us out of love, he can defeat us because when we're not walking in love, it opens us up to everything the enemy has and wants to do; but if we will continue to walk in the fruit of love, no matter what is happening, we will win every time.

Part of continually walking in love is being careful what you hear. If what a preacher says sets you out to war against someone, or if listening to a message riles you up in a bad way, you should stop listening to them because love has no ill will toward its neighbor. We do not wrestle against flesh and blood (Ephesians 6:12). We stand strong against the enemy by walking in love with others because love never fails, never comes to an end, and will always prevail.

I've experienced times when I've had to walk in "much" love. Recently, I was at a store, and somebody yelled at me and then, somebody butted in front of me in line. I just stood there, minding my own business. I could see on this lady's face standing near me that she was wondering what I was going to do about it. I just said, "I've got bigger things to do than to get mad at this man. If anybody wants to butt in front of me, go ahead. I'm just going to stand here and wait my turn." I then went to get something to eat, and this young lady got so sassy with me for no reason, so what did I do? I didn't act out, which is what my flesh wanted to do. Instead, I ate my meal and at the end, I just said, "Thank you," and gave her a big tip. Did she deserve that? No, but love gives even when a person doesn't deserve it. I'm sharing this with you because I want you to know that I don't just teach this, I have to walk in love too, and it's not always easy.

We must choose to put on love. Colossians 3:14 says, "And above all these things put on charity [agape love], which is the bond of perfectness." We put it on by getting the Word in us and letting it grow the fruit of love in us, so we can walk it out. God is love, so the Word of God is love that will produce more love in us. The more we walk in agape love, the more His love will abound in us and come out of us to others.

It's so important for the body of Christ to be taught about God's love on a regular basis, so they can be helped and encouraged to grow in their love walk. This would definitely stop a lot of people from acting the way they do and from being fooled by what the world says love is supposed to be. God's love is not lust. It is always giving the best to those around us.

A person who walks in love is a person who walks in victory. How I respond to others should never be based on circumstances. It should always be based on what the Word says.

When I get squeezed, it's agape love that is coming out of me, whether I'm talking, writing, or posting. The same should be said of you.

We all want to see the signs, wonders, and miracles of God happening today, but if we have no love, the Word says...

> ## 1 Corinthians 13:1-3 (NIV)
>
> **¹If I speak in the tongues of men or of angels, <u>but do not have love, I am only a resounding gong or a clanging cymbal</u>.**
>
> **² If I have the gift of prophecy and can fathom all mysteries and all knowledge, and if I have a faith that can move mountains, <u>but do not have love, I am nothing</u>.**
>
> **³ If I give all I possess to the poor and give over my body to hardship that I may boast, but <u>do not have love, I gain nothing</u>.**

It says without love,

- **we are only a clanging cymbal.**
- **we are nothing.**
- **we gain nothing.**

The Amplified Classic says we are "a useless nobody."

I'm so grateful that my wife, Rhonda, has received such a great revelation of God's love because it has helped me grow so much in this fruit. I don't know if I'd be as strong as I am today if it wasn't for my love walk because I've had a lot of opportunities to get mad at a whole lot of people.

I am so thankful to God that He has taught me what to sow and what not to sow. Galatians 6:7 says, "Whatever a man sows, he shall reap." I plan on sowing love because I want to receive love. I don't plan on sowing judgment because I don't want to receive judgement. It matters what we sow. We need to sow what we want to receive!

Some people will come and want to talk about the church they left and how awful it was, but my wife and I won't do it. You cannot get us to talk bad about a minister. Now, we will talk with them about restoration, how great God is, the healing power of God, but we will not talk negatively about others because we're not going to sow that. We're going to stay in love, and we'll do our best to get them back in love, too. We're not ignoring the facts of what has happened or is happening, but our talking about it won't do anything but get us out of love. Our confession should be, "I'm walking in love, and I will not take offense." If you really believe that, say it and do it, so you can continue to walk in love and see your life change for the better.

Below is a good prayer we can pray for others and also pray for ourselves when it comes to walking in love.

Ephesians 3:14-19

14 For this cause I bow my knees unto the Father of our Lord Jesus Christ,

15 Of whom the whole family in heaven and earth is named,

16 That he would grant you, according to the riches of his glory, to be strengthened with might by his Spirit in the inner man;

17 That Christ may dwell in your hearts by faith; that ye, being rooted and grounded in love,

18 May be able to comprehend with all saints what is the breadth, and length, and depth, and height;

19 <u>And to know the love of Christ, which passeth knowledge, that ye might be filled with all the fulness of God</u>.

It's knowing the love of God that will lead us into the fullness of God. We are the elect (chosen) of God, holy, and beloved. That's who we are. We need to grow in this abounding love and walk in it because it is our foundation that enables us to walk in all the other fruits of the Spirit.

AGAPE LOVE WILL TAKE CARE OF THE FOLLOWING:

ADULTERY AND FORNICATION:

These works of the flesh are well known; they involve sex outside of marriage. Any sex that is not a husband with his wife or a wife with her husband, is sin. This area of sin is very common for those who are not born again but should not be happening within those in the Body of Christ. Love, agape love, the fruit we are talking about, will remove this sin, this work of the flesh from our lives. How? When we walk in this God kind of love, we will not let our flesh insist on its own rights. This fruit of love is not self-seeking. When this fruit is fully grown in our life, we will consider our spouse before we consider our fleshly wants or needs. It will also consider our love for God and His love for us, and we will not want to displease our Father because He is a jealous God, even over our bodies. Also, as a believer who walks in love, we would not even want to hurt someone who is not our spouse by getting them entangled in sin. When the fruit of love is working in us, it will drive out the desire to yield to this sensual appetite that would cause us to yield to fornication or adultery. Love is the greatest, so this fruit will drive out one of the most intense desires of our flesh. The more we grow the fruit of love in our lives, by meditating on it, gaining knowledge of it, the less our flesh will be in charge. It seems to me that if we come to a full knowledge of God's love in us, it will push out the desire of sexual sin. Love will stop adultery and fornication!

HATRED:

People who yield to the work of the flesh known as hatred hold grudges and harbor deep resentments with roots of bitterness. You can have hatred against an individual or even against an entire people group. The cure is still the same, the love of God. The love of God in us is not rude or unmannerly and does not act unbecomingly. When you have the love of God, this amazing fruit, working in you to full capacity, you will not hate, despise, reject, or even talk bad about a person or a group of people. The love of God is ever ready to believe the best of everyone. It is able to cause us to forgive people, not based on feelings we have towards them but based only on the love of God that we are walking in. This love never fails or comes to end and so, when hatred tries to pop up in our lives, this agape love will displace it. If hatred ever tries to get a root in you, dig deeper into the subject of love and meditate on the scriptures we have covered so that God's love will prevail and the nasty, fleshly desire to hate will have to leave. I have watched this with my own eyes. Someone on my staff was at a gathering held by a member of our church, whose husband did not attend our church. When my staff member went to shake the husband's hand, he turned his back to her. It was hard to watch, but she handled it very well but then, wow! This man later received Jesus in his heart and was born again. I watched an interaction they had years after their first encounter, but this time, this man, who was now a child of God, didn't just shake her hand, he hugged her. The love of God in us changes everything. If we want to fix all the hatred in the earth, it will not be through education or by protesting, it will be by the new birth and the love of God shed abroad in our hearts. Love will get rid of hatred!

EMULATIONS:

What are emulations? It is to burn with jealousy. This person desires to be superior in every situation and often creates a rivalry and will put other people down to gain the ascendant position they desire. They do whatever it takes to get what they want, no matter who it hurts. This should not be a part of the born-again believer. The love of God, the agape in you will not let you do this to people. The love of God in us, according to I Corinthians 13:4, never boils over with jealousy; it is not boastful, vainglorious, or haughty. All these feelings are part of someone who displays emulations. Love, God's love in us, is not self-seeking, but someone who walks in the work of the flesh called emulations, is definitely self-seeking. The cure for emulations is the love of God. Grow this fruit, and this work of the flesh will have no chance to remain in your life. This love will push emulations out!

STRIFE:

When strife is present in someone's life, there is contention, conflict, and discord. The Word clearly says that where there is strife and envy, there is every evil work (James 3:16). This seems to be telling us that these two, strife and envy, may be the root of all the works of the flesh because where they are manifested, every evil work is manifested. We should not let any works of the flesh be a part of our life, especially strife. So, if I will deal with strife by growing in love, maybe dealing with the rest of the works of the flesh will get a little easier. Again, we are talking about how the fruit of love will remove this heinous work of the flesh.

The love of God in us is not touchy or resentful, and someone who is operating in strife, is definitely touchy and resentful. Agape will push these out, so we will not be touchy or resentful and will not operate in this fleshly thing called strife. Someone who creates and walks in strife doesn't really care about the truth, which is totally opposite of someone who walks in love. Remember, love rejoices when right and truth prevail. One of the great things about this fruit of love is that it bears up under anything and everything that comes our way. It is a foundation, which is the opposite of someone in strife who always wants to tear away at the foundation of things. They like things to be in an uproar all the time because they love the drama. Love believes the best of everyone, and strife believes the worst of everyone.

Strife is something that is so predominant in our society. People's opinions, their harshness, their disdain for others, will try to get on you because the flesh loves strife, and the devil knows it. The devil wants this work of the flesh operating in our lives because it opens the door for him to bring every evil work. I remember when we were remodeling our first church building, our volunteers were getting tired from working so many late nights and became very snappy with each other, so one of our church members posted the love chapter (1 Corinthians 13:4-7, AMPC) in every area where work was being done. The volunteers started quoting these verses to each other, which got them back into walking in love again, so they could get the job done. In whatever we do, even in doing the work of God, we are to keep ourselves in check, so we can continue to walk in love with everyone. So, meditate on love so you can grow in the love of God and then, strife will not have a chance to develop or stay in your life. Love will completely drive out strife!

FRUIT OF JOY

The second fruit is joy which in the Greek is "chara" (Strong's G5479), and it means the exultation of spirit that comes from the presence of God. Rick Renner defines it as "a Spirit-given expression that flourishes best when times are strenuous and daunting and tough". So, God is telling us that in these strenuous, daunting, and tough times, we are to rejoice; and we all can by choosing to walk in the joy He has placed within our born-again spirit.

I've heard people say, "If mama ain't happy, ain't nobody happy." I say that mama just needs to get born again and filled with the Holy Ghost, then get in the Word, and grow in the fruit of joy because we can't be playing this "mama ain't happy" game and letting it be an excuse for mama to get her way.

We are to let this joy in us rise up.

Jeremiah 15:16 Thy words were found, and I did eat them; and thy word was unto me the joy and rejoicing of mine heart...

Colossians 1:11 Strengthened with all might, according to his glorious power, unto all patience and longsuffering with joyfulness [chara].

It's the Word of God and the Holy Ghost that strengthens us with chara (joy). The more I get into the Word, the more I pray and get in the spirit, the more the fruit of joy will start displaying itself in my life.

1 John 1:4 And these things write we unto you, that your joy may be full.

Reading the Word of God, and taking it in, will bring us joy. So, when God's Word is big on the inside of you, you ought to do some rejoicing. You should have some joy about you.

The more joy you have, the more unshakable you will be and, like Paul, can say, "None of these things move me," (Acts 20:24). You can continue to walk in joy because you know when a bad situation comes, the Lord is going to work it out.

There are so many people today, including ministers and preachers, who can get so demanding, and it's not godly. It's devilish and sensual, thinking everyone should treat them special. I remember, some years ago, my wife and I were at a restaurant that had just opened up. There was a bunch of teenagers working there, and it was a mess because they had no direction. The old McDonald's manager in me wanted to get up, put an apron on, and help them because nobody seemed to be in charge, and the customers were yelling about not having their food. I walked up to one of the teenage girls working there just to calm her down because she looked like she was about to cry. I said to her, "I'm sorry all these people are getting so mad, but it's going to be okay. This is only your job for now, so hang in there and smile." She looked at me and did smile and then, she went to work on getting my order out. I didn't ask for that favor. I just wanted to encourage her, but God was working it out for me because I was walking in the fruit of joy with her. She was so grateful that someone was being nice that she got our food out right away.

It's so important to walk in the fruit of joy. We have this joy in us that we can give to others, and other people need to receive the joy we have. Ask the Lord to help you, to give you more revelation concerning joy, so you can walk in it, especially in this squirrely world we live in. Joy is contagious; so, when you walk in joy, it will get off on those around you.

When we walk in joy, it will bring glory to God by showing people we serve a God of joy.

> **2 Corinthians 7:4** Great is my boldness of speech toward you, great is my glorying of you: I am filled with comfort, I am exceeding joyful in all our tribulation.

Even in tribulation and trials, you can be joyful knowing God will provide you a way out. You can't always control what comes at you, but you can control how you respond to it, so respond with joy, knowing God will lead you to victory.

> **James 1:2** My brethren, count it all joy when ye fall into divers temptation.

Even when temptations come, you can be joyful. That means when the devil comes with something, or our flesh wants to get out of control, we can still be joyful because we know we can resist whatever it is. It is in joy that we will reap the answer and the victory.

So, when someone bumps into you, what do they get? First and foremost, they should get agape love followed by joy. Having joy means putting a smile on your face instead of looking like you've been sucking on lemons. There are so many people today that look so sad and want everybody else to be sad with them; but we can't do that because, as believers, we have traded in our tears and sorrow, so we can reap in joy (Psalm 126:5). I choose joy!

JOY WILL TAKE CARE OF THE FOLLOWING:

WITCHCRAFT:

This is the use of medicine to escape, especially when someone has a broken heart, or they feel destroyed in their soul. They have a lot of pain, and they are desperately trying to medicate it. We know that doesn't work, but our flesh likes it, craves it, and wants us to continue doing it, even as a believer. The fruit of joy will push this work of the flesh right out of your life. When we get the Word of God in us and find His fullness of joy, our lives will completely change. When we lean into joy, it will cause our broken heart to be healed and the need to self-medicate will go away. We will no longer find ourselves relying on medication or illegal drugs to have the joy of the Lord, which is our strength. The addictions that people have can be very difficult in the natural to get over. Once you are born again, this joy is now on the inside of you, and you can learn to tap into it instead of tapping into drugs or alcohol to escape. Instead, you can live in the moment with joy. Whether that moment is good or filled with challenges, it won't matter because the joy of God will be working in you. With joy, you can sing on purpose, and I believe you can laugh on purpose. Laughter is an expression of joy, so express that fruit of your born-again spirit on a regular basis, and just laugh! People might even think you are a little crazy. They might even ask you, "What are you doing?". Just tell them, "I am expressing my joy; it's a fruit of my born-again spirit, and you should join me!" Joy will absolutely stop the work of the flesh called witchcraft!

WRATH:

When you have wrath actively working in your flesh, you are one situation away from blowing up like a volcano. Why is this person like this? It seems to be just an overall unhappiness. They just don't seem to like life, feel mistreated, underappreciated, and are very much self-focused. No one seems to be able to do anything right. They never seem to be happy with anything. They might consider themselves perfectionist and even feel like nobody around them seems to know how to do anything right. Truthfully, they are just people who need the Lord, or if they are already born again, they need to get full of joy. It seemed to me that joy is the answer for this work of the flesh because these people who are unhappy, tend to make everyone around them unhappy, or at the least, nervous, because you never know when they are going to explode. If this person would get into the Word and let joy come to them, it would remove the anxiety in their life and their need to explode on people. They would realize that by putting their trust in God, they can now relax. When you know He will take care of you and your problems, joy comes. Where there is joy there is no wrath. Joy will absolutely push out wrath!

DRUNKENNESS:

Like witchcraft, I think drunkenness is used by people who don't want to deal with life's problems. People who regularly get drunk or high are trying to get over something. Many people start drinking or taking drugs at a young age to fit in and then, with some, it starts a habit or an addiction. While people get drunk for various reasons, it seems like most continue to do it just to deal with the pain of life. What is the answer? The joy of the Lord. There will be no need to get drunk with wine when you can get "drunk" (saturated) with the Spirit of the living God. When you get full of joy, you are full of God. When you laugh with the joy of the Lord, your troubles seem to melt away. Joy is a fruit. Joy is an expression. Joy is powerful. Being drunk with wine won't solve anything. Instead, it will cause a lot of problems and a lot of loss in your life, but being full of joy will cause you to excel in this life because joy is a manifestation of your faith. 1 Peter 1:8 (TPT) "…but through believing in him you are saturated with an ecstatic joy, indescribably sublime and immersed in glory." What a way to live! Get full of the joy of the Lord. Joy will absolutely get rid of drunkenness!

FRUIT OF PEACE

The third fruit is peace which in the Greek is "eirene" (Strong's G1515). This word is similar to the Hebrew word "shalom." According to Rick Renner, it expresses the idea of "wholeness, completeness, tranquility of the soul that is not affected by circumstances or outward pressure". It's having order in the place of chaos, a calm and inner stability that results in a peaceful manner without trauma.

It's interesting that love, joy, and peace are the first three fruits of the spirit listed and the ones most people know. I think they come first because they're the most predominant. The other six fruits are also important for us to walk in, but it seems that these first three help us to walk in the other six.

We all need peace and should teach our children about the fruit of peace. We should all confess on a regular basis, "I have great peace and undisturbed composure."

Peace can also be a weapon. Jesus used peace to quiet the storm. Jesus said, "Peace be still," and the winds were calm (Mark 4:39). So, peace is not only a weapon, but it's also a fruit that comes from our born-again spirit that we can walk in every day.

> **John 14:27** Peace I leave with you, my peace I give unto you: not as the world giveth, give I unto you. Let not your heart be troubled, neither let it be afraid.

This is not the same peace that the world has because their peace only happens when everything around them is okay. This peace Jesus gave us will keep us in peace whether everything around us is okay or not. It is the same peace that Jesus Himself walked in while He was on the Earth.

Our world is not at peace, and that's why everyone seems to get irritated and agitated so easily, and they want everyone else to be irritated and agitated with them. If you don't wallow with them, they think you don't care; but we can still care without going there with them because acting that way won't help the situation. As Christians, we are to stick with the Word and walk in peace, so we can change things for ourselves and help others, who have no peace, change things too. With God's peace, my heart will not be troubled or afraid because peace will kick out all fear. Fear is the absence of peace.

Ephesians 4:3 **Endeavouring to keep the unity of the Spirit in the bond of peace.**

Peace keeps us in unity with God and that is so important if we want to walk in His blessings.

Romans 8:6 **For to be carnally minded is death; but to be spiritually minded is life and peace.**

So, you could say that someone who is carnally minded, does not have life or peace. The only way to stop walking carnally is to renew your mind with the Word of God, to read, study, and meditate on it. Confess scriptures concerning peace, so His peace will get bigger inside you and then, you can sow peace to others.

Philippians 4:7 **And the peace of God, which passeth all understanding, shall keep your hearts and minds through Christ Jesus.**

The Weymouth translation says that the peace of God will be a "garrison to guard your heart and mind." Thank God for His peace.

Colossians 3:15 **And let the peace of God rule [umpire] in your hearts, to the which also ye are called in one body; and be ye thankful.**

One of the things my wife and I started doing when we first began pastoring, was to carry peace wherever we went to minister. In tough situations, it was difficult to know what to say, and also difficult for those we were helping to make decisions, especially if there was confusion, screaming, and everybody was a mess around them. When we got there, we would always loose the peace of God in the room by faith and expect it to manifest. It helped so much because God's peace would push out the chaos.

> **James 3:18** **And the fruit of righteousness is sown in peace of them that make peace.**

This says we are to be the peacemaker and not the troublemaker. This doesn't mean we let people run over us. Jesus is the Prince of peace, and He never got run over. Why? Because He is also the lion of the Tribe of Judah and Proverbs 28:1 says, "We are to be bold as a lion." When we walk in peace, we won't get run over because peace will be our weapon to calm the storms.

So, when someone bumps into you, what do they get? Agape love should come out of you followed by joy and then, peace.

PEACE WILL TAKE CARE OF THE FOLLOWING:

LASCIVIOUSNESS:

Someone who displays this work of the flesh has extreme indulgences, which may manifest in overeating, overspending, and a life that is just totally out of control. When you deal with this operation of the flesh, there is no restraint. You don't care what anyone thinks. If you want it, you are going to get it, do it, and have it, no matter the consequence. There is no moderation in your life; a little dab of anything will not do. You want it all how and when you want it. What is absent in this person's life? Peace. Their mind is undisciplined; they let it think on whatever it wants and then, they act on it. When there is peace in a person's life, it is because they have kept their mind on the Lord. When Jesus is your peace, when you walk in the peace that He left you, then you will stabilize, and you will moderate. You will become a person full of peace, and it will drive out lasciviousness. You can even speak peace to your flesh. When it wants to do something that it shouldn't, like overeat, or overspend, you can talk to it, and tell it to be still, just like Jesus talked to the storm. Peace will always take care of lasciviousness!

STRIFE:

When we walk in peace, we will not let conflict, discord, or quarrels happen. When I was an accountant in Indianapolis, I began to practice having a "no strife zone." This was my first job out of college, and although I appreciated the work ethics my boss taught me, she was tough and had a mouth on her that could cuss in rhyme. She scared all the employees, including me. When someone made a mistake, she would get right in their face; but I decided when it came to my work area, it would be a place of peace. I would play Christian music softly and pray in a whisper as I worked. It took some time, but I started noticing that when my boss came near my area, she would catch herself cussing and would stop. However, this one day, she got so mad that she really lost it. She came to my desk and started yelling and cussing at me. Looking back, I know it was the Holy Ghost and the peace that I walked in that caused me to stand up and firmly say to her, "Don't you ever cuss at me again," and then I told her to leave my area until she could talk respectfully to me, and she did. I didn't realize it then, but I had used God's peace as a weapon to calm the storm that was happening at my desk, and it worked! I was so surprised by what I had done that I started packing because I just knew it was all over and she would fire me. It ended up that I didn't get fired and how she talked to me after that got better. In fact, before I left for Bible school, she was back in church. I really loved her, but I sure didn't love her mouth.

Having a "no strife zone" at my accounting job really made a difference. We all need to decide that we will not enter into strife no matter what. Does that mean you can do what I did to your boss? Only if the Holy Ghost rises up in you to do it. Otherwise, you just might get fired. Just stay calm and at peace and follow the leadings of the Holy Ghost. When we choose not to participate in strife, we are protecting our fruit tree from being corrupted, so our fruit will continue to grow. We are also inviting God into the situation. Peace will always drive out strife.

ENVYINGS:

Remember, where there is strife and envy, there is every evil work. So, envy is a big issue because if we have it, we are opening the door to every evil work. A person who deals with envy resents another's blessing so much that they attempt to take that blessing away. It is not the same as jealousy which is fear of losing something to someone. This one seems so vile, because not only do you resent the person, but you also, literally, want and are willing to take away their blessing. When you feel like you should have something that someone else has, you have got to get rid of the envy by getting into a place of peace, so that you don't and won't want to take what they have. Meditate on peace and when you do, you will realize that God can bless you with the same or better. Peace is so important in this area, just like the Apostle Paul who said that it didn't matter where he was or what he had, he learned to be content or at peace in every situation. When you have this fruit called peace working, you will be satisfied, and it won't take something to satisfy you because your peace comes from within. So, keep your mind on the Lord and He will keep you in perfect peace. This peace will always get rid of all envy.

REVELLINGS:

As a reminder, when someone deals with this work of the flesh, they always needs to be entertained. They can't sit still. They need noise. They need activity. Why is that? It's because they don't want to be alone with their own thoughts. When your life is like this, and you are dominated by this work of the flesh, there is no silence, no stability, and no rest. Your flesh will keep you so busy that you don't have to deal with the problems of your soul; but when someone gets born again, the Prince of Peace moves in. When a believer begins to study the Word of God, peace begins to manifest because their mind becomes stayed on Him. When we find out that Jesus left us His peace, and we walk in the fruit of peace, all this need for activity will cease. We won't need things to constantly fill up our lives. We will be ok, just us and the Lord. Then, the activities we do will be enjoyable because we are not doing them to fill a void in our life to appease our flesh, but we are doing them because we want to enjoy this good life God has given us. Peace will always take care of revellings.

QUICK VIEW OF THE FRUITS OF LOVE, JOY, AND PEACE AND WHICH WORKS OF THE FLESH THEY WILL KEEP UNDER:

	LOVE	JOY	PEACE
ADULTERY	X		
FORNICATION	X		
UNCLEANNESS			
LASCIVIOUSNESS			X
IDOLATRY			
WITCHCRAFT		X	
HATRED	X		
VARIANCE			
EMULATIONS	X		
WRATH		X	
STRIFE	X		X
SEDITIONS			
HERESIES			
ENVYINGS			X
DRUNKENNESS		X	
REVELLINGS			X

Chapter Nine Questions

1. In your own words, explain the fruit of the Agape love of God. What does it look like when it is in operation in your life?

2. Take one of the works of the flesh that love displaces and explain how you can implement this in your own life with your own struggles.

3. In your own words, explain the fruit of joy. What does that look like when it is operating in your life?

4. Take one of the works of the flesh that joy displaces and explain how you can implement this in your own life with your own struggles.

5. In your own words, explain the fruit of peace. What does the peace of God look like when it is operating in your life?

6. Take one of the works of the flesh that peace displaces and explain how you can implement this in your own life with your own struggles.

Chapter
Nine
Confessions

The Fruit of Love:

✻   I will let all I do be done in love. (1 Corinthians 16:14)

✻   I will put on love which will produce perfect harmony. (Colossians 3:14)

✻   I will love others because God is love. (1 John 4:8)

✻   I will walk in love because perfect love casts out fear. (1John 4:18)

✻   I will love others because God first loved me. (1 John 4:19)

Chapter
Nine
Confessions

The Fruit of Joy:

✻   **I choose joy because a merry heart does good like a medicine.** (Proverbs 17:22)

✻   **The joy of the Lord is my strength.** (Nehemiah 8:10)

✻   **I will spend time with God because in His presence is fullness of joy.** (Psalm 16:11)

✻   **I have joy because I delight myself in the Lord.** (Psalm 37:4)

✻   **I will be joyful always because this is God's will for me.** (1 Thessalonians 5:16-18)

Chapter Nine Confessions

The Fruit of Peace:

✻ Because I keep my eyes on Jesus, He will keep me in perfect peace. (Isaiah 26:3)

✻ Because I love your Word, I walk in peace and do not stumble. (Psalm 119:165)

✻ God is not the author of confusion but of peace, so I will walk in peace. (1 Corinthians 14:33)

✻ I will seek peace and pursue it. (1 Peter 3:11)

✻ I walk in the same peace that Jesus did, so I will not be troubled or afraid. (John 14:27)

chapter 10: fruit of the spirit
longsuffering, gentleness, goodness

FRUIT OF LONGSUFFERING

Longsuffering in the Greek is "makrothumia" (Strong's G3115), which means "patient restraint, being slow to anger or despair, patient, bearing patiently with the frailties and the provocations of others, bearing up also through all the troubles and difficulties of life without murmuring or complaining".

I know some people who like to make those around them suffer long by their complaining, and this fruit will help you deal with that by not joining in with what they are doing. It will give you patience with people like that without murmuring and complaining with them. Patience is needed as we come to understand that no one is perfect or has it all together all the time.

The fruit of patience is one that I'm not naturally good at. My flesh wants to tell somebody one time only to do this or that, and it doesn't like waiting for it to get done. I have to, on purpose, choose to walk in this fruit every day; and the more I do, the more it grows in me, and the more patience I have with others. We should all walk in patience because God is patient (longsuffering) with us.

I've heard people say, "Well, don't pray for patience because that's when the Lord will give you something to be patient about." The Lord doesn't do that. The devil is the one who brings afflictions and troubles. We don't have to pray for patience because this longsuffering fruit is already in us, but we must choose to walk in it no matter what is happening around us.

So, when someone bumps into us, what do they get? They should get love, followed by joy, and peace, and then, longsuffering. When something is going on, we should be the one in the room displaying patience (longsuffering).

LONGSUFFERING WILL TAKE CARE OF THE FOLLOWING:

HATRED:

When we walk in longsuffering (patience), we won't hold a grudge or deep resentment against others. We won't get down in the mud with those who come against us, nor will we say mean things about them. Walking in hatred will reap us the whirlwind of that because it opens the door for the devil to attack us even more.

No matter who or what is messing with us, we can't let our flesh respond. Saying, "Wrong me once, shame on you; wrong me twice, shame on me," is the same as saying, "I'm going to get you." That's not in the Bible, and it's not speaking the Word. The devil is not an idiot; he knows how to get people out of walking in the fruit of the Spirit. So, instead of getting irritated at those around you, irritate the devil by being longsuffering and not murmuring or complaining.

When we let go of hate, we will forgive others; but if we stumble, just stop, and forgive that person(s) immediately. God told Peter to forgive 70 times 7 which is 490 times (Matthew 18). That's a lot! Most of us would say that's too much! What this number is really saying is that we are never to stop forgiving others. We are to obey the Word and forgive, always!

Colossians 3:12-13

[12] **Put on therefore, as the elect of God, holy and beloved, bowels of mercies, kindness, humbleness of mind, meekness, longsuffering;**

[13] **Forbearing one another, and forgiving one another, if any man have a quarrel against any: even as Christ forgave you, so also do ye.**

Forgiving others will keep unforgiveness from growing into a root of bitterness in your heart. Forgiving doesn't mean you forget what happened, but it does means you no longer think on it, bring it up, or hope the Lord will get them. And when the memory of it does come, it no longer riles you up against someone. God forgave you, so you should forgive others. I'm not saying it's easy, especially when you've given so much, done the right thing, and thought the best of somebody and then, they turn around and get you; but the Bible says you are to do it, so that means God has given you the power to do it.

I remember, in the beginning of the church, somebody did me wrong, so I decided I was going to change the way I pastored. I would no longer get close to anybody to help them. Instead, I would just give them the Word and let them grow up that way. That approach only lasted two weeks which was two weeks longer than it should have.

We cannot stop doing the right thing and obeying the Word just because somebody hurts us. Nobody is immune to hurt. We all get hurt, but how we respond to that hurt matters. We are to forgive. This is not something we can do in our own strength, but when we do take that step to forgive, God will be there to help us. Longsuffering will get rid of hatred.

WRATH:

Someone who yields to this work of the flesh is always just on the edge of an explosion. They seem to be very volatile. They are quick to anger. That is why the fruit of longsuffering will drive out this work of the flesh.

When you are longsuffering, you are slow to anger and patient with people, even in stressful situations. We looked at James 1:19-20, which says to be quick to hear, slow to speak, and slow to wrath; and if we will be a doer of this scripture and yield to the fruit of longsuffering, wrath will not have a part of our life. This part of our flesh will have no chance to manifest, but if it tries, you will know how to yield to the fruit of longsuffering so it can't. You are to be quick to hear when you deal with wrath. You must, on purpose, listen to people in every situation because you are not always right. Letting them get it out and tell you how they are feeling will keep the situation from turning explosive.

Next, be slow to speak. Don't speak too quickly. Don't speak from an emotional place. Longsuffering doesn't provoke others. Longsuffering will deal patiently, even when others are trying to provoke your flesh. A soft answer turns away wrath, but you can only give the right answer if you are slow to speak, and you can even ask the Holy Spirit how to respond in every situation. He is your helper, and He will help you navigate even the most combustible situations. He will help you to throw water on a situation instead of gasoline.

When you do the first two, quick to hear and slow to speak, then, the last one will happen for you. You will be slow to wrath, slow to take offense, and slow to get angry. That tells me the opportunity for wrath is still there, but we can choose to pass it up. James finishes the thought of the Holy Spirit about wrath and how to avoid it by saying that the wrath, which we yield to from our flesh, doesn't produce God's righteousness, or it doesn't produce any godly results. Yielding to the fruit of longsuffering, being patient with people in every situation, will cause wrath to be pushed out of your life. Another thought that is important is that any time we show wrath to someone, we are usually demeaning them and elevating ourselves above them, and that is not godly. We must make up our mind to yield to longsuffering, which is in our born-again spirits. Longsuffering will get rid of wrath!

SEDITIONS:

This work of the flesh is always creating drama. Someone who yields to their flesh in this area is always part of some kind of commotion and will help to keep things in a constant uproar. The people who let their flesh dominate them in this area are professional complainers and think those over them are not right, so they are very defiant to those who are in charge. Thank God, He has given us the ability to yield to this fruit of the Spirit instead of this work of our flesh. The fruit of longsuffering removes seditions because longsuffering means we have patient restraint. It also means that we can go through troubles and difficulty without complaining. When longsuffering has its full manifestation in us, we are the ones who are bringing peace and keeping drama out of the situation. We carry this peace because we have developed this fruit. When this fruit manifests in us, the commotion ceases, and cooler heads prevail. With longsuffering, we can do what the Word of God tells us to do by praying for those who are in authority over us and submitting to their authority. Praying from a place of longsuffering, from our righteous position, will get things changed God's way instead of trying to do it in the flesh. Longsuffering will get rid of seditions!

FRUIT OF GENTLENESS

Gentleness in the Greek is "chrestotes" (Strong's G5544), which means "mildness of temper, calmness of spirit, unruffled, treats everybody with kindness, compassionate, considerate, sympathetic, and gentle; somebody who is adaptable to others".

As a born-again believer, we need to get to the place where we are comfortable around everyone, especially our brothers and sisters in the Lord. I've learned to be comfortable no matter who I'm around, whether they're considered important or not, because everybody is important to God. I didn't start out there. I used to be in awe of certain people who, I thought, were better than me. It took a long time in God for me to see we're all the same. We just have different assignments and gifts. So, when we walk in the fruit of gentleness, we're going to be comfortable around everybody.

Romans 12:10 Be kindly affectioned one to another with brotherly love; in honour preferring one another.

The fruit of gentleness will cause us to prefer others. What does that mean? It's putting others first, in front of you, and preferring them over yourself. My wife, Rhonda, is so good at this. She is always preferring me and giving me the best she has.

When she and I teach marriage classes, we tell couples they should prefer their spouse. Preferring is important, but we have to make sure we're doing it in the right way. What do I mean by that? I remember when we first got married, we didn't have much money, so we believed for a vacation in the Smokies. When we were blessed with the finances to go, we went to this restaurant to eat. Since it was our first trip to the Smokies together and a restaurant we went to, we would go to that restaurant every time we vacationed there. We did that for years. It wasn't my favorite, but I was preferring my wife because she is so sentimental. On one of our vacations there, we were walking out of that restaurant, and I said, "Okay, we went to your favorite restaurant, now let's go to one of mine next meal." She looked at me and said, "It's not my favorite restaurant, it's yours." Here we were, going to a restaurant that neither of us wanted to go to because we were preferring one another instead of communicating with one another. That was the last time we went to that restaurant. It was good we weren't being selfish, but communicating our preferences would have kept us from going to that restaurant all those years.

We are to prefer others as Jesus prefers us.

> **Philippians 2:7-8**
>
> **⁷ But made himself of no reputation, and took upon him the form of a servant, and was made in the likeness of men:**
>
> **⁸ And being found in fashion as a man, he humbled himself, and became obedient unto death, even the death of the cross.**

Jesus, in gentleness and humbleness of heart, preferred every person on the Earth by dying on the cross for us.

So, when someone bumps into us, what should they get? They should get love followed by joy, peace, longsuffering and then, gentleness.

GENTLENESS WILL TAKE CARE OF THE FOLLOWING:

VARIANCE:

When we walk in gentleness, we will no longer be bitter and mean spirited, consumed with self-interest, or wanting chaos rather than admitting wrong. And to say, "It's just my personality," or "That's just the way the Lord made me," or "That's just the way my family acts," is a bunch of baloney. If you are born again, you are now in the family of God and that's not how God's family is supposed to act. Gentleness will get rid of variance.

EMULATIONS:

This work of the flesh is not only jealous but can also cause malice to someone to get what it wants. This work of the flesh causes someone to put others down to get want it wants. In other words, this person is getting theirs no matter the cost to someone else. When we begin to grow in the fruit of the Spirit, through meditating on the Word of God, gentleness will begin to manifest and push out emulations. Gentleness treats everyone with kindness and compassion and will not allow us to be vindictive or mean to someone so we can get what we want. We will also start trusting God even more when we realize that people are not holding us back, and even if they have something we want or even deserve, they are not our enemy. We will do what the scripture says and honor and prefer them. Can you go from being so mean and having malice towards someone to preferring them? Yes, but only with the fruit of this spirit working in your life. The fruit of gentleness will cause you to be considerate and compassionate, and it will cause you to show God's amazing love to someone you once thought was a rival, who had something you wanted. Gentleness will get rid of emulations!

HERESIES:

When we walk in gentleness, it will stop us from having a clique behavior and thinking we're better than everybody else. When I first started the church, I could see some of that happening. It took me back to the cliques in high school where you were either in or you were out. It was awful, and I wasn't going to have that in the church. The Lord doesn't like cliques. He is a God of inclusion and not exclusion. We have worked very hard, through the years, to keep that out of the church and to be a friendly and loving church so all who come will feel welcomed. I love it when new people say to me, "Your church is so friendly and loving." That's what we want because that's what God wants. Amen! Gentleness will get rid of heresies.

FRUIT OF GOODNESS

Goodness in the Greek is "agathosune" (Strong's G19). It's "the zeal of truth, the desire to abstain from the appearance of evil, an uprightness of soul that abhors evil". It also means being good to someone. It is a person who is generous, big hearted and charitable. As believers, we should abhor evil, and be good, generous, and big hearted toward others.

When I walk in the fruit of goodness, I am allowing it to grow in my life. And as this goodness continues to grow in me, it will begin to push out the lusts of the flesh. And as I keep letting this goodness work on the inside of me and come out of me to others, the more able I am to keep my flesh under.

It's like keeping your lawn looking good. If a lawn is not treated for weeds, no matter how many times the weeds are cut, they will grow back. We have to pull them out by the root. It's the same when we try to correct something in our flesh. We have to get to the root of it by walking in the fruit of goodness and growing in the Word of God. When we do, the works of the flesh will die at the root just like the fig tree that Jesus cursed (Mark 11).

Jesus walked in goodness.

> **Acts 10:38** How God anointed Jesus of Nazareth with the Holy Ghost and with power: who went about doing <u>good</u>, and healing all that were oppressed of the devil; for God was with him.

Jesus went about doing good. The word "good" is a derivative of the same root word as goodness, so this verse is saying that Jesus walked in goodness. He went about doing good deeds, performing service benefits, and being philanthropic (a person who donates time, money, experience, skills, and talent to help create a better world). Jesus was a philanthropist!

Walking in the fruit of goodness includes finances; but for us to bless others, we must be first be blessed. Jesus was financially blessed. Remember when the three wise men came to baby Jesus bringing gold, frankincense, and myrrh. Most people think they came with just a little of each because of how we portray it at Christmas, but they came with camels loaded down because they were coming to see a king, and they wanted to make sure they were in good with this king who had His own star in the sky over Him. Jesus had money! So much that when God sent His family to Egypt for two years, it was more than enough to live on. In Jesus' ministry, He had a treasurer who was skimming. A person can't take money from a treasury if it's not full because it would be missed. The more goodness that is produced in us, the more good we will want to do for others.

> **Galatians 6:10** As we have therefore opportunity, let us do good unto all men, especially unto them who are of the household of faith.

This is also talking about being blessed so we can be a blessing to others.

> **Romans 15:14** And I myself also am persuaded of you, my brethren, that ye also are full of goodness, filled with all knowledge, able also to admonish one another.

If you are born again, you should be full of goodness, so you can go around doing good for others. Grow in goodness by walking it out. That's how goodness will grow in us.

It's easy to tell when someone is walking in the fruit of goodness and when they are not. When some things are going on in my life and I get a little fleshy (selfish, feisty and such), my wife will very sweetly say to me, "You need to go spend some time with Jesus." She is right. We're all better when we spend time with Jesus. We're all better when we walk in the Word. We're all better when we walk in the Spirit. Doing these things will enable us to grow in the fruit of goodness and all the other fruits too.

> **2 Thessalonians 1:11 (NLT)** So we keep on praying for you, asking our God to enable you to live a life worthy of his call. May he give you the power to accomplish all the good things your faith prompts you to do.

This is another "blessed to be a blessing" scripture. The fruit of goodness is very active. I like the way the NLT version says it, "May he give you the power to accomplish all the good things your faith prompts you to do." Our church has done so many good things as God has led (prompted) us to do them, and it's good to be able to do good for others. God wants us blessed so when our faith prompts us to do something good, we are able to do it.

Let's walk in the fruit of goodness instead of making excuses for wrong behavior. We can't blame our job or profession, our background, or our personality for bad behavior because we can choose to walk in goodness now that we are born again. If you're having trouble walking in this fruit, get in the Word and study goodness; meditate on goodness scriptures and speak them out and then, start being good to others. This isn't something we just do at church. We should be good to others all the time until we go home to be with the Lord. That way, no one has to lie at our funeral and say what a good person we were when the truth was, we really acted like a fool.

So, when someone bumps into us, what should they get? They should get love followed by joy, peace, longsuffering, gentleness and then, goodness.

GOODNESS WILL TAKE CARE OF THE FOLLOWING:

ADULTERY:

Remember, the act adultery doesn't just happen one day out of nowhere. It first starts in the mind as a thought, then a picture, until it becomes an action. The act of porneia begins when we put ourselves into a compromising situation, when we look at things we shouldn't, and when we talk about things and jest about things we shouldn't. The fruit of goodness will combat this evil tendency of our flesh. This fruit will cause us to invoke the scripture in our lives of avoiding even the appearance of evil. This fruit, in full operation, will stop us from being places we shouldn't. This fruit will help us keep only good, godly company. Even though the world may scoff at you for being strict about these things, this fruit will actively make sure you are abhorring evil and displaying only the goodness of God. If you yield to this fruit, it will keep your marriage strong. It may cause those in the world, who don't understand, frustration with you, but it will lead you to a good life and a good marriage. Goodness will always displace adultery!

UNCLEANNESS:

When someone yields to this work of the flesh, they are unclean, especially in their minds. They are crude and insensitive to others, first in their mind and then, it becomes an action. So many times, we see things in the news about a seemingly normal person doing something crazy, and we wonder how they could have done that. That unclean, lewd thing they did started in their mind and eventually showed up in their life because they didn't get rid of this work of the flesh. Even if someone has a strong will power, it is not enough to overcome the strength of their flesh. Thank God that He has given us the ability, because of our new birth, to do away with those hideous works of the flesh. Goodness causes us to have a zeal in the truth. If we will begin to meditate on the things God said, we can drive out this work of uncleanness. When uncleanness is working in someone, if they will yield to goodness, it will cause them to begin to hate that evil lurking in their mind, and they will combat it with the sword of the Spirit, which is the Word of God, and cast down that stronghold, that pattern of thinking that is in their flesh. They will even change their once crude personality and become a reflection of Jesus. Thank God for this fruit called goodness. Goodness will always displace uncleanness!

STRIFE:

Where there is strife, there is every evil work. When our flesh is allowed to be contentious, we are in conflict with everyone, and are always causing disunity. We are operating in strife, and it leads to every kind of evil work. Strife is everywhere today. It is fermented on news casts, on social media, in politics, at school. and in the workplace. It is literally everywhere, and the devil is as pleased as he can be that so many people yield to their flesh every day in this area. When they yield, especially as a Christian, it opens the door for the devil to slide in. If we, instead, will yield to the fruit of goodness, which is to have an upright soul that abhors evil, then strife will be far from us. If goodness is working in me, I will be big hearted instead of wanting to be in conflict or be contentious with someone. It is interesting that this fruit causes me to be charitable to people. I don't have to agree with people, but rather disagree agreeably. Thank God this fruit of goodness is available to drive out this evil called strife. Goodness will always displace strife!

HERESIES:

When your flesh is allowed to operate in heresies, it will tell you that you are superior to others. This work of the flesh is the beginning of prejudice. When someone operates in prejudice, it is because they think they are superior, whether that is because of money, education, nationality, physical appearance, or whatever they believe causes them to be better than someone else. This fleshly work the King James translates as heresies is everywhere today because the devil is always pushing people to yield to their flesh in this area but thank God for the new birth. Thank God for the fruit of the Spirit called goodness. What does this fruit do to combat this feeling of superiority, this prejudice? The Bible clearly teaches us to love our neighbors as we love ourselves. To do good to others. This fruit will help us fulfill the royal law that Jesus gave us. When we walk in the fruit of goodness, it will cause us to, literally, do good to the people that our flesh used to tell us we were better than. We will understand that everyone is important to God, believer, and unbeliever alike. It will cause us to love them and treat them as someone who God cares about because He does. We are to do good to everyone, we are to be big hearted, and we are to be generous to everyone, without partiality. We can only do this by the fruit of goodness. We are to imitate Jesus who went about doing good. The connotation of this is that Jesus was a philanthropist. So, someone you used to put down, ignore, or devalue, you will now want to do something good to bless them, love them, and see God's best come into their lives. Goodness will always displace heresies!

QUICK VIEW OF THE FRUITS OF LONGSUFFERING, GENTLENESS, AND GOODNESS AND WHICH WORKS OF THE FLESH THEY WILL KEEP UNDER:

	LONGSUFFERING	GENTLENESS	GOODNESS
ADULTERY			X
FORNICATION			
UNCLEANNESS			X
LASCIVIOUSNESS			
IDOLATRY			
WITCHCRAFT			
HATRED	X		
VARIANCE		X	
EMULATIONS		X	
WRATH	X		X
STRIFE			
SEDITIONS	X		
HERESIES		X	X
ENVYINGS			
DRUNKENNESS			
REVELLINGS			

Chapter
Ten
Questions

1. In your own words, describe the fruit of longsuffering. What does it look like when it is operating in your life?

2. Pick one of the works of the flesh that the fruit of longsuffering displaces and that most relates to your life and describe how this fruit will help you overcome.

3. In your own words, describe the fruit of gentleness. What does it look like when it is operating in your life?

4. **Pick one of the works of the flesh that the fruit of gentleness displaces and that most relates to your life and describe how this fruit of gentleness will help you overcome.**

5. **In your own words, describe the fruit of goodness. What does it look like when it is operating in your life?**

6. **Pick one of the works of the flesh that the fruit of goodness displaces and that most relates to your life and describe how this fruit will help you overcome.**

Chapter
Ten
Confessions

The Fruit of Longsuffering:

✳	With patience, I will be quick to listen and slow to speak. (James 1:19)

✳	I will walk in patience because I know in due season I will reap if I do not faint. (Galatians 6:9)

✳	I will overlook an offense because God's wisdom in me gives me patience. (Proverbs 19:11)

✳	I will stay in unity as I walk in peace. (Ephesians 4:3)

✳	God is longsuffering with me, so I will be patient with others. (2 Peter 3:9)

Chapter
Ten
Confessions

The Fruit of Gentleness:

✻   **I will let my gentle spirit be known to all.
(Philippians 4:5)**

✻   **I will, in gentleness, comfort others.** (Isaiah 40:1-2)

✻   **I will be gracious and show compassion to others
because God is gracious to me.** (Isaiah 30:18)

✻   **I will lead the unsaved and backslidden to repentance.
(Romans 2:4)**

✻   **I will walk in gentleness because it is a kind answer
that will turn away wrath. (Proverbs 15:1)**

✻   **I will be kind to others and quick to forgive because
Christ has forgiven me.** (Ephesians 4:32)

Chapter Ten
Confessions

The Fruit of Goodness:

✻   **I will overcome evil with good. (Romans 12:21)**

✻   **I will cling to what is good, so that I can be good to others. (Romans 12:9)**

✻   **As I walk in goodness, I am confident that I will see the goodness of the Lord. (Psalm 27:13)**

✻   **When I trust in the Lord and do good, I dwell in safety. (Psalm 37:3)**

✻   **I will speak what is good and not what is evil for the benefit of those who listen. (Ephesians 4:29)**

chapter 11: fruit of the spirit
faithfulness, meekness, temperance

FRUIT OF FAITHFULNESS

Faith is better translated faithfulness. In the Greek, it is "pistis" (Strong's G4102), which means "someone who can be trusted and confided in, unswerving loyalty to a person or plan, someone who is punctual in performing promises".

Many people can have a form of faithfulness in their flesh based on who they are and how they were raised, and that's great, because I would rather have somebody, even in the natural, who is faithful rather than a Christian who is unfaithful. Everybody, born again or not, should be trustworthy, on time, and work hard. I was all those things when I was an accountant, even though I was backslidden. I would get there five minutes before my boss arrived, work hard, and then leave five minutes after my boss left.

Faithfulness in the natural is good, but the fruit of faithfulness the Bible is talking about is what the Spirit of God produces in us. This faithfulness is part of God's character that you can't get on your own. You have to be born again to receive it. His faithfulness will change your life because it is not something you can do in your own strength. The faithfulness given by God to you in your born-again spirit, will enable you to continually walk in faithfulness.

Jesus did. He gave up everything for us. He went to the cross to pay for our sins, but He didn't stop there. He took stripes on His back, so we could be healed, but He didn't stop there. He became poor so we could become rich, but He didn't stop there. He left us His peace, but He didn't stop there. He also sent us another Comforter, the Holy Ghost, to teach us, but it is up to us to do our part because as a born-again believer, we are in a two-way covenant. Everything He has is ours, but everything we have is supposed to be His. We must be faithful to give Him what we have, withholding nothing. Our Sundays are His, but so is every day of the week. Whatever we have and whatever we do should be His. We need to be faithful and give all that we have and all that we are to Him, so we can do what He asks of us.

1 Corinthians 4:2 **Moreover it is required in stewards, that a man be found faithful.**

This verse is talking about finances, but it also pertains to the things God has asked us to do. No matter what God gives us, it's required that we be found faithful, and lean on Him because we can't do it on our own. We must go to God and get His plan downloaded in us, so we can do it in His power instead of trying to do it on our own. When we try to do it ourselves, sooner or later our power will run out when adversity comes and then, our flesh won't want to do it anymore, which means sooner or later we will crash and burn. When we do it in God, we will complete it because His power is enabling us to do it. That's why when somebody says to me, "You are so faithful!" I immediately respond, "Well, glory to God. He is the one who enables and helps me to be that. I just cooperated, so He could do it through me."

Be faithful in all you do. I worked hard when I was an accountant and did alright, but after I got filled with the Holy Ghost, I became a better accountant because God knows accounting. Whenever I would have an accounting problem I couldn't figure out, I would go home and ask the Lord to help me, and He would show me exactly what I needed to do to fix the problem. He could make my balance sheet balance better than I ever could. He made me look like a genius. My boss would say, "Wow, you figured it out." I would respond and say, "Praise God!" I always made sure I gave the Lord the glory because He's the one who did it through me. God knows about everything. He even knows how to cook. The Bible says that Jesus cooked up some fish, and I'm sure those fish tasted awesome. No matter what you do, He can help you do it better.

Paul found Timothy faithful and would send Timothy on his behalf.

> **1 Corinthians 4:17** For this cause have I sent unto you Timotheus, who is my beloved son, and faithful in the Lord, who shall bring you into remembrance of my ways which be in Christ, as I teach every where in every church.

In Matthew 25, the parable of the talents talks about being faithful with money. God uses money a lot to check on our fruit of faithfulness. To one servant, this master had given five talents; the servant turned it into ten talents and the master was pleased.

> **Matthew 25:21** His lord said unto him, Well done, thou good and faithful servant: thou hast been faithful over a few things, I will make thee ruler over many things: enter thou into the joy of thy lord.

We are to be faithful stewards over our finances, so we can become faithful stewards over the mysteries of God. If God cannot trust us with money, He's not going to trust us with His true riches, the anointing. Don't think it strange when our enemy brings in false things to destroy our faithfulness. That's why the devil tries to get in the church and stop us from talking about money; he is trying to remove this very important testing ground concerning tithing and giving. The devil knows that the Lord is tied to His Word, and if He can get the church to stop tithing and sowing finances, then the Lord can't bless them.

> **Luke 16:10-11**
>
> 10 He that is faithful in that which is least is faithful also in much: and he that is unjust in the least is unjust also in much.
>
> 11 If therefore ye have not been faithful in the unrighteous mammon, who will commit to your trust the true riches?

These verses are talking about being faithful in the "least," which is unrighteous mammon (money). When it comes to prosperity, money is part of it, but it's not the "it." If a person sees money as the it, then they've got dollar signs for pupils and love money. I don't love money. I use money to serve God. I don't serve it. Money is just a tool and is necessary for life and in the work of the ministry. Preachers who teach prosperity are teaching the Word of God. I teach prosperity in the church because it is in the Word of God and I believe it, but the true riches being talked about is not about us being a millionaire. True riches are the anointing (power of God), the presence of God, the manifestations of the Spirit, the weighty things of God. God said that if we can't be faithful with money, He can't give us the weighty stuff. It's up to us to be faithful, so we can receive His true riches.

Luke 16:12-13

¹² And if ye have not been faithful in that which is another man's, who shall give you that which is your own?

¹³ No servant can serve two masters: for either he will hate the one, and love the other; or else he will hold to the one, and despise the other. Ye cannot serve God and mammon.

This is two-fold. This is being faithful with money and also in what God has called us to do.

I remember when I was on my way to Bible School, my mom asked me, "Where are you going to work?" I said, "Anywhere but McDonald's." I had worked at the golden arches to pay my way through college, and I was glad I was done with that. Then, the Lord said, "If you don't work at McDonald's, you'll miss half your training." What He said didn't make sense to me since my accounting degree would get me better pay and better hours to pay my way through school. So, what did I do when I got there? I got me a good paying accounting job because I didn't want to go back to McDonald's. I made more mistakes in one week on that accounting job than I ever did at the accounting job I had just left back home, so I quit before my boss could fire me. Why did I make so many mistakes? It was because I was out of the will of God and the anointing wasn't there for me to do accounting. After I ate those words I had said to my mom, with a little salt, I repented to the Lord and got me a job at the golden arches. It still seemed ridiculous to me, but God is smarter than I am, and I just didn't know that yet.

On my job at McDonald's, especially in my second year, I began to put into practice what I was learning at Bible school, and I used the verses in Luke 16 to do it because I had decided

I would be faithful with that which was another's. The owner of the McDonald's I worked at owned seven or eight other stores, drove a Corvette, and seemed to have plenty of money, but that didn't matter to me. God put me here, so I was determined to learn the things God wanted to teach me. I started by believing that the owner would make more money at this store than he ever had. I treated that store like it was mine. Whenever the owner would call, my boss would put her hand over the speaker and holler at me, "Mark, what are you believing for today?" She asked that because each day I would believe for a certain amount in sales, and we would hit it every time. I started teaching the workers around me to believe too. I would say to them, "Let's believe God together." We did and God did. It meant we had to work harder because more customers were coming in; but no matter how busy we got, I made sure we had good, hot, tasty food. I would never serve anything to a customer that I wasn't willing to eat myself. That's just the way I felt about it. I took it personal like it was my store. Much of what God taught me at McDonald's, I still use today.

My wife, Rhonda, would do the same when she worked as an insurance adjuster before she entered the ministry. She would send people out to prove fraud, so the company wouldn't have to pay any false claims, which saved the company a lot of money. People who worked there would say that she treated the company's money like it was hers, and she did because she was determined to do what was right while she was watching over what belonged to someone else.

What were we doing? We were walking in the fruit of faithfulness and being good stewards of what belonged to another and now God has given us our own. So, no matter where you work, or what you do, be a good steward over what you've been given, and treat it like it's yours, so you can receive your own someday. We are to be faithful with God's stuff and to that which is not our own, so God can give us His true riches.

The church building we're now in, was all God. He did it, and my wife, Rhonda, and I do our best to be faithful with what we've been given. As I am faithful with what God has given me, including church finances, I will receive the true riches; His power, more of His anointing. I want to see people who have diseases instantly healed. I've seen it in part, but I want to see more of it. I want to see people who are messed up come in and, after a moment in the presence of God, be changed forever, but to experience that, I must be faithful.

I really do want to see the presence and the power of God moving more in the church, and if being faithful with money will get us there, then I'm going to do it. It's not just about sowing to get stuff. It's about obeying God. It's about putting Him first. It's about being faithful with what He has given us, so we can check the reins of our heart. This is a principle we all need to be taught. Even though it's just money, money has become a big stumbling block to a lot of people causing them to pull away from obeying what the Word says about tithing, giving, and managing money, which will then pull them further away from the anointing.

The devil knows that God has chosen to operate within His Word, and that won't change. God doles out the anointing and His precious gifts to those who are faithful to His Word. People who teach and believe otherwise are listening to a deceiving spirit. We have to stay with the Word for God to be able to bless us. Ask the Holy Ghost to reveal God's truth to you concerning faithfulness.

So, when someone bumps into us, what should they get? They should get love followed by joy, peace, longsuffering, gentleness, goodness and then, faithfulness.

FAITHFULNESS WILL TAKE CARE OF THE FOLLOWING:

ADULTERY:

Adultery is being unfaithful, first to the Lord, because we belong to Him, and then, to your spouse. When someone commits adultery, it is not just the act of sex, it is, at the very core, the breaking of a covenant. I don't know that most people really understand how God detests this work of the flesh called adultery. How do we commit adultery against the Lord? James 4:4 (AMPC) says, "You [are like] unfaithful wives [having illicit love affairs with the world and breaking your marriage vow to God]! Do you not know that being the world's friend is being God's enemy? So whoever chooses to be a friend of the world takes his stand as an enemy of God." Most translations begin this verse by saying, "You adulterers and adulteresses;" the Lord takes it very seriously when we have illicit love affairs with the world; He calls it adultery. He is also very serious about a man or a woman breaking their covenant with each other. How do we get rid of this nasty work of the flesh, this desire to cheat on God and on our spouses? It is called the fruit of faithfulness. This fruit causes us to be trusted, to have an unswerving loyalty to a person or a plan. One thing we all know is that God is faithful to us. There is no denying that. He will never lie to us or make a promise that He won't keep; if He said He will do something, we can just count it as done. That is faithfulness. This fruit of faithfulness is available in our born-again spirit, and as we develop this fruit, it will push out the desire to commit adultery. We will not lie to our spouse, we will only be where we say we will be, and we will not befriend people we should not befriend. We will make sure, in our faithfulness, not to share ourselves with those we shouldn't, including confiding in people intimate details of our lives that should only be reserved for our spouse. The fruit of faithfulness is powerful, and it will dispel any desire to be unfaithful. Faithfulness will displace adultery!

IDOLATRY:

Idolatry is creating a substitute for God and treating it like God in our lives. Idolatry is more than just worshipping a statue of Buddha in your house. It's giving your complete, undivided attention, devotion, passion, love, and commitment to a person, project, or object above God. It could be putting your friends first, or being a workaholic, or letting sports or your new car be the most important thing to you. We can still be passionate about such things, but when we let something come before God, it is out of place. God will not share His place with anyone or anything. The Bible says, "We are to have no other gods [idols] before Him" (Exodus 20:3). That means God must be number one. Everything must come after God, including our career, family, politics, money, hobbies, sports, and so on. The Lord wants us to have fun and enjoy our life, but that only happens when we let God be number one.

When we walk in faithfulness, we will keep our focus on Jesus. James 4:4-5 talks about God's children acting in adultery and idolatry. James 4:5 (NLT) says, "Do you think the Scriptures have no meaning? The Bible says God is passionate, and that the spirit He has placed within us should be faithful to Him." God is jealous over us, and He doesn't want us to have anything or anyone ahead of Him because that is idolatry. Remember the warning of 1 Corinthians 10:14 that says to stay away from idolatry, which is loving or venerating anything more than God. Faithfulness will drive out idolatry.

SEDITIONS:

When someone yields to seditions, they are yielding to rebellion and drama. They are revolting against the authority that God has put in their lives. This person, sometimes knowingly or sometimes unknowingly, is participating in an insurrection. Even their attitude is wrong. The words that incite others are from this hideous work of the flesh known as seditions. We can't embrace this foul thing because it is meant to steal, kill, and destroy. That is where the fruit of faithfulness comes in. It will push this rebellion (something the devil loves) far from us. When you are faithful, you stand firm where and with whom God has called you. You will not be offended, and you will not be moved. You will only move and speak at the instruction of the written and spoken Word of God. God, and the people He puts over us in the Lord, can count on us, because we yield to this fruit called faithfulness. The person who has developed this fruit knows it is a requirement from the Lord to be good stewards over the mysteries of God. Being faithful is something others should be able to observe in us. Being faithful in every part of our walk with God will help with this very subtle yet nasty work of the flesh called seditions. Faithfulness will displace seditions.

FRUIT OF MEEKNESS

Meekness in the Greek is "praiotes" (Strong's G4236). This one we don't focus on too much because people equate this fruit of the Spirit with weakness, especially when it comes to men, i.e., a woman doesn't want a wimpy guy, she wants a man. Jesus, when He walked the earth as a man, was meek, but He wasn't weak. Bible meekness is not weakness. It is "mildness, an even balance of all tempers and passions". It is remaining in control no matter what comes your way. It's being steady as you go, without having ups and downs. Someone who is even balanced attracts others to them.

To walk in meekness, we must guard our mouth and actions, so we don't find ourselves falling back into walking in the flesh, which can happen to any believer at any given moment. It happened to Peter. One moment he was in the spirit saying that Jesus was the Christ, the son of God, and then a few verses later he was saying he wouldn't let Jesus die, and Jesus rebuked him by saying, "Get behind me, Satan." If we continually walk in the fruit of meekness, this doesn't have to happen to us.

Meekness (humility) is the absence of feeling superior to others. It's an attitude of the heart that we must all walk in. Those who exhibit true humility are able to come under those who are over them in the Lord. Their focus is not on recognition or rank, but just service. Humility is something the Lord Jesus, our example, displayed. It is so vital in our walk with the Lord that Jesus gave us a personal invitation to come and learn from Him.

Matthew 11:28-30

28 Come unto me, all ye that labour and are heavy laden, and I will give you rest.

29 Take my yoke upon you, and learn of me; for I am meek and lowly in heart: and you shall find rest for your souls.

30 For my yoke is easy, and my burden is light.

Jesus is saying, "Come, let me teach you." How will He teach us? Through His Word and through the great teacher, the Holy Spirit.

In Luke 14:7-11, Jesus used an example of someone going to a wedding and where they should sit. He told them not to take the best seat thinking they were so important because if someone more important came in, they would be asked to move to a lower seat. Jesus was using a wedding as an example, but this pertains to the Kingdom of God and life in general. You ought to take the lower seat and be content and then, if someone wants to move you to a more important seat, they will come and get you. This is saying not to think yourself too important because you might find yourself being humiliated in front of everyone if you are paraded to a lower seat.

You must choose humility because it is not automatic. When you truly humble yourself, God will exalt you and with that, so many graces become available to you, especially the grace needed to resist the devil. Psalm 149:4 says, "He crowns the humble with victory." Our prayer should be, "Lord, teach me to be humble, so I can find rest for my soul."

Jesus was humble and displayed it perfectly. In Matthew 21:5, Jesus, the King of kings and Lord of lords, for His triumphal procession, didn't come in riding a white stallion. Instead, He showed meekness by riding in on the colt of a donkey, which was considered a beast of burden and the common man's mode of transportation. Jesus, on purpose, positioned Himself this way, humble and lowly, to demonstrate meekness to us.

The meekness that Jesus walked in and wants us to walk in is strength under control. It is about how we treat others. Meekness is not passivity. Those who are meek are people of power and influence, who, consciously and intentionally, keep their strengths under control while demonstrating humility, kindness, and tranquility.

Moses was meek. Numbers 12:3 (AMPC) says, "Now the man Moses was very meek (gentle, kind, and humble) or above all the men on the face of the Earth." Moses was the meekest of all men on the planet during his time, and the most used by God of anyone at that time. God spoke with Moses face to face because he was a friend, and God mightily used Moses, the meekest man of all, to deliver His people out of bondage. That's strength under control. Psalm 37:11 says, "The meek shall inherit the earth, and shall delight themselves in the abundance of peace."

There are so many benefits to walking in meekness.

Isaiah 29:19 **The meek also shall increase their joy in the Lord, and poor among men shall rejoice in the Holy One of Israel.**

The meek shall increase in joy, which makes sense because meekness is being mild tempered, gentle, kind, not provoked to anger, or easily irritated, so if you are not angry or irritated, you would be more joyful, more carefree.

The meek shall eat and be satisfied because they are yielding to the Lord (Psalm 22:26).

The meek shall be guided in judgement so they can make wise decisions, and they will be taught the ways of the Lord (Psalm 25:9).

The Lord shall lift up the meek (Psalm 147:6).

By walking in meekness, we are assured victory, protection, and that we will receive all that salvation is (Psalm 149:4, Zephaniah 2:3).

Meekness positions us to help others.

Galatians 6:1 **Brethren, if a man be overtaken in a fault, you which are spiritual, restore such a one in the spirit of meekness; considering yourself, lest you also be tempted.**

We have all received help, if not from a person, definitely from the Lord, so we should freely give help to others. How do we start? It begins with us having an attitude of humility and submission in receiving the Word of God, which is able to save our souls (James 1:21). Being meek will help us lay aside uncleanness and wickedness, so that when we help others, we will not give into any temptation to sin.

Titus 3:2 **To speak evil of no man, to be no brawlers, but gentle, showing all meekness unto all men.**

When others see us walking in meekness, it will be an example to them and show that we are there to help and not hinder them.

Meekness is critical in evangelizing those not born again, helping those who have been hit with a stupid stick, and restoring the backslidden. If we want to reach others, we must allow the fruit of meekness to flow out of us to them. Our part is to tell them who Jesus is, what the Word says about them and their situation, and what Jesus has done. Then, it's on them to acknowledge the truth (Word of God) and give themselves to repentance.

Restoring others is not always easy because the person we're trying to help may be a bit fussy and give us a bunch of foolishness by questioning everything we say, but we can't react to what they say or do. We must, with wisdom, walk in the spirit of meekness and be even tempered, so it will push their foolishness away.

> **James 3:13** Who is a wise man and endued with knowledge among you? Let him show out of a good conversation his works with meekness of wisdom.

The NLT says, "If you are wise and understand God's ways, prove it by living an honorable life, doing good works with the humility that comes from wisdom."

The Message says, "Do you want to be counted wise, to build a reputation for wisdom? Here's what you do: live well, live wisely, live humbly. Mean-spirited ambition isn't wisdom."

Because we have allowed the Spirit of God to correct us, we now have the ability to live an honorable life, not because of will power but because of God's power; and because we decided to walk in the spirit of meekness for ourselves, we can now help others.

So, when someone bumps into us, what should they get? They should get love followed by joy, peace, longsuffering, gentleness, goodness, faithfulness and then, meekness.

MEEKNESS WILL TAKE CARE OF THE FOLLOWING:

LASCIVIOUSNESS:

Someone who yields to this work of the flesh is constantly out of control. This can happen in any area, such as eating, spending, drinking, or anything else that comes to mind. If you live with this work of the flesh in any area of your life, you lack restraint, so anything goes. Thank God there is a solution for this and that is to be born again, so you can start living by the fruit of your recreated spirit. The fruit that will help this craziness is meekness.

Jesus was the meekest man who ever lived on the Earth, and one would have to say, the most in control of His flesh.

When you walk in the spirit and the fruit begins to manifest from your born-again spirit, you can expect meekness to show up and move out this nasty lasciviousness. There are a few scriptures I want to remind you of concerning meekness. Isaiah 29:19 says that the meek shall increase their joy. I think the reason most people have yielded to lasciviousness is because they have no joy. Meekness which produces joy and will push out lasciviousness. According to Psalm 22:26, the meek will eat and be satisfied. Remember, the Lord said to come, taste, and see that He is good. So, when you are satisfied by the Lord and walk in the fruit of meekness, your fleshly cravings will be kept under. Meekness will get rid of lasciviousness.

HATRED:

When someone yields to this work of the flesh, they hold grudges, harbor deep resentments, and have a root of bitterness in them. This person not only hates but gets others to hate with them. We know that to hate is to murder in the eyes of God (1 John 3:15), but the fruit of meekness will get hatred out of our lives forever. We can look at Jesus and Moses and see how meekness got rid of hatred.

Jesus was persecuted, lied about, and hated by the religious, but during His trial, beatings, and death on the cross, He only showed the fruit of meekness. Jesus said for us to come and let Him teach us about meekness. Why? So we can combat this evil thing called hatred. I'm sure Jesus was tempted to hate and to retaliate, but He let meekness win out.

Although Moses wasn't perfect like Jesus, he did walk in meekness, because the Word says Moses was the meekest man on the Earth. Moses had plenty of opportunities to choose to live in anger because of his dealings with those stiff-necked people he was trying to lead to a better life. He could have been angry at Aaron and Miriam when they opposed his new wife but instead, his meekness was shining through when he prayed for Miriam and asked God not to hold it to her charge.

Titus 3:2 says we should not speak evil of any man, nor brawl with people, but instead, be gentle by showing meekness to all men. This wonderful fruit of meekness is available to every born-again believer. Wouldn't the church, our community, and our nation be a better place if we all yielded to this wonderful fruit called meekness? Meekness will get rid of hatred.

VARIANCE:

This work of the flesh, when yielded to, will cause someone to be quarrelsome. This person will look for controversy, always thinking they are right and that what they believe and say is the only way. They are basically saying it is their way or the highway. Thank God for meekness. Cultivating this fruit will get rid of this ridiculous work of the flesh called variance.

What will meekness do to displace variance? Meekness will cause us to be mild and have an even balance of passion and temper. A person who displays meekness is in control of all their passions. Once again, Titus 3:2 says that a meek person is not a brawler, or combative, or causing controversy. When you yield to the fruit of meekness, it will take away the desire to brawl and to cause controversy. Instead, you will get over yourself and realize you are not always right. Meekness gives opportunity for us to develop understanding from God; and with God's understanding, you will act in wisdom in dealing with other people and their opinions, whether those opinions are right or wrong. Remember, Psalm 25:9 says the meek are guided in judgement. You will not only be able to make right decisions but also be able to bring solutions to any problem. Meekness will get rid of variance.

WRATH:

Meekness will get rid of wrath. When someone displays this work of the flesh, they are a volcano ready to erupt. Just like a natural volcano can sit idle, so can a person who yields to wrath, but when they blow, destruction will come creating a steady, hot flow to anyone in their path. It is not godly, and no one likes to be around this kind of person during an eruption of their unsanctified behavior. Once again, God has made a way to remove wrath by walking in the fruit of meekness. When we display meekness, we are kind, gentle, and humble. If someone is born again, there is no excuse for being a walking, talking volcano ready to erupt. Meekness will get rid of wrath.

STRIFE:

Meekness will get rid of strife. When someone walks in strife, they are willing to upset anyone and everyone to get what they want, but walking in meekness will put a stop to that. Meekness will keep us from getting into arguments and opposing others and will position us to resolve issues instead of stirring things up.

Strife is particularly evil. James 3:16 says that where there is strife, there is every evil work. Wow! That is a big statement. Strife causes everyone to be in such discord that there can be no agreement. Strife causes total chaos all the time. A person who causes strife feels superior to others and doesn't care about anyone's feelings. They are willing to live in constant drama as long as they get what they want. God hates strife, and we should hate it too. The cure, once again, is the fruit of meekness that will produce joy, peace, sound judgement, and humility. When Jesus rode a young donkey on His triumphal entry, He chose the meek route and not the "Hey, look at me" route. How does this help get rid of strife? It helps because you are humbling yourself in each situation you face; and rather than saying, "Hey, look at me," you are more concerned with others. When someone yields to strife, they tear things apart, but someone walking in the fruit of meekness puts things back together. Galatians 6:1 talks about restoring a person in the spirit of meekness, so if you can restore a person, you can restore a situation. Meekness removes strife because it brings peace and restoration. Meekness is the answer for anyone who can't seem to stay out of strife. Meekness will get rid of strife.

FRUIT OF TEMPERANCE

Temperance in the Greek is "egkrateia" (Strong's G1466) which means "moderation, restraining from unhealthy passions, appetites, and desires". It is someone who is disciplined and has self-control. It is similar to will power but much better because temperance (self-control) comes from the spirit realm instead of the soul realm.

1 Corinthians 9:24-25

24 Know ye not that they which run in a race run all, but one receiveth the prize? So run, that ye may obtain.

25 And every man that striveth for the mastery is temperate in all things. Now they do it to obtain a corruptible crown; but we an incorruptible.

It says, "Every man that strives for the mastery is temperate." The Apostle Paul, by the Holy Ghost, is telling us that if we are serious about finishing our course, we need temperance in our lives. He likens it to getting a prize or crown for an athletic event. For us, it is receiving an eternal crown at the Judgement Seat of Christ for doing what the Lord has asked us to do.

It goes on to say…

1 Corinthians 9:26-27

26 I therefore so run, not as uncertainly; so fight I, not as one that beateth the air:

27 But I keep under my body, and bring it into subjection: lest that by any means, when I have preached to others, I myself should be a castaway.

If you want to go higher in God, and be more useful to Him, you need to keep your body under. In Romans 12:1-2, Paul tells us to offer our bodies as a living sacrifice to the Lord; and in Romans 8:13, he tells us to crucify our flesh to keep it under. Titus 2:1-2 says, "But speak thou the things which become sound doctrine: that the aged men be sober, grave, temperate, sound in faith, in love, in patience." So, being temperate is right up there with faith and love. Temperance (self-control) must be a part of your life if you are going to be used of God and last. Temperance is needed to finish your course with joy.

Paul preached temperance.

Acts 24:24-25

24 And after certain days, when Felix came with his wife Drusilla, which was a Jewess, he sent for Paul, and heard him concerning the faith in Christ.

25 And as he reasoned of righteousness, temperance, and judgment to come, Felix trembled, and answered, Go thy way for this time; when I have a convenient season, I will call for thee.

In these verses, Paul ministered to Felix about faith in Christ, specifically on righteousness, temperance, and judgement. Felix, obviously, must have felt convicted hearing this but instead of turning to the Lord, he sent Paul away.

Paul spoke to Felix about temperance and is also telling us we must be temperate. In 2 Peter 1:6, we are told to add to our faith virtue, knowledge, temperance, patience, godliness, brotherly kindness, and love. When we add these, which includes temperance, to our faith life, we will not be barren or unfruitful. To successfully walk out this life in Christ, we need temperance because without it, our flesh will run wild.

There are many things in this life that are good unless they are taken to an excess. Anything that you can't put down, can't live without, and have to have lest you go crazy, then temperance is lacking, and that fruit must be developed in your life. Proverbs 25:16 (NASB2020) says, "Have you found honey? Eat only what you need, so that you do not have it in excess and vomit it." Honey is good; it is sweet and even good for you, unless you eat too much and then, it can become a real mess. Proverbs 25:28 (NASB2020) says, "Like a city that is broken into and without walls so is a person who has no self-control over his spirit." In other words, when temperance is not found in your life, it is like leaving all the gates into your life open and then, you are headed for destruction because with your doors wide open, the devil will come to steal, kill, and destroy. Thank God, we have the fruit of temperance to combat the evil tendencies of our flesh.

When we walk in temperance, we will keep our body under and never over-indulge. It is good to always keep your flesh in check, so it never has preeminence in your life. Excess in your flesh is never good, but being full of God is the best. I love Ephesians 5:18 because it says to never to be drunk with natural wine (alcohol) but instead, be filled with the Spirit. With the new birth and by walking in the fruit of temperance, we can get rid of excesses in every area of our lives.

We have to decide to obey God if we are going to finish our course, so we don't end up on the sidelines with our faith shipwrecked, like Paul said, by the Holy Ghost, when he warned those on the ship (Acts 27). We must understand and take to heart this warning and be temperate in all things.

We should all want to walk in temperance, so we can finish our course and hear, "Well done, good and faithful servant," and obtain a crown at the judgment seat of Christ that we can lay at Jesus' feet. We can all achieve this but to get there, moderation of all things good has to be a part of our lives. How do we do that?

Food is always a good example of being moderate. Eating is a good thing, but instead of devouring an entire coconut cream pie at one sitting, which some of us would love to do, we can be moderate and put the fork down after one piece. Being moderate is that simple but it's not always easy.

Money is another good example of being moderate. Money is a tool that we all need in our lives but that doesn't mean we should spend beyond our means. God wants us to have nice things, but not if it took a credit card debt to do it because instead of those jeans costing $75, they're now costing $500 when you add in the interest paid. Temperance keeps us from doing such extremes. I'm not saying you can never use a credit card. Many people do and then pay it off at the end of the month. There are also times when emergencies happen (which would not include blue jeans), and we charge it; but when we do, we should believe God that we will pay it off quickly. Let's stay with the Word and walk in temperance (moderation), so we can walk in victory and receive the blessings of God.

It's also important to understand that temperance (moderation) never applies to sin. If you think sin is okay in moderation because you only do a little and it doesn't have a hold on you, that is wrong thinking. Sin is sin and always leads to death. Most people have this wrong thinking because Philippians 4:5 says, "Let your moderation be known unto all men," but the Greek word for "moderation" here is not "egkratei" which means temperance. It is "epieikes" (Strong's G1933), and would have been understood as brotherly kindness. Then the verse would read, "Let your brotherly kindness be known unto all men." So, let me make it perfectly clear. Temperance is not sinning in moderation. It is keeping your body under and being in total control over your flesh, so you will not sin.

We should also be temperate in helping others.

Romans 14:17-21

> **[17]For the kingdom of God is not meat and drink; but righteousness, and peace, and joy in the Holy Ghost.**
>
> **[18] For he that in these things serveth Christ is acceptable to God, and approved of men.**
>
> **[19] Let us therefore follow after the things which make for peace, and things wherewith one may edify another.**
>
> **[20] For meat destroy not the work of God. All things indeed are pure; but it is evil for that man who eateth with offence.**
>
> **[21]It is good neither to eat flesh, nor to drink wine, nor any thing whereby thy brother stumbleth, or is offended, or is made weak.**

This says that although eating meat is okay when we do it in faith, if eating it will cause offense to the person we are with because they think it's wrong to eat it, we should refrain from eating it. Why? Because we are helping a brother, so he will not stumble. Preferring someone else is a sign of maturity and the more we grow in this, the higher up we will go, and, also, the more responsibility we will have to those around who are watching us.

The fruit of temperance will help us to walk in love with others. We're supposed to be preferring the brethren (Romans 12:10). Even as a witness to the lost, we're supposed to be living in a temperate way so as not to offend them or let them offend us. Let temperance work in your life!

So, when someone bumps into us, what should they get? They should get love followed by joy, peace, longsuffering, gentleness, goodness, faithfulness, meekness and then, temperance.

TEMPERANCE WILL TAKE CARE OF THE FOLLOWING:

UNCLEANNESS:

Uncleanness is the work of the flesh that makes you morally unclean. It causes you to be out of control, especially concerning thoughts that turn into actions in the sexual realm. One of the best definitions of temperance is self-control. Someone who deals with uncleanness has no control because they have let their mind and imaginations run wild. Improper sexual thoughts and fantasies will eventually lead to fornication or adultery. The fruit of temperance is being in control, and it will remove uncleanness, especially when we renew our mind with the Word of God. The Apostle Paul, when he was on trial in front of Felix, expounded about temperance, this self-control (Acts 24:25) while also talking about righteousness. It must have come as a great revelation to Paul about keeping your body under and unclean thoughts at bay, so he talked about it at a most pivotal time in his life. Also, it may be that Felix, the governor, dealt with such things, and Paul was trying to give him an answer for his problems. Temperance will rid us of uncleanness.

LASCIVIOUSNESS:

Since lasciviousness is wild, out of control living, you could easily see how temperance would fix that. If you wanted to control this work of the flesh, you must walk in godliness by doing what Paul said in 1 Corinthians 9:25 and that is to be temperate in all things. In context, Paul was talking about athletes who are in total control of their body, their exercise, their food, their sleep, etc., everything that is necessary to win a prize. Paul was saying that we, too, must be temperate, or self-controlled, like an Olympic athlete if we are going to win the prize.

One thing I know is that the works of the flesh are meant to take you out of the race. We are all running a race to receive a prize at the judgement seat of Christ, where we will all stand one day. Temperance is key to finishing your race. We are told by Peter to add temperance to our lives, so we won't be barren or have no fruit when we come to the end of our race on the Earth (2 Peter 1:5-11). When we yield to the fruit of temperance (self-control), we will keep this work of the flesh called lasciviousness out of our lives, and we will not have to deal with some of the other works of the flesh that are lurking right behind this one. Temperance will rid us of lasciviousness.

WITCHCRAFT:

Since we know that witchcraft is self-medicating, overindulging in legal or illegal drugs to medicate the problems of life, we can see how temperance (self-control) would remove this evil work of the flesh called witchcraft. If we are self-controlled, we won't need to medicate our broken heart or try and relieve stress through overmedicating. Being temperate in all things will cause us to stop mistreating our bodies and allow the Lord to heal and deliver us from all bondage. When temperance kicks in, it's like telling your flesh, "I have the Holy Spirit to help me, and I don't need a pill, a bottle, a hit, or anything else to self-medicate." I also think that once we begin to walk in temperance, we can help others that have this same problem in their flesh. It is our flesh that we must crucify, and not our spirit. Our spirit is perfect and has been recreated in the likeness and the image of God, but your flesh was not. We have to let God heal our soul as we renew our mind. That's when walking in the fruit of temperance will eradicate the need for speed or any other drug. Temperance will rid us of witchcraft.

QUICK VIEW OF THE FRUITS OF FAITHFULNESS, MEEKNESS, AND TEMPERANCE AND WHICH WORKS OF THE FLESH THEY WILL KEEP UNDER:

	FAITHFULNESS	MEEKNESS	TEMPERANCE
ADULTERY	X		
FORNICATION			
UNCLEANNESS			X
LASCIVIOUSNESS		X	X
IDOLATRY	X		
WITCHCRAFT			X
HATRED		X	
VARIANCE		X	
EMULATIONS			
WRATH		X	
STRIFE		X	
SEDITIONS	X		
HERESIES			
ENVYINGS			
DRUNKENNESS			
REVELLINGS			

FRUIT OF THE SPIRIT:

We have looked at the nine fruits of the spirit, and they all are available to you. We also talked about what fruit is needed to take care of each work of the flesh. This is not an exhaustive list but what the Lord has revealed to me that I wanted to share with you. I encourage you to identify which works of the flesh you're still yielding to, and the fruit you need to study in the Word of God to obtain greater revelation, so you can walk in that fruit and keep your flesh under. It is powerful that God gave us this fruit in our born-again spirit. It is now our responsibility to develop in each fruit and remove all the works of the flesh, so we can live free from these works that are meant to destroy our lives. This fruit of the Spirit is amazing and powerful! Listing the fruit of the Spirit in the Bible wasn't just meant for you to memorize, but for you to learn about each one so you could walk in them and let them change your life. Let the change begin now!

Chapter Eleven Questions

1. In your own words, explain the fruit of faith (faithfulness). What does it look like when it is operating in your life?

2. Choose one of the works of the flesh that the fruit of faith (faithfulness) displaces and that most relates to you and explain how it will help you keep that particular work of the flesh under.

3. In your own words, explain the fruit of meekness. What does it look like when it is operating in your life?

4. Choose one of the works of the flesh that the fruit of meekness displaces and that is most relatable to you in your personal life and explain how it will help you keep that particular work of the flesh under.

5. In your own words, explain the fruit of temperance (self-control). How does it look when it is operating in your life?

6. Choose one of the works of the flesh that the fruit of temperance displaces and that is most relatable to you and explain how it will help you keep that particular work of the flesh under.

Chapter
Eleven
Confessions

The Fruit of Faithfulness:

✳ I will be faithful in both the small and big things, and I will be faithful with money, so God will commit to me His true riches. (Luke 16:10-11)

✳ I will be faithful like Timothy so that God can send me to help and train others. (1 Corinthians 4:17)

✳ I will be faithful with the things you give me, money, assignments, and whatever you say. I will be faithful so I can hear well done. (Matthew 25:21)

✳ I will obey God and His Word. I will not have illicit love affairs with the world. I will only be God's friend and not a friend of this world. (James 4:4)

✳ I will remain faithful, so I can receive the true riches of God. (1 Corinthians 4:2)

Chapter Eleven Confessions

The Fruit of Meekness:

* Because I walk in meekness, I shall eat and be satisfied. (Psalm 22:26)

* Because I walk in meekness, I am blessed and will inherit the Earth and will delight in an abundance of peace. (Matthew 5:5, Psalm 37:11)

* I will walk as Jesus walked, in humbleness of heart. (Matthew 11:29; Titus 3:1-2)

* I will walk in meekness in my conduct because those who do are considered wise and understanding. (James 3:13)

* As I walk in meekness, the joy of the Lord will increase in my life. (Isaiah 29:19)

Chapter
Eleven
Confessions

The Fruit of Temperance (Self-Control):

✳   I will walk in temperance to obtain the prize at the end
    of my race, a crown that I can lay at Jesus' feet. (1
    Corinthians 9:24-25, Revelations 4:10-11)

✳   I will fight by keeping my body under subjection, so I
    will not become a castaway. I will finish my course. (1
    Corinthians 9:26-27)

✳   I will live soberly and uprightly before God by denying
    ungodliness and worldly lusts. (Titus 2:12)

✳   I will live by the Spirit and put to death the things of
    my flesh. (Romans 8:13)

✳   I will add temperance to my faith so that I will not be
    barren but will produce much fruit. (2 Peter 1:6)

chapter 12: benefits of righteousness

We have seen how walking in the fruit of the Spirit will keep our flesh from acting out. Another key to closing the door to sin and living a sin free life is understanding our righteousness. Knowing you have been made righteous will give you a whole new perspective on what Jesus provided and will completely change how you see your position as a born-again believer. It will cause you to realize that you're not looking up at sin as it beats you down, but your seated in heavenly places with Christ Jesus looking down and refusing sin because it and the devil are under your feet.

Righteousness is defined as right standing with God. It's being made right with God, and the Bible calls righteousness a free gift that Jesus provided to all who are born again.

Romans 3:24 (AMPC) [All] are justified and made upright and in right standing with God, freely and gratuitously by His grace (His unmerited favor and mercy), through the redemption which is [provided] in Christ Jesus.

The Message translation says it this way.

Romans 3:24 (MSG) Out of sheer generosity he put us in right standing with himself. A pure gift. He got us out of the mess we're in and restored us to where he always wanted us to be. And he did it by means of Jesus Christ.

Thank God Jesus paid the price for us and all we have to do is receive His finished work and walk in it.

Someone might say, "I'm born again, but I don't feel righteous." I don't always feel righteous either but being righteous is not a feeling. God's Word says that everybody, who is born again, has received the free gift of righteousness, so we are righteous whether we feel like it or not. Let's look at this verse in the New Living Translation.

Romans 3:24 (NLT) Yet God, in his grace, freely makes us right in his sight. He did this through Christ Jesus when he freed us from the penalty for our sins.

Notice, God, with underserved kindness, declares that we are righteous (right in His sight). It's not a matter of how you feel but what Jesus, in His loving kindness, did for you. If you will walk in this free gift of righteousness you received when you were born again, the feelings will come. So, how do you do it? By getting a revelation of the righteousness you have received.

As I've taught the Word of God to people for all these years, since 1990, I've come to realize that people have a problem seeing themselves like God sees them. That's part of the reason why sin is such a big problem, even for Christians. By getting a revelation of our righteousness, it will cause us to see ourselves as God sees us and then, sin will drop off because righteousness is not something you do, it's who you are. Jesus made you righteous.

In the beginning, Adam and Eve had perfect fellowship with God until they disobeyed. When they sinned, man fell from grace. Although the consequences of their disobedience brought sin and death into the Earth, God immediately set a plan into motion to restore mankind back to Himself. God sent Jesus Christ, who was with Him in Heaven from the beginning, to Earth. God's miraculous plan was for Jesus, who was all God, to be born of a virgin and walk the earth as a man, so He could, as the sin-free lamb, pay the price for our redemption on the cross and bring us back into fellowship with God. Jesus paid the ultimate price by giving His life for you and me.

In 2 Corinthians 5:21, it tells us that Jesus became sin so we could become the righteousness of God in Christ Jesus. That means if you've received Jesus as your Lord and Savior, when God looks at you, He no longer sees sin because the blood of Jesus has washed you clean. Jesus did the work, but we reap the benefits. His righteousness cleansed you from all guilt, pain, and shame, so you could stand clean before God. It doesn't matter what someone did before they were born again because the old is gone and has been done away with. You are now a new creation in Christ Jesus.

Jesus restored fellowship between God and those who have received Him as Lord. As a child of God, you now have access to Almighty God and can boldly go to the throne of grace 24/7. And if you sin, you've got an advocate, a lawyer named Jesus, who will represent you. And I can guarantee that this attorney has never lost a case, and He won't lose yours.

THE FRUIT OF RIGHTEOUSNESS

As we take this gift of righteousness and walk uprightly in it every day, we'll find there's no better way to live because the fruit of righteousness will manifest in the following ways.

1. **Your prayers will be powerful and effective.**

> **James 5:16 (AMPC)** ...The earnest (heartfelt, continued) prayer of a righteous man makes tremendous power available [dynamic in its working].

> **1 Peter 3:12** For the eyes of the Lord are over the righteous, and his ears are open unto their prayers: but the face of the Lord is against them that do evil.

If you're thinking, "I guess I'm not righteous enough because I wouldn't exactly call my prayer life powerful," you've missed the whole point. You don't have to become righteous; if you are born again, you are righteous. So, if the fruit of prayer is not showing up in your life, just begin to acknowledge that you are righteous. Say it right now! "I am the righteousness of God in Christ Jesus." Say it loud, and often, so the devil can hear you and you can hear it too because that's who you are.

I believe that when it dawns on you that you are righteous, it will not only help you live free from sin and its effects, but you will pray with power.

When you know who you are in Christ, you will know that God hears your prayers, and that the army of Heaven is behind the Word prayed, believed, spoken and acted upon. You will know that things are moving and shaking because you prayed. Knowing you are righteous will make you bold.

2. You will be empowered to rule and reign as royalty in this life.

Look at what Romans 5 tells us.

> **Romans 5:17 (AMPC)** For if because of one man's trespass (lapse, offense) death reigned through that one, much more surely will those who receive [God's] overflowing grace (unmerited favor) and the free gift of righteousness [putting them into right standing with Himself] reign as kings in life through the one Man Jesus Christ (the Messiah, the Anointed One).

There is no sin big enough to dominate you if you will reign as a king in this life through Jesus Christ. Kings don't let anything push them around, and you shouldn't let the devil push you around either. Kings have what they want and lack for nothing. When a king says, "Jump!" those around him ask, "How high?" That's how it will be for you when you take your righteous position and rule and reign over the enemy. God expects you to rule and reign over him and all the evil he brings. Are you ruling over temptation? You should be. Pull out your scepter and reign over sin in your life. You can because Jesus gave you dominion.

3.   You will continue to grow up by eating the meat of God's Word.

Look at what Hebrews tell us.

> ### Hebrews 5:13-14 (NKJV)
>
> [13] For everyone who partakes only of milk is unskilled in the word of righteousness, for he is a babe.
>
> [14] But solid food belongs to those who are of full age, that is, those who by reason of use have their senses exercised to discern both good and evil.

Are you ready to move up, out of the spiritual nursery, and get off the milk bottle? We all start out as babies both in the natural and in the spiritual realm, but when a child gets older, it's troubling if they still want a milk bottle or their steak cut into little pieces. When we grow past milk and begin eating the meat of God's Word, we're better able to say, "No" to temptation and sin.

Baby Christians who are not willing to get off the spiritual bottle and move to the meat of the Word, have not yet grasped their righteousness, which means sin is likely dominating them.

4.   You will be strong and courageous.

Individuals who don't have a revelation of their righteousness will walk in sin consciousness. What's the solution? Isaiah 41 tells us.

> **Isaiah 41:10** Fear thou not; for I am with thee: be not dismayed; for I am thy God: I will strengthen thee; yea, I will help thee; yea, I will uphold thee with the right hand of my righteousness.

God says He will uphold you with the right hand of His righteousness, and all you have to do is accept what Jesus has already provided for you. You cannot earn it. You cannot buy it. But you can have it. It's a free gift. You are righteous, so act like it!

Don't let sin or fear creep into your life in any way, shape, or form. Jesus wasn't afraid of anything, and you don't have to be afraid either. Jesus commanded the winds and the waves to stop. When people ran out of food, He multiplied it. "But that's Jesus," someone might say. Yes, but when you speak His Word, you can also declare that circumstances and situations change. God said He would uphold you with His righteousness, so be bold.

5. You will refuse to be a slave of sin.

Nothing good comes from sin. It may bring pleasure for a short while, but it quickly turns into an ugly picture with a dead end. Look what the Apostle Paul said.

Romans 6:16-23 (AMPC)

16 Do you not know that if you continually surrender yourselves to anyone to do his will, you are the slaves of him whom you obey, whether that be to sin, which leads to death, or to obedience which leads to righteousness (right doing and right standing with God)?

17 But thank God, though you were once slaves of sin, you have become obedient with all your heart to the standard of teaching in which you were instructed and to which you were committed.

18 And having been set free from sin, you have become the servants of righteousness (of conformity to the divine will in thought, purpose, and action).

19 I am speaking in familiar human terms because of your natural limitations. For as you yielded your bodily members [and [c]faculties] as servants to impurity and ever increasing lawlessness, so now yield your bodily members [and [d]faculties] once for all as servants to righteousness (right being and doing) [which leads] to sanctification.

20 For when you were slaves of sin, you were free in regard to righteousness.

> **²¹ But then what benefit (return) did you get from the things of which you are now ashamed? [None] for the end of those things is death.**
>
> **²² But now since you have been set free from sin and have become the slaves of God, you have your present reward in holiness and its end is eternal life.**
>
> **²³ For the wages which sin pays is death, but the [bountiful] free gift of God is eternal life through (in union with) Jesus Christ our Lord.**

When you know you're no longer a slave to sin, you'll never again say things like, "I cannot control myself," or "I got into trouble because I'm sort of wishy-washy," or "I can't get over this or that," or "It's just my personality," or "I can't help myself," because the truth is, yes, you can! You have been set free, so walk free. Walk in your righteousness!

6. You will receive correction and be better for it.

Good parents correct their children, and God is no different. If you are God's child, He will correct you. If you receive that correction and adjust your life accordingly, you'll walk in righteousness. What you cannot afford to do is pretend like God is not dealing with you and continue to do those things that are wrong. In that case, the righteousness that legally belongs to you will not work in your life, and sin will continue to dominate you. Look at the instruction Hebrews 12 gives us.

> **Hebrews 12:11** Now no chastening for the present seemeth to be joyous, but grievous: nevertheless afterward it yieldeth the peaceable fruit of righteousness unto them which are exercised thereby.

God corrects us because He loves us. He doesn't punish us, but when we do wrong, He doesn't wink and say, "Oh well! Those stupid humans will never get it." No. God doesn't do that. He trains us as any good parent on Earth would. As every good parent will testify, bad behavior that goes undisciplined will cause great trouble for your children later.

The Amplified Classic says it this way,

> **Hebrews 12:11 (AMPC)** For the time being no discipline brings joy, but seems grievous and painful; but afterwards it yields a peaceable fruit of righteousness to those who have been trained by it [a harvest of fruit which consists in righteousness—in conformity to God's will in purpose, thought, and action, resulting in right living and right standing with God].

God will discipline, teach, and train us with His Word and by His Spirit. He loves us and does not send sickness, disease, calamities, or disasters to correct or teach His children. John 10:10 says that Jesus came to give us abundant life, and it's the devil who steals, kills, and destroys. James 1:17 says that every good and perfect gift comes down from the Father above.

An example is that God has probably corrected you as you've been reading this book. Every time you've thought, "Ouch," or "Yeah, that's me," or "That's true," or "I'm guilty of that," that was the Word correcting you. Every time you've known in your heart, "I need to change that area of my life," that was the Holy Spirit convicting and prompting you to change. And though that can be painful, if you will make the adjustments needed, you'll save yourself a whole lot of trouble and gain the "peaceable fruit of righteousness."

Even now, you may be standing at a fork in the road. Will you choose to break away from sin and follow righteousness? The choice is yours alone, but once you make that choice, God will help you walk it out. You and I could never overcome sin on our own; we must have the help of the Holy Spirit to teach, train and coach us through life.

Let's look at Romans 6 in The Amplified Classic that explains more about how righteousness sets us free from the acts of sin.

> **Romans 6:17-18**
>
> [17] But thank God, though you were once slaves of sin, you have become obedient with all your heart to the standard of teaching in which you were instructed and to which you were committed.

> **[18] And having been set free from sin, you have become the servants of righteousness (of conformity to the divine will in thought, purpose, and action).**

If you're thinking, "Where do I sign up to become a servant of righteousness?", you start by obeying the teachings of God's Word, transforming your thoughts to His thoughts, which are higher than our thoughts, and lining up with God's purposes, actions, and ways, which are higher than our ways. Again, you do this with the help of the Holy Spirit.

We cannot overcome temptation and sin by willpower; it must be done by God power. If we rely on willpower, we will become weak and fail; but when we allow God's power to work in our lives, we will be set free from sin and the desire to sin. Of course, we will still have our flesh to contend with and the devil, who will still try to entice us with the lusts of the flesh, but we will no longer be a slave to sin. Because we have been empowered and changed by the righteousness of God in Christ, we will no longer yield our bodies to its desires; instead, we will be a slave to righteousness.

> **Romans 6:22 (AMPC)** **But now since you have been set free from sin and have become the slaves of God, you have your present reward in holiness and its end is eternal life.**

This says you have the reward of holiness, and its paycheck is eternal life with God in Heaven, but the reward of holiness is so much more. It will help you to live free from the bondage of sin here and now.

Let me encourage you to meditate on the following scriptures to better lodge the truth of righteousness deep in your heart.

> **2 Corinthians 5:17-21**
>
> **[17] Therefore if any man be in Christ, he is a new creature: old things are passed away; behold, all things are become new.**
>
> **[18] And all things are of God, who hath reconciled us to himself by Jesus Christ, and hath given to us the ministry of reconciliation;**

¹⁹ To wit, that God was in Christ, reconciling the world unto himself, not imputing their trespasses unto them; and hath committed unto us the word of reconciliation.

²⁰ Now then we are ambassadors for Christ, as though God did beseech you by us: we pray you in Christ's stead, be ye reconciled to God.

²¹ For he hath made him to be sin for us, who knew no sin; that we might be made the righteousness of God in him.

1 Corinthians 1:30-31

³⁰ But of him are ye in Christ Jesus, who of God is made unto us wisdom, and righteousness, and sanctification, and redemption:

³¹ That, according as it is written, He that glorieth, let him glory in the Lord.

Romans 10:1-10

¹ Brethren, my heart's desire and prayer to God for Israel is, that they might be saved.

² For I bear them record that they have a zeal of God, but not according to knowledge.

³ For they being ignorant of God's righteousness, and going about to establish their own righteousness, have not submitted themselves unto the righteousness of God.

⁴ For Christ is the end of the law for righteousness to every one that believeth.

⁵ For Moses describeth the righteousness which is of the law, That the man which doeth those things shall live by them.

> [6] But the righteousness which is of faith speaketh on this wise, Say not in thine heart, Who shall ascend into heaven? (that is, to bring Christ down from above:)
>
> [7] Or, Who shall descend into the deep? (that is, to bring up Christ again from the dead.)
>
> [8] But what saith it? The word is nigh thee, even in thy mouth, and in thy heart: that is, the word of faith, which we preach;
>
> [9] That if thou shalt confess with thy mouth the Lord Jesus, and shalt believe in thine heart that God hath raised him from the dead, thou shalt be saved.
>
> [10] For with the heart man believeth unto righteousness; and with the mouth confession is made unto salvation.

The more revelation you have of righteousness, the better off you'll be. Maybe you've felt that up until now, your Christian walk has been the right walk, but a hard walk. Let me encourage you that this righteousness will make hard things easy. If you'll position yourself to rule and reign through the righteousness Jesus has given you, you'll no longer continually struggle with sin, sickness, poverty, or any work of the devil. Righteousness is how we are able to walk in the position ordained for you as a son and daughter of the Most High God.

Another important key is to renew your mind, so it agrees with what the Word of God says. This we will talk about in the next chapter.

Chapter
Twelve
Questions

1. What is righteousness, and how do we receive it?

2. What happens when we know that we are righteous in Christ, and how does it affect our confidence?

3. Explain what it means for your prayers to be effective.

4. **How will ruling and reigning in this life help the sin problem?**

5. **What happens when you are unskilled in the word of righteousness?**

6. **Why does correction benefit you concerning sin?**

Chapter
Twelve
Confessions

✳ I will not fear for You are with me. I will not be dismayed for You are my God. I am strengthened and helped because God upholds me. (Isaiah 41:10)

✳ I have been set free from sin and have become a servant of righteousness. I walk in God's divine will, thoughts, and purposes. (Romans 6:18)

✳ God corrects me because He love me. I will yield to His correction because it will produce the peaceable fruit of righteousness in me. (Hebrews 12:11)

✳ Because of God's generosity freely given, He has made me right with Him and has restored me. (Romans 3:24)

✳ I am seated in heavenly places, and I refuse to sin because it and the enemy are under my feet. (2 Corinthians 5:21, Ephesians 2:6, 1:22)

chapter 13: our mind is a terrible thing to waste

Your mind is powerful. It can nip sin in the bud or set the stage for temptation to run rampant and drive you to destruction. In fact, your mind is a battlefield and it's where you fight most of your battles. Whatever you set your mind on is eventually what happens in your life.

After all, a person doesn't just go to Walmart one day and fall into adultery. A person doesn't just drive the kids to school one morning and suddenly decide to rob a bank on their way home. That's not how it happens. That's not the process of sin. Sin starts in the mind; it begins with a single thought that builds from there. Sin and lust are conceived in the mind.

That's why the Bible tells us that if we will train our mind not to think on things we shouldn't think on, we can close the door on sin before it even starts. In fact, the Bible is pretty clear that if we will keep our mind focused on God's Word and follow the leadings of the Holy Spirit, victory and success will be ours.

> **Joshua 1:8 (NKJV)** This Book of the Law shall not depart from your mouth, but you shall meditate in it day and night, that you may observe to do according to all that is written in it. For then you will make your way prosperous, and then you will have good success.

If you keep your mind focused on God's Word and purpose to do it, you will walk in prosperity, health, and wisdom, and fulfill what God has called you to do.

God is not trying to spoil your good times. God wants you to be free from sin and be the best you can be, to have the best family and best job. God wants you to be happy, wealthy, and wise, and His Word will show you how to do it as you walk uprightly.

SAVING YOUR SOUL

We talked earlier about how we receive a new nature, that our spirit, or inner person of the heart, becomes new. Our spirit isn't just fixed a little when we're born again, it is completely made new; but our mind remained the same as they were before we were born again, so they need to be retrained according to God's Word.

Let's look at it this way. Maybe you have heard it said that your mind is like a computer, and that's true; but when it comes to being born again, nothing happens to your mental computer. No reset button is pushed, no new program is downloaded or installed. Even though, practically speaking, you are in desperate need of new software and technical assistance, so your mind can be filled with new information and a new way of thinking, that doesn't happen when your spirit is born-again. Learning to think like God thinks is a process of adjusting what and how you think, which the Bible calls "renewing your mind. "

This is where I feel a lot of people miss it and remain stuck in a life of sin. People get born again, even filled with the Holy Spirit, but they don't do anything with their soul realm (mind, will and emotions). They continue to live, think, and talk just like they did before they were born again.

The word "soul" can be hard for people to understand. For instance, people will say, "Wow, 10 souls got saved today!" Yes, 10 people did get saved but what they really meant to say was 10 people received Jesus as their Lord and Savior. They were born again, and received a brand-new spirit, His divine nature, but their body and soul remained the same, so they need to be disciplined, controlled, and retrained in the things of God.

As a pastor, I've often seen the anointing of God deliver people in our church services from drugs, pornography, alcohol, gambling, stealing, lying, cheating and habits that have been dogging them. But then, most don't realize that in order to continue walking in their victory, they need to renew their mind. Only then, can they be free and remain free.

Without a doubt, the anointing will remove the addiction, but addictions are not only physical; they can also be mental or emotional. So, until a person gets their mind renewed, the sin problem won't be fixed.

You see, before we were born again, our old nature thought like the world, acted like the world, and followed in the footsteps of our father the devil. Why did sin dog us?

Ephesians 2:3 Among these we as well as you once lived and conducted ourselves in the passions of our flesh [our behavior governed by our corrupt and sensual nature], obeying the impulses of the flesh and the thoughts of the mind [our cravings dictated by our senses and our dark imaginings]. We were then by nature children of [God's] wrath and heirs of [His] indignation, like the rest of mankind.

Bottom line, before being born again, our mind was a mess because it was programmed by this world. We didn't think right because we were influenced by the devil, who is the god of this world system. We were unable to resist these influences, but now that we are born again and have a new spirit and the help of the Holy Ghost, we can resist by renewing our mind with the Word of God.

You might be thinking, "Well, I'm telling you right now that my mind was not controlled by the devil;" but the truth is that before you were born again, your mind was governed by this world's system rather than by God and His Word. You didn't know how to combat your evil tendencies, so you just yielded your thoughts to the enemy, the god of this world (2 Corinthians 4:4).

It's important for us to realize the tremendous influence the enemy had over us before we were born again, so we can understand why we must renew our mind. Before we were born again, all we could do was follow after our flesh because our nature had not been changed. We were of this world with our mind set on gratifying our flesh. We thought about sin, got a picture of it in our mind, and then set out to satisfy what our flesh wanted. Whatever it craved, we said "Yes" because our mind had been set to sin.

Romans 8:4-8 (AMPC)

4 So that the righteous and just requirement of the Law might be fully met in us who live and move not in the ways of the flesh but in the ways of the Spirit [our lives governed not by the standards and according to the dictates of the flesh, but controlled by the Holy Spirit].

5 For those who are according to the flesh and are controlled by its unholy desires set their minds on and pursue those things which gratify the flesh, but those who are according to the Spirit and are controlled by the desires of the Spirit set their minds on and seek those things which gratify the [Holy] Spirit.

6 Now the mind of the flesh [which is sense and reason without the Holy Spirit] is death [death that comprises all the miseries arising from sin, both here and hereafter]. But the mind of the [Holy] Spirit is life and [soul] peace [both now and forever].

7 [That is] because the mind of the flesh [with its carnal thoughts and purposes] is hostile to God, for it does not submit itself to God's Law; indeed it cannot.

8 So then those who are living the life of the flesh [catering to the appetites and impulses of their carnal nature] cannot please or satisfy God, or be acceptable to Him.

Here's the battle. Your mind wants to set its sights on what feels good to the flesh, and it doesn't plan to let anything get in its way. That's why your mind has to be taught to think differently. If you don't retrain and renew your mind, then you're in for a real knock-down drag-out with the devil. That's why a lot of Christians, who love God, are still sinning, even though they really don't want to sin.

We have to face facts. Knowing something is wrong and doing something about it are two totally different things. What am I telling you? If you want to do something about sin, you must reprogram your mind. In fact, Romans 8 makes the choice clear. Either you will refocus your mind on God's Word and pleasing Him, or you will keep your mind set on the things of this world and gratify the cravings of your flesh at every turn.

Romans 8:6 lays out what happens if you make the wrong choice because it said that the mind of the flesh without the Holy Spirit is death. When our mind is left to think on its own, without the help of the Holy Spirit, it will lead to destruction. Why? Because without the Word and the Spirit of God, the human mind produces sin, and sin always produces a paycheck of death.

If you're thinking, "I'm still alive, and I've sinned plenty." Well, I'm glad you're still alive because it gives you more time to choose to walk uprightly and in the goodness of God. If you will look back at the point where you got off into sin, I'm sure you'll find that it has produced some sort of death in your life. Did it end a relationship, a marriage, a business, a ministry, or something else? That's death. Sin may be fun for a season, but it always comes to an end. I'm so thankful for God's mercy, and how He waits for us to come to Him and repent.

Let's look at Romans 8:6 (AMPC) again.

> **Romans 8:6 (AMPC)** Now the mind of the flesh [which is sense and reason without the Holy Spirit] is death [death that comprises all the miseries arising from sin, both here and hereafter]. But the mind of the [Holy] Spirit is life and [soul] peace [both now and forever].

How many of you want some soul peace? We all do. Verse 7 went on to say that the mind of the flesh, with its carnal thoughts and purposes, is hostile to God, which means an unrenewed mind is hostile to God, and that's not a good place to be.

Like a lot of kids, I heard the stories of the Bible as a little boy, but I didn't have much practical teaching from God's Word; so even though I was born again and loved God, by the age of 12,

I got off into doing what I wanted to do. I still loved God and respected Him, but I no longer served Him. And honestly, back then, I didn't really understand a lot of what I had read in the Bible. By my early 20s, I was a very liberal thinker and embraced many things that I oppose today. Why? Because even though I was born again, my mind was still contrary to the Word of God. I had heard very little of God's Word and understood even less. My mind couldn't think like God. I didn't know or understand what God thought because I never renewed my mind with the Word of God.

What happened to me is the same story for a lot of people. Although they love God, they never renewed the space between their ears, their mind. That's sad because what we do with our mind will determine whether or not we will be successful in our walk with God.

We have to choose to renew the mind because if left alone, it will oppose God. Romans 8:8 says, "…those who are living a life of the flesh…cannot please or satisfy God or be acceptable to him." Make no mistake. These words were not written to sinners but to Christians in the early church and are also for the church of today, which includes you and me.

Wouldn't it be wonderful if all we had to do was call someone down to the altar in a service and pray that all their sinful tendencies would just disappear? That would certainly be a microwave or drive-thru kind of fix, but most things are not that way with God. God is a good God, and He wants to fix things, but we have a part to do. In fact, there are many things that God has for us that we will never receive unless we do our part. God will always do His part. His side is already done, but there's a God side and a man side to receiving from God, so what you do does matter.

As a pastor, I see Christians who have been in church for decades who have failed to renew their mind; and, unfortunately, they are the ones who either fall right back into sin or wrestle and struggle with sin for the rest of their lives. If we don't renew our mind, we will continue to have the same ugly, impure, lustful, mean, unkind, unholy thoughts that will produce the same ugly, impure, lustful, mean, unkind, unholy desires and actions that we had before we were born again.

It's no wonder why so many Christians have such a problem with sin. Just by living in this world, we're continually faced with things that try to entice and tease the lusts of our flesh. So, if you want to live in victory, and I know you do or you wouldn't be reading this book, you must renew your mind. If you're going to break free, stay free and walk free from sin, you've got to think differently than you did before. And you can because God said you could.

So, how do we do it?

HOW TO RENEW YOUR MIND

God's Word shows us how we can renew our mind, so we can think differently.

Writing to the Christians in Rome, the Apostle Paul lays out a key scripture for us.

> **Romans 12:2 (NKJV)** **Do not be conformed to this world, but be transformed by the renewing of your mind, that you may prove what is that good and acceptable and perfect will of God.**

The word "transform" in the Greek means a metamorphosis, and that's exactly what our mind needs. We need to transform our mind in the same way that a caterpillar transforms into a butterfly. Our mind needs a radical change! The process of going from a caterpillar to a butterfly creates something altogether different. Caterpillars aren't all that good looking, but butterflies are beautiful. I believe Paul was telling them and us that it's time to turn into something beautiful. God wants to take our mind, which pushes us into sin, and transform it into something of beauty.

Psalm 23:3 (NKJV) says, "He restores my soul." We hear the word "restore" a lot of times when people talk about restoring old cars or old furniture. It means to bring an object back to its original state of beauty. Restoration is not automatic. It takes a lot of hard work, but eventually the original beauty shines through.

James 1:21 (NKJV) tells us how to begin the restoration process on our mind in James 1:21, "Therefore lay aside all filthiness and overflow of wickedness, and receive with meekness the implanted word, which is able to save your souls." James is explaining that the key to renewing our mind is to receive God's Word with a meek and teachable spirit.

As you give the Word first place in your life by reading, studying, meditating, and acting on what it says, it will begin to transform your life. Your thoughts will change your words, and your words will change your actions. This is where the rubber meets the road. So many people, who love God, never find the pathway to victory because they don't renew their mind and act on the Word. It's not enough to love God; we must also obey God. When we obey

God and do what He says, that's when victory will be ours.

I cannot count the number of people who have been in my office over the years in tears saying, "I don't understand how I fell into sin. I love God." I don't question their love for God, but it takes more than loving God to walk in victory. We have to obey His Word.

THE BATTLEFIELD OF THE MIND

You're at war, whether you realize it or not, and the battlefield is right between your ears. It's a battle to walk in the light instead of darkness. It is a battle to obey instead of disobey God. It's literally a battle between good and evil, and you get to decide the winner.

If you haven't figured it out already, you cannot afford to think like you did, and here's why. If you continue to think like you used to, then you will act like you did before you were saved. In fact, one of the biggest triggers causing you to sin is the thought patterns you developed while you were living and practicing sin, and it's those thought patterns that need to be changed by the renewing of your mind.

A born-again person, who does not renew their mind, is at a tremendous disadvantage because the enemy continually attacks them with wrong thoughts. It's sad, but it's true. No wonder people are frustrated, feeling defeated, and still living in sin. What is the answer? A great transformation must take place by renewing our mind, so we can use our God-given weapons to defeat the enemy.

This is another key scripture that will point the way to victory.

2 Corinthians 10:4-5

4 (For the weapons of our warfare are not carnal, but mighty through God to the pulling down of strong holds;)

5 Casting down imaginations, and every high thing that exalteth itself against the knowledge of God, and bringing into captivity every thought to the obedience of Christ.

Did you notice the word "stronghold"? It refers to a fortified place where people in days gone by would build forts high on a hill to be protected from enemy attack. That's what the devil tries to do to us; he wants us to build strongholds, fortified places, and wrong patterns of thinking in our mind to destroy us.

These strongholds and patterns of thinking come through imaginations, thoughts, arguments and reasonings. A stronghold is any thought pattern in your mind that opposes the Word of God. Whether we call them strongholds or patterns of thinking, we all have them; and if we don't deal with them, they will keep us from walking in God's highest and best.

Someone might be thinking, "He's just talking about people who struggle with alcohol, or drugs, or pornography, or have some huge problem, right?" No. We all have thoughts that oppose the will and purpose of God in our lives, and if we don't get rid of them, they will develop into strongholds, so this applies to all of us.

In a book called *Dressed to Kill*, author Rick Renner shares this about strongholds.

> **"Individuals who have these kinds of strongholds in their lives are in bondage both mentally and emotionally. Sometime in the past the enemy located an open door in their lives. Then after passing through that entrance into their minds, he began the process of taking their thoughts captive through his lies. The result is always the same: Strongholds are built that acts as a prison, preventing these individuals from breaking free to fulfill their God-ordained purpose on this earth."**

How serious is this? It's very serious. If a believer never does anything about renewing their mind, these strongholds will prevent them from obeying and fulfilling their God-ordained purpose.

If we don't learn to take captive thoughts that oppose God's Word, then one day these negative thoughts will take us captive. We must arrest these thoughts and take them prisoner before they trap us into a wrong way of thinking that will keep us bound to sin for life. Armed with the Word of God, we are to cast down every high thing that exalts itself against the knowledge of God and bring into captivity every thought, every single one, to the obedience of Christ.

Notice how the Amplified Bible translates Paul's instructions to us.

2 Corinthians 10:4-5 (AMPC)

[4] For the weapons of our warfare are not physical [weapons of flesh and blood], but they are mighty before God for the overthrow and destruction of strongholds,

[5] [Inasmuch as we] refute arguments and theories and reasonings and every proud and lofty thing that sets itself up against the [true] knowledge of God; and we lead every thought and purpose away captive into the obedience of Christ (the Messiah, the Anointed One).

Paul tells us to overthrow and destroy strongholds by refusing to think any thought that opposes God's Word. Whatever God says and declares about a thing is what we should say and declare about a thing.

When it comes to thoughts, you don't have to receive and meditate on every thought that pops into your head. You don't have to take it! You can refuse it because every thought that comes into your head isn't yours. The devil will pester you with all kinds of thoughts about sin, sickness, poverty, and death, and anything else that is contrary to God's Word. If you have something physically wrong in your body, the devil will plant a thought like, "You're probably going to die." When you are struggling with your finances, have you ever thought, "What if I can't pay my bills, and I go broke?" Can you see what the devil is trying to do? He's trying to plant a bad thought in your mind, so you'll begin to believe and talk that thought. That's called a stronghold; and if not dealt with, it will produce the wrong results.

The good news is, God has given you authority over your life and what happens to you. He's given you many precious promises, and He expects you to use your faith to obtain them; but what the devil wants is for you to agree with him, so he can ruin your life.

How do we know if a thought is from God or the devil? Because God's thoughts are written down in the Bible from Genesis 1 to Revelation 22. Everything we need to walk in victory is in His Word for us to read, so no more garbage in when it comes to your mind. As we put in God's Word, it will remove the garbage. As we make God's thoughts our thoughts, we'll find ourselves on the road to victory. If a thought goes against God's Word, it's from the devil. If it steals, kills, or destroys, it's from the devil. Those are the thoughts we are to cast down. If a thought doesn't agree with God's Word, take it prisoner and then, kick it out of your mind.

Tell that thought, "You're not allowed here, so go!" Then, replace those negative thoughts with the truth of God's Word.

Have you ever thought, "I'm a failure," or "I'm just a loser," or "I'll never amount to anything"? If you're married, maybe you can't stop thinking about that guy or gal at work. Maybe you're someone who is overcome with thoughts of pornography or addictive substances. Whatever wrong thoughts you might be having, just ask yourself, "Do these thoughts oppose God's Word?". If the answer is "Yes," take them captive. Arrest them. Toss them out. Refuse to think them. Replace them with what God says such as…

"God always leads me to victory; I am more than a conqueror."

"I am dead to sin, so…

- **I will think good thoughts about my spouse and not that person at work.**

- **I will meditate on the Word which will drive out the lusts of my flesh (Pornography, addictive substances, and so on)."**

You can't just let wrong thoughts go crazy and run wild in your mind because if you do, they'll eventually become strongholds. Thoughts will make pictures and will then create reality if you don't deal with them. When I say, "Dog," most people will get a mental picture of a dog. When I say, "Cat," you get a picture of a cat. When I say, "A million dollars," you get a picture of a pile of cash. Words build pictures and imaginations in our mind. It's the same with wrong thoughts, so you can't afford to let negative thoughts hang around.

What do you do when negative thoughts come to your mind? Talk to them. When I was flying overseas and the plane began bouncing around, the devil shot plenty of thoughts my way including, "You're going to die. The plane is going down." Did I give in to those fearful thoughts? Did I start imagining my funeral and wondering what it would be like? Did I begin to cry? Did I say goodbye to my loved ones? No. I opened my mouth and said, "With long life will God satisfy me and show me His salvation" (Psalm 91:16). "I will live and not die and proclaim the works of the Lord" (Psalm 118:17). In other words, when the devil fired shots at me, I fired back with the truth of God's Word.

That's how you take thoughts captive. Your mouth speaking the Word takes a thought captive and releases your faith to cleanse your mind. That's also how you can arrest thoughts of sin and temptation that come across your mind. You must do this to back off thoughts of temptation or, before you know it, you'll be sitting in your pastor's office with your head in your hands saying, "Oh, my God, how did I fall into this sin? How did it happen?"

Begin meditating on what God has to say about your situation. For example, if you have a thought of worry, begin to meditate on scriptures like 1 Peter 5:7 (NKJV), which says "Cast all your care upon Him, for He cares for you." Begin to say from your heart, "I refuse to worry because my God cares for me. He takes care of my cares, so I am carefree."

If you have thoughts concerning anger issues, confess scriptures on the love of God. If you have trouble with sin in any area, confess "In Him" and "In Christ" scriptures because when you're conscious of your oneness with Jesus Christ, it's hard to be conscious of sin at the same time. As we continually confess our union with Jesus Christ, sin has to drop off.

Let me give you a tool that has worked for me many times. In fact, let's do this now. Begin to count to 10 in your mind. Then, when I say, "Praise the Lord," you repeat it out loud after me. Here we go. Count: 1, 2, 3, 4, 5. Say, "Praise the Lord." What happened to your counting when you said, "Praise the Lord!"? Did you stop counting? Yes, of course, you did! Your brain had to unhook from the counting to connect with your vocal cords to speak. Likewise, even though the devil may pester you with wrong thoughts, if you'll speak God's Word out loud, your brain will unhook from those wrong thoughts and quote the Word.

This has been a tried-and-true method for me to short circuit negative thoughts. Just open your mouth and say what the Word says about your situation and short circuit those wrong thoughts that come. You have to get serious about this. Don't let even one wrong thought go unchecked. It's that serious. Not controlling your thoughts would be like not dealing with cancer and letting it spread and destroy everything in its path.

If you're wondering, "How long do I have to resist thoughts of sin and temptation?" The answer is, as long as it takes. You've got to be stronger than the enemy. You've got to demonstrate more perseverance than the devil does knowing he's a defeated foe. Best yet, if you continue to resist the enemy, James 4:7 says, "…he will flee." The word "flee" is to run in terror, which means with God's Word, you'll put the devil on the run.

The one thing you cannot do is ignore negative thoughts. If you do, they can really put you in bondage. Worries can fly at you so fast and furious that you end up in a tailspin of panic. You also cannot pray away thoughts, nor can someone else pray them away for you. The only way to get rid of wrong thoughts is to take them prisoner by speaking God's Word. And the only way we can successfully change our thinking is to renew our mind with the Word of God. We transform our mind by taking every thought contrary to God's Word captive. We need to cast down every wrong thought, imagination or mental picture that does not line up with God's Word and replace it with the truth of God's Word.

GIVE YOUR MIND A BATH

God's Word will give our mind a bath. Ephesians 5:26 says, "That he might sanctify and cleanse it with the washing of water by the word." This scripture is talking about washing the church with the Word because the Word is the cleansing agent that is applied to whatever needs cleaning.

John 17:17 (NKJV) **Sanctify them by your truth. Your word is truth.**

John 15:3 **Now ye are clean through the word which I have spoken unto you.**

You and I must let the truth cleanse our mind, and only God's Word can do that.

We must allow God's Word to sanctify us, to set us apart from the lusts of the flesh. When we continuously live a life that is sanctified, we won't yield to what our flesh wants. God gives us the ability to take His Word and use it like a washcloth with soap and water to scrub our mind clean from sin.

Another scripture that talks about the mind is found in Hebrews.

Hebrews12:3 **For consider him [Jesus] that endured such contraction [hostility] of sinner against himself, lest ye be wearied and faint in your minds.**

Did you know that you can become weary and faint in your mind? The devil will try to wear you out to the point that you faint mentally.

There have been two times in my life I've fainted physically, and it's like you just suddenly lose all power. You can imagine the heyday the devil would have if he could get you to lose all power and control mentally. Sin would not only be knocking at your door but would move in. But did you notice that this scripture also shows you how not to faint? It says those who get weary faint because they fail to consider Jesus. They're not focused on the way of escape God has provided for them. So, this tells us that if we will keep our mind on Jesus, we won't get weary and faint.

Isaiah 26:3 goes further and says that God will keep you in perfect peace when your mind is focused on Him. The New Living Translation says, "You will keep in perfect peace all who trust in you, all whose thoughts are fixed on you!" That's your solution. Keep your mind on Jesus. Keep your thoughts fixed on Him, and He will keep you in perfect peace because this peace has nothing in common with sin.

Another step in renewing your mind is to accept the promises of God concerning your mind. How do you accept a Bible promise? You hear it, believe it, and confess it over yourself to release it. Romans 10:17 says that "Faith comes by hearing the Word of God," and one of the best ways to hear the Word is to hear it coming out your own mouth. Notice what the Bible says in Mark.

> **Mark 11:23 (NKJV)** **For assuredly, I say to you, whoever says to this mountain, 'Be removed and be cast into the sea,' and does not doubt in his heart, but believes that those things he says will be done, he will have whatever he says.**

When thoughts fly against your mind that don't line up with God's Word, open your Bible and find out what God says about the situation and then, speak His Word aloud, so His Word will renew and retrain your mind.

Here are two verses God has spoken about your mind to help you.

> **1 Corinthians 2:16** **...We have the mind of Christ.**

Begin to say, "Because Jesus lives in me, I have the mind of Christ. I think His thoughts, which are found in His Word.

> **Philippians 2:5** **Let this mind be in you which was also in Christ Jesus.**

Begin to say, "I have the same mind set as Christ Jesus." Even if your current thoughts don't even remotely seem like thoughts that Jesus would think, say this verse anyway and watch what happens.

If you will begin to measure and weigh your thoughts, the Holy Spirit will help you by bringing to your attention those thoughts that don't line up with God's Word.

Philippians 4 says you can keep yourself from thinking wrong thoughts. In fact, the Bible even tells you what to think on.

> **Philippians 4:8 (NKJV)**
>
> **Finally, brethren, whatever things are true, whatever things are noble, whatever things are just, whatever things are pure, whatever things are lovely, whatever things are of good report, if there is any virtue and if there is anything praiseworthy—meditate on these things.**

This is the ultimate God-ordained Bible test for thoughts. The Holy Spirit has spelled out exactly what we should think about. That means when a thought comes that doesn't meet the Philippians 4:8 test, kick it out and refuse to think on it. Think God's way and you'll find yourself no longer bound to sin.

Chapter
Thirteen
Questions

1. What does it mean to "renew your mind" and why should you renew your mind?

2. How do you overcome strongholds in your mind? What are we to do with wrong thoughts/strongholds?

3. How do you know if a thought is from God or the devil?

4. **How do we keep our mind from leading us into sin?**

5. **What are some things that we should think on?**

Chapter
Thirteen
Confessions

✷   I will meditate on and be a doer of the Word of God, so that my way will be made prosperous, and I will have good success. (Joshua 1:8)

✷   I will not be conformed to this world, but I will be transformed as I renew my mind with the Word of God so I can prove what is the perfect will of God. (Romans 12:2)

✷   I will only think on those things that are true, noble, just, pure, lovely, and things that are of a good report. I will think on those things that have virtue, and things that are praiseworthy. These are the things I will meditate on. (Philippians 4:8)

✷   I will cleanse and sanctify my mind with the washing of the Word. (John 15:3, 17:17)

✷   I have the mind of Christ because I think His thoughts which I find in the Word of God. (1 Corinthians 2:16)

chapter 14: multiplan to attack sin

The Bible doesn't list only one key to our freedom because there's not just one single thing to know or to do; there's not simply one switch we flip to eliminate sin in our lives. We've talked about many of the "how-to" keys that will enable us to break free and stay free from sin, but there's more. And the more supernatural tools you know about and learn how to use, the more empowered and equipped you will be to walk in the freedom that God has provided.

Walking with God is just that. It's a walk with many things to learn along the way. That's why God gave us 66 books in the Bible, so we could know. God doesn't waste words, so I know there are different keys that work for different people at different times in their lives. Which keys do you need to know about? All of them, so you can be ready to use the one you need. Let's continue by looking at what we have been given to attack sin.

THE ANOINTING

One of the most important supernatural helps available is what the Bible calls the anointing, the manifest presence of God. This manifest power can be sensed in the spirit, in the inward person of the heart; but it can also be tangible. Whether you sense the anointing inwardly or outwardly, it's still the power of God that delivers His promise of freedom into your life.

Jesus boldly proclaimed the anointing was upon Him to preach the gospel to the poor, heal the broken hearted and deliverance to the captives.

> ### Luke 4:18-19
>
> **[18]The Spirit of the Lord is upon me, because he hath anointed me to preach the gospel to the poor; he hath sent me to heal the brokenhearted, to preach deliverance to the captives, and recovering of sight to the blind, to set at liberty them that are bruised,**
>
> **[19]To preach the acceptable year of the Lord.**

It says that Jesus came to set at liberty those that were bruised, so what does "bruise" mean? It is having a sore spot left over from an injury. I'm sure you've noticed that the devil likes to poke at sore spots in your life, and it hurts when he does. The enemy will constantly poke at those areas where you have yielded to the lusts of your flesh, but the good news is, the anointing will liberate those who are bruised or have been hurt by sin.

Let me encourage you to come in contact with the power of God as often as possible. Get into as many church services as you can where the presence of God is manifested. Worship God at home until His presence fills the room. If you want emancipation from the bondage of sin that you're in, you must yield yourself to God's power and anointing.

In 2 Corinthians 3:17 (AMPC), it says, "Now the Lord is that Spirit, and where the Spirit of the Lord is, there is a liberty (emancipation from bondage, freedom)." When you allow the anointing, the presence of God, to invade your life and come into contact with your flesh, freedom will be yours.

This anointing we are talking about always destroys bondage. Isaiah 10:27 says, "the yoke shall be destroyed because of the anointing." That means the sinful junk we all deal with can be destroyed by coming in contact with the power of God. We all need the power of God, but His anointing and power are not stand-alone solutions. If we want to walk in victory over sin, we need to keep ourselves in the Word of God and continually seek the presence of God. That means we need to attend churches that pursue the presence of God, not only in teaching, but also in practice.

The anointing has changed my life, and I know it will change yours. It's the anointing that comes to destroy the bondage that's held us in sin. Isaiah 42:7 says, "To open the blind eyes, to bring out the prisoners from prison, and them that sit in darkness out of the prison house." The anointing will break off any chains that bind you, so you can walk out free from the prison house of sin.

Make no mistake. Jesus broke the power of bondage in your life when He went to the cross over 2,000 years ago. The door to the prison house has been unlocked and is now wide open. All you have to do is believe that it's God's will for you to be free and then, by faith, walk in this freedom.

Other than physically dying, there's no way to completely get rid of the lusts of your flesh, but the manifest presence of God will go a long way in equipping you to resist the devil. Regular doses of the power of God will help you keep your flesh in check. We need the anointing, and we need it on a regular basis.

Acts 2:17 says, "And it shall come to pass in the last days, saith God I will pour out of my spirit upon all flesh…". In this instance, the scripture is talking about the Holy Spirit being poured out on all mankind. I believe this scripture also shows us how the Holy Spirit will help us keep our flesh under because God's Spirit is not only in you as a born-again believer but can also come on you. For example, on the day of Pentecost, the Bible says the Spirit of God came on each one of the people in the Upper Room like cloven tongues of fire. This fire of God forever changed 120 people that day.

Prior to the day of Pentecost, Peter had denied Jesus three times. Then, the fire of the Holy Ghost changed him so much that day that he was bold enough to stand up and preach to everyone who would hear him. The fire of God caused Peter's flesh to go from hiding in the Upper Room to proclaiming the gospel message on the streets of Jerusalem. The fire, or power of God, on your flesh will change you so thoroughly that you will act differently.

Malachi 3:2-3 talks about how Jesus will come like a refiner's fire and fuller's soap and clean you up. After you are born again, you are clean on the inside, but your flesh that's inclined to sin still needs work. So, thank God for His fire that brings change to our lives.

I've watched many people come to church and get on fire for God but then, slowly drift away and eventually return to their sinful life. One reason they slid back into sin was because they left the fire. They thought they could conquer sin on their own, but they were wrong. If we could handle sin on our own, we wouldn't need God. The truth is that we will never get to a place where we don't need God and His power.

Will just one dose of the power of God be enough to set you free from sin? Maybe. But to stay free, you'll need to partake regularly. Get in the manifest presence of God as often as you can because, again, 2 Corinthians 3:17 (AMPC) says, "…Where the Spirit of the Lord is, there is liberty (emancipation from bondage, freedom)."

I want to encourage you to get in a church where God's Word is taught, and His Spirit is allowed to move and given free course to manifest. It's important to regularly position yourself in church services where the people know how to worship God and the power of God is in demonstration. It will forever change you from the inside out.

Notice how Paul teaches about how the power of God works from the inside out in our lives.

Romans 8:8-13 (NKJV)

8 So then, those who are in the flesh cannot please God.

9 But you are not in the flesh but in the Spirit, if indeed the Spirit of God dwells in you. Now if anyone does not have the Spirit of Christ, he is not His.

10 And if Christ is in you, the body is dead because of sin, but the Spirit is life because of righteousness.

11 But if the Spirit of Him who raised Jesus from the dead dwells in you, He who raised Christ from the dead will also give life to your mortal bodies through His Spirit who dwells in you.

12 Therefore, brethren, we are debtors—not to the flesh, to live according to the flesh.

> **¹³ For if you live according to the flesh you will die; but if by the Spirit you put to death the deeds of the body, you will live.**

Verse 11 in The King James says:

> **Romans 8:11** **But if the Spirit of him that raised up Jesus from the dead dwell in you, he that raised up Christ from the dead shall also <u>quicken your mortal bodies by his Spirit that dwelleth in you</u>.**

I want to focus on Verse 11, which tells us something many people seem to miss. I've heard many Bible teachers share from this verse about how the power of God quickens our mortal bodies to heal us. That's true and thank God for it; but did you know, in this setting, Paul is actually talking about living free from sin?

Verse 11 tells us that the same Spirit, the Holy Spirit, that raised Jesus from the dead is in you through the new birth and is quickening your mortal flesh. What does "quickening" mean? It means to make alive. How awesome is that?! The Holy Spirit is inside you and comes on you to make you alive to God and dead to sin. How will you ever be able to mortify the deeds of your flesh? By allowing the power of God to quicken your flesh, you can live the good life God has planned for you.

How much better can it get? While you simply enjoy the presence of God, the Holy Spirit is working on the inside as well as on the outside to help you keep your flesh under. Keep in mind that this is the same power that raised Jesus from the dead and translated Him from one kingdom to another. It's the same power that transported you from the kingdom of darkness into the kingdom of light and empowered you to live free from sin.

THE TRUTH THAT MAKES YOU FREE

If you look over your life and think, "What's wrong with this picture? I've been continually struggling with sin." Then, it's time for you to turn your attention to the Word of God because John 8:32 (NKJV) says, "You shall know the truth, and the truth shall make you free." God's Word will make you free!

What's your part? Your part is to know the truth. What does that mean? Let me answer this way. Jesus is the Word made flesh who lived among us (John 1:14). So, when you know the Word of God, you will know the Son of God. John 8:36 says, "If the son therefore shall make you free, ye shall be free indeed." Jesus wants to set you free from the sins, bad habits, and junk that tries to keep you in bondage.

Let's look at what Hebrews 4 tells us.

> **Hebrews 4:12 (NKJV)** **For the word of God is living and powerful, and sharper than any two-edged sword, piercing even to the division of soul and spirit, and of joints and marrow, and is a discerner of the thoughts and intents of the heart.**

The Word of God is alive and powerful and sharper than even a double-edged sword. Only God's Word is able to divide between your soul and spirit, so you can discern between what God is telling you and what your mind and emotions are telling you. Only the Word of God is powerful enough to help you separate your mental thoughts from your heart purposes.

What a powerful tool to help us combat sin. The Word of God can perform surgery and help us identify attitudes, patterns, and behaviors that need to change, so we can get out of the mess of sin and bad habits we are in. God's Word will guide us out of sin into a life that is full and pleasing to the Lord.

Hebrews 1:3 says the Word of God is the power of God, and it's that power that you need in your life. Willpower is great, but a strong will is not enough to permanently deliver you from sin. Self-help programs can be good too, but they are not enough. They won't get you to the finish line. You need God's Word abiding in your heart and demonstrated in your life, so that the truth of His Word can make you everything you need to be.

WORDS MATTER

If I tell you that by making one small change, you can radically change your life for the better, would you make the change? Sure, you would. If you'll line up your words with God's Word, your whole life can turn around, and you will be heading in the right direction.

The truth is, if you talk like a sinner, sin is what you'll have. You shouldn't be saying things like, "I just cannot help myself," "I give up," "I never do anything right," "I've tried to defeat sin, but I keep failing," "I just cannot seem to say no." Do you see these words in the Bible? No. Did Jesus talk like that? No. Then you shouldn't talk like that either. Proverbs 18:21 says that death and life are in the power of the tongue, so what you say matters.

James 3 tells us that if we will learn to control our tongue, we can control our whole body.

> **James 3:2-6 (NKJV)**
>
> **² For we all stumble in many things. If anyone does not stumble in word, he is a perfect man, able also to bridle the whole body.**
>
> **³ Indeed, we put bits in horses' mouths that they may obey us, and we turn their whole body.**
>
> **⁴ Look also at ships: although they are so large and are driven by fierce winds, they are turned by a very small rudder wherever the pilot desires.**
>
> **⁵ Even so the tongue is a little member and boasts great things.**
>
> **See how great a forest a little fire kindles!**
>
> **⁶ And the tongue is a fire, a world of iniquity. The tongue is so set among our members that it defiles the whole body, and sets on fire the course of nature; and it is set on fire by hell.**

Notice that Verse 2 says, "If anyone does not stumble in word, he is able to bridle the whole body." Then, notice how it explains that the horse is controlled by a bit in its mouth (Verse 3), and the ship is controlled by a small rudder (Verse 4). Your tongue is just like that. Is it creating a world of iniquity for you or steering you to victory over sin?

Let's look at how The Amplified Classic translates this passage.

James 3:2-6 (AMPC)

² For we all often stumble and fall and offend in many things. And if anyone does not offend in speech [never says the wrong things], he is a fully developed character and a perfect man, able to control his whole body and to curb his entire nature.

³ If we set bits in the horses' mouths to make them obey us, we can turn their whole bodies about.

⁴ Likewise, look at the ships: though they are so great and are driven by rough winds, they are steered by a very small rudder wherever the impulse of the helmsman determines.

⁵ Even so the tongue is a little member, and it can boast of great things. See how much wood or how great a forest a tiny spark can set ablaze!

⁶ And the tongue is a fire. [The tongue is a] world of wickedness set among our members, contaminating and depraving the whole body and setting on fire the wheel of birth (the cycle of man's nature), being itself ignited by hell (Gehenna).

We need to speak God's Word of freedom and victory over our lives daily to see freedom and victory come to pass in our lives. The Bible says…

- **I am the righteousness of God in Christ Jesus (2 Corinthians 5:21)**
- **Old things have passed away and all things have become new (2 Corinthians 5:17)**
- **I can do all things through Jesus Christ who strengthens me (Philippians 4:13)**
- **I am the head and not the tail (Deuteronomy 28:13)**
- **I have the mind of Christ (1 Corinthians 2:16)**
- **I triumph in every situation in Christ Jesus (2 Corinthians 2:14)**

Revelation 12:11 says that we overcome the devil by the blood of the Lamb and by the word of our testimony. Jesus has already done His part and provided His own blood to defeat the works of the devil and set us free. Now, we must give the word of our testimony and declare and decree God's Word in our lives. That's how we overcome temptation, sin, and everything else the devil throws our way.

FRIENDS

As a pastor, I've watched people get born again, filled with the Holy Spirit, and get on fire for God; but then, two or three months later they're not around anymore. Why? They didn't learn from God's Word what it takes to live free.

Let's face it. People make mistakes. People do sin; nobody is perfect. But that's why we have 1 John 1:9 written to Christians. When we sin, we need to run to God and ask forgiveness, and He is faithful and just to forgive us. As Christians, we need to be quick to ask for forgiveness and quick to forgive others. We also need to help people who have sinned; sometimes, we need to pick them up and restore them.

> **Galatians 6:1 (NKJV)** Brethren, if a man is overtaken in any trespass, you who are spiritual restore such a one in a spirit of gentleness, considering yourself lest you also be tempted.

This verse tells us to pick up people who have fallen into sin, restore them, and leave them stronger. This verse also tells us to be wise about their temptation, so we will not become tempted ourselves.

Along the same line, 1 Corinthians 15:33 says, "Be not deceived…" When the Bible says don't be deceived, it's like a neon light flashing to warn you. You will fall into a trap if you don't get the next part of this verse, which says "…evil communications corrupt good manners." The Amplified Classic puts it this way, "Do not be so deceived and misled! Evil companionships (communion, associations) corrupt and deprave good manners and morals and character."

You could be the most moral person around and be on fire for God, but if you hang around people who don't want to serve God and think sin is fun, it will take its toll on you. Yes, we should reach out and help people who fall into sin, but those we help don't need to become our best buds.

Don't misunderstand me. I'm not saying we should have the attitude of, "Don't touch me," but we cannot start hanging around sin in order to help them. We need to pull them up to our walk with God and not lower ourselves down to their walk in the flesh.

If we see a Christian in sin, should we get out our sword and cut them down by saying, "You big sinner"? No, of course not. We should lovingly restore that person with the same nonjudgmental attitude Jesus had when He said, "Neither do I condemn you, but go and sin no more."

For those who have just been born again, let me encourage you to make friends with believers who can help you grow strong. Find someone who's been walking with God for a while and let that person mentor you. I'm so glad that when I came back into the church at 23 years of age and was delivered out of the life I was living, someone grabbed me and said, "Hey, let me show you the way."

When I first started pastoring, I had a small congregation of 15 to 20 people that I bugged morning, noon, and night. I was on the phone checking on them because I wanted to be there for them. I wanted to invest in their lives and do everything I could to help them grow, but these days, with a large congregation, it's no longer possible. The Bible says that iron sharpens iron, so it's important to be around strong Christians who will sharpen you. Become friends with people of like precious faith who will sharpen and encourage you.

The Bible is very clear. We all need to be careful in choosing our friends. This also means that parents are responsible for knowing their children's friends. Don't let a child tell you that it's none of your business; they are your children and God has made them your business. Using caution in picking the right friends isn't just good advice for our children, it's good advice for everyone. We all need to pick our friends carefully, so we can live the good life God has ordained for us.

Chapter
Fourteen
Questions

1. What will the anointing do?

2. Reading about how Jesus used the anointing to set those who have been bruised free, is there a bruise in your life that you need to be set free from?

3. What are some things you can do in your life to make sure that you stay in the refiner's fire, so that your body becomes quickened, dead to sin but alive to God?

4. **What are your plans to set yourself up for success to stay in the Word of God so you can continue to be set free and not fall back into sin?**

5. **Are there friends in your life who the Lord is asking you to distance yourself from? Are there friends who you need to draw closer to? Who is someone that you can share with them what the Lord has done in your life?**

Chapter Fourteen Confessions

* Because I am born again, I am in right standing with God. (Romans 3:24)

* I am the righteousness of God in Christ Jesus (2 Corinthians 5:21)

* Because I partake of the solid food of the Word of God, I am able to discern good from evil. (Hebrews 5:14)

* I purposely enter into God's presence to receive His fire that destroys any yokes of bondage and helps me keep my flesh under. (2 Corinthians 3:17)

* The same Spirit that raised Jesus from the dead dwells in me and is making my mortal body alive again. (Romans 8:11)

* The Word of God lives in me, and it divides between my soul and spirit and between my thoughts and God's thoughts. (Hebrews 4:12)

chapter 15: living free

In the beginning of this book, we talked about how Jesus ministered to the woman caught in the act of adultery (John 8). While everyone else judged and condemned her to death, Jesus had a whole different attitude. He didn't condone her sin, but neither did He condemn her.

In my book "No Longer Condemned", I talk about how condemnation from past sins can weigh you down and beat you up until you feel ashamed, unworthy, and unfit; but nevertheless how Romans 8:1 says "There is therefore now no condemnation to those who are in Christ Jesus". I believe "No Longer Condemned" would be a great additional resource to read to help you leave sin and condemnation in the past where they belong.

Jesus told the woman, "Go and sin no more." These are life-changing words He spoke. Even more amazing is the God-given power behind these words that will help you and me do the same. Jesus was telling this woman, and all of us today, that it's possible to go and sin no more, that you can break free, stay free, and live free from sin.

If you've received Jesus as your Savior, you're not like everybody else walking around on this Earth. The moment you were born again, something happened on the inside of you. You were filled with God Himself, and the more you allow what's on the inside of you to show up on the outside, the more you will walk, talk, and act differently.

The devil wants to keep you tied to your past, but it's too late. We've exposed his trickery and deceit with the truth of God's Word that says Jesus defeated sin on the cross and removed our sins by washing them away with His blood. God has raised us up to sit in heavenly places in Christ Jesus. It is a finished work, so now the choice is yours. Will you receive and walk in the redemption Jesus has purchased for you? You are no longer a sinner held captive by sin. You are a child of God and a joint heir with Jesus, and no devil in Hell can stop you from taking your place, so start acting like it.

Jesus came to Earth not only to redeem us but to show us how to live, and it's time we follow His example. Jesus knew who He was and that He had power over the devil and sin and had dominion in the Earth. When He spoke to storms, they calmed. When He spoke to fevers, they broke.

Jesus gave us His power over the devil and sin. Luke 10:19 says that He gave us authority over all the power of the enemy, so now He expects us to use that authority. He expects us to declare and decree His Word, so the Holy Spirit can demonstrate it through us; and He expects us to exert dominion over our own mind and body. We can do this because of the new nature we have on the inside of us. We are the temple of the Holy Spirit, and we can now walk in the spirit. We have received the free gift of righteousness. We are armed with the Word of God as our weapon, and we're guided through life by the Holy Spirit. God has given us every supernatural tool needed to win over sin.

SUPERNATURAL RESTORATION

God cares about His children so much that He wants us to do more than just conquer sin; He wants us to recover what sin has stolen from us. God restored the children of Israel as they came out of Egypt (Exodus 12), He restored David (2 Samuel 11-12), He restored the prodigal son (Luke 15), and God will restore you.

When the children of Israel came up out of Egypt, which was a type of sin, they recovered all that God had long ago promised Abraham, Isaac, and Jacob in His covenant with them.

Through miraculous intervention, God brought the Israelites out of slavery. They would have left with nothing except they had a covenant with God and that was everything. God brought them out with silver and gold, and there was not one sick or feeble person among them (Psalm 105:37). Just like God delivered the Israelites from bondage and restored their health, wealth and all the enemy had stolen, He stands ready to do the same for you and me right now!

In this Old Testament account, God restored His children and in so doing, showed us what redemption looks like. He showed them His goodness and led them to the land of promise, which He had promised to restore to them because it belonged to them; and that land still belongs to them today. Unfortunately, a great number of Israelites got their eyes off the promise because they believed the enemy was too big, and they ended up staying in the wilderness another 40 years. Those who were in unbelief died in the wilderness and never saw the Promised Land, but those who believed did see it come to pass.

What is your Promised Land? Maybe your Promised Land looks impossible to you at the moment. Maybe the enemy looks too big like they did in the eyes of many Israelites, but God's Word is full of great and precious promises that will enable you to take hold of every godly thing you need or want. These blessings are not for when you get to Heaven; they are available in the here and now, so don't let the same thing happen to you that happened to the Israelites. Don't get bogged down in unbelief. Make up your mind that you will partake of everything God has promised you and then, let God restore to you everything sin has stolen from you.

 If you say, "That sounds great, but I got myself into this sin. It was my fault, so how can I expect God to restore anything to me?" It's what He does. God is a restorer. Psalm 107:20 says God will deliver us from all our destructions, so hold on to the promise of restoration because God wants to restore you.

In 1 Samuel 30, King David and his men returned to find the place burnt down, and the women, children and all their possessions gone. Things looked bleak all around.

1 Samuel 30:2-4

2 And had taken the women captives, that were therein: they slew not any, either great or small, but carried them away, and went on their way.

> **³ So David and his men came to the city, and, behold, it was burned with fire; and their wives, and their sons, and their daughters, were taken captives.**
>
> **⁴ Then David and the people that were with him lifted up their voice and wept, until they had no more power to weep.**

Maybe you have experienced this kind of devastation in your life where all you could do was weep. Maybe you have felt like the wind was knocked out of you. The verse below says there's only one thing to do at a time like this.

> **1 Samuel 30:6 And David was greatly distressed; for the people spake of stoning him, because the soul of all the people was grieved, every man for his sons and for his daughters: <u>but David encouraged himself in the Lord his God</u>.**

David had been the hero when all was well, but when things went from bad to worse, the people wanted to stone their great leader. So, what did David do when it looked like things couldn't get any worse? David encouraged himself in the Lord, his God.

When it feels like you were punched in the stomach and grieving over mistakes gone by, you've got to make up your mind to start encouraging yourself in the Lord. Maybe your sins and bad choices have stolen from you. Maybe temptation and sin has caused you to wreck your whole life or the life of another. Maybe you've lost your spouse, or your job, or your whole family. Maybe you've lost your reputation or years of enjoying life. It doesn't matter what it is. It's never too late. God can restore what you've lost if you will trust Him and follow Him.

Even when things look bad concerning family, health, financial, or even in relationship situations, you've got to get up and encourage yourself in the Lord. It's nice when other people encourage you, but you cannot always depend on others. David had to grab himself by what I like to call "the nape of the neck" and say, "Soul, you will encourage yourself. Why are you so disquieted within me; you will yet praise God" (Psalm 42:5).

Encourage yourself in the Lord like David did. God has brought you this far; and even though you got off track, God can bring you from where you are to where you need to go. God is not finished with you, so don't give up.

The temptation, sin, or devastation you have faced was sent by the devil to destroy you, but you're still standing. Restoration may look impossible, but with God, nothing is impossible. That's why you can encourage yourself because you have a God who restores.

What did David do next? He asked God for advice, which is always a good idea.

> ### 1 Samuel 30:7-8
>
> **7 And David said to Abiathar the priest, Ahimelech's son, I pray thee, bring me hither the ephod. And Abiathar brought thither the ephod to David.**
>
> **8 And David enquired at the Lord, saying, Shall I pursue after this troop? shall I overtake them? And he answered him, Pursue: for thou shalt surely overtake them, and without fail recover all.**

David went before the Lord and basically asked, "What shall I do? Shall I go after this army? What's the game plan?" That was wise of David because every battle we face is not the same. The Word of God will always cause us to win, but we still need to be led by the Spirit of God and get the plan for each battle. There were times when David went after the enemy, and other times when he stood still and saw the salvation of the Lord, which means letting God taking care of it.

So, what did God tell David to do? He said, "Pursue." What do you suppose God is telling you to do? David didn't sit by silently, and he didn't just sit down and sing, "Kumbaya [Arise and come], my Lord, kumbaya." No. He asked the Lord what to do; and when God told Him to pursue, he did and recovered all that had been stolen from him because the Lord was with Him. I believe the Lord is telling you the same thing. Don't wait for the devil to attack you again with temptation or sin. Pursue! Pursue your place in God. Pursue a sin-free life. Pursue restoration of what sin has stolen from you.

Be strong in the Lord every day. Be blessed in the Lord every day. The Bible says, "The just shall live by faith," so put faith to work in your life and continually speak God's Word over every situation in your life. If you do, you won't have to fight so many adversaries all the time, and the ones that do show up won't be such a big deal to overcome.

Restoration of all things in our lives is not automatic, so we need to quit saying, "Well, if it's God's will for me, it will just happen, and if it's not His will, then it won't." That's not how it works and that's not in the Bible. The Bible says that it is God's will for everyone to be saved but is everyone you know saved? No. So, who determines if the will of God is done in your life? Your spouse? Your pastor? No. The Holy Ghost can't even make it happen. The choice is yours alone. The Word and Spirit of God will guide you into all truth and empower you to walk in the truth, but you must do the walking.

If you say, "How do I know it's God's will for things to be restored to me? John 10:10 says it's the devil who comes to steal, kill, and destroy, but Jesus came to give us abundant life. God sent Jesus to give a full and amazing life to all who will believe on Him and receive it. Throughout the Epistles, the Word makes it clear that God wants good things for us.

Luke 15 tells the story of the prodigal son. This young man took his inheritance and squandered it all on wild living (lasciviousness). When he spent all his money, there was famine in the land, and he didn't have anything to eat, so he came to himself and decided to go home. Verse 21 says that the son said to his father, "Father, I have sinned against heaven and in your sight, and am no longer worthy to be called your son," but the father lovingly and compassionately received his son and restored him to sonship. Father and son were reunited. The family was reunited. With the ring that was put on his finger, the son's authority and wealth were restored. This father's restoration of his son is a demonstration of how God wants to restore us.

People who have sinned against the heavenly Father, and come back, often have this same attitude that the prodigal son had and will say, "I don't deserve anything," and they're right. They don't. But the father in Luke 15 looked past what the son deserved, and so does our heavenly Father look past what we deserve. God wants to restore us in every area of our life, and the best evidence of this is found in Jesus' own words.

Luke 4:18-19 (NKJV)

[18] "The Spirit of the LORD is upon Me, Because He has anointed Me To preach the gospel to the poor; He has sent Me to heal the brokenhearted, To proclaim liberty to the captives And recovery of sight to the blind, To set at liberty those who are oppressed;

| **¹⁹ To proclaim the acceptable year of the LORD."**

What is the "Acceptable year of the Lord"? It is Jubilee!

Leviticus 25:9-10, 13 (NKJV)

⁹ Then you shall cause the trumpet of the Jubilee to sound on the tenth day of the seventh month; on the Day of Atonement you shall make the trumpet to sound throughout all your land.

¹⁰ And you shall consecrate the fiftieth year, and proclaim liberty throughout all the land to all its inhabitants. It shall be a <u>Jubilee</u> for you; and each of you shall return to his possession, and each of you shall return to his family.

¹³ 'In this Year of Jubilee, each of you shall return to his possession.

Every 50 years the trumpet would sound, and the people would shout, "Jubilee! Jubilee!" That meant if family members were taken as a result of debt, they would be restored during Jubilee. Possessions sold because of debt, would be restored during Jubilee. On this day of atonement, the people would be returned to their possessions and their families. Think about it. If someone took your house, when the Jubilee trumpet sounded, you could knock on the door and say, "Jubilee, give me my family back. Give me my house back. You may leave now. Did you hear the trumpet? It's Jubilee!"

So, what did Jesus mean when He said He was here to preach the acceptable year of the Lord (Luke 4:19)? Jesus was telling us that He is our Jubilee! When Jesus paid the ultimate price for us on the cross, atonement came to us once and for all. Now, Jubilee is every single day for us.

That means it's Jubilee for you! So, pursue what you've lost because God is in the restoration business. Jesus Himself preached the acceptable year of the Lord, so it's time to recover all that you've lost. It doesn't matter what you've lost or how you lost it, God can return it. Even if you deserved to lose something, God wants to bring it back to you. Jesus came to set us free and restore whatever we've lost.

Maybe you were married and got divorced and both of you have remarried. Does that mean you should go back to your first wife? Absolutely not. God won't rearrange the lives of four people because you've now figured out that you made a mistake. Maybe you've been married three times and you just got born again and filled with the Holy Ghost, and, for the first time, things are going well, so you're thinking, "I really messed up. I need to go back and fix it. No. Don't do that unless the Holy Spirit leads you to do it. In a situation like that, you shouldn't go back; but God can restore marriage to you with someone else. In other words, God won't necessarily restore the same person back to you, but He will restore marriage to you. He'll restore family to you. Just keep going forward from where you are now and follow the Holy Ghost.

Maybe you didn't do well in raising your children when they were young. It's not too late. I've watched God rearrange lives and restore families when it appeared to be impossible.

Maybe you feel like drugs and alcohol have stolen years from your life. Joel 2:25 says that God will restore the years to you that the locusts have eaten. It doesn't matter how much time has passed. God has a way of restoring things.

The Shunammite woman who helped the prophet, Elisha, (2 Kings 4) is a good example. Her son had died, and Elisha raised him from the dead. Then, later in 2 Kings 8, the prophet told the woman that a famine was coming, so she left her land and traveled to the land of the Philistines. Then, seven years later when the famine ended, she returned to her homeland and petitioned the king to get her land back. God had positioned her at the right place with her son, while the prophet's assistant, Gehazi, told the king everything Elisha had done and how he had raised the boy from the dead. When the king realized the miracle that had occurred with the boy, he immediately restored the woman's land to her. And because God is in the restoration business, he moved on the king to also give the woman all the money that was made off her land during the time she was away.

If you're thinking, "But she didn't deserve it. That's not fair." Maybe not, but favor isn't fair. If you don't want to walk in God's favor, I'll take yours because favor is better than fair, and the righteous are encompassed about with this favor (Psalm 5:12).

Let God restore you like He did the Israelites, David, the prodigal son, and the Shunammite woman. No matter what you've lost, God will restore it to you if you can believe for it, obey the Word, and follow the leadings of the Holy Spirit.

RUN YOUR RACE

God wants you free and restored in every area of your life. God's plan is a "happily ever after" for you and your whole family. However, in order to finish strong, you must realize that you're not running a sprint, you're running a marathon.

We need to determine right now that we will walk in the divine nature we've been given until we go to Heaven or Jesus returns. We want to make it to the end, so we can hear Jesus say to us, "Well done, good and faith servant," and walking free from sin is a big part of it.

Hebrews 12 tells us what we must do to focus on running and winning our race.

Hebrews 12:1-2

1 Wherefore seeing we also are compassed about with so great a cloud of witnesses, let us lay aside every weight, and the sin which doth so easily beset us, and let us run with patience the race that is set before us,

2 Looking unto Jesus the author and finisher of our faith; who for the joy that was set before him endured the cross, despising the shame, and is set down at the right hand of the throne of God.

As Heaven cheers us on, each of us has a race to run and to run it well, we must lay aside weights and sins that ensnare us. Why? So, we can run with endurance and cross the finish line.

Imagine a marathon runner lined up at the starting line. The gun fires, but the runner can barely make it down the lane because of dragging a 25 or 100-pound weight. Even if you've never been a runner or an athlete, it's pretty easy to figure out that if you're carrying extra weight, it will slow you down and make you ineffective in your race.

With this in mind, let's look at Hebrews 12:1-2 in The Amplified Classic.

Hebrews 12:1-2 (AMPC)

[1] Therefore then, since we are surrounded by so great a cloud of witnesses [who have borne testimony to the Truth], <u>let us strip off and throw aside every encumbrance (unnecessary weight) and that sin which so readily (deftly and cleverly) clings to and entangles us</u>, and let us run with patient endurance and steady and active persistence the appointed course of the race that is set before us,

[2] Looking away [from all that will distract] to Jesus, Who is the Leader and the Source of our faith [giving the first incentive for our belief] and is also its Finisher [bringing it to maturity and perfection]. He, for the joy [of obtaining the prize] that was set before Him, endured the cross, despising and ignoring the shame, and is now seated at the right hand of the throne of God.

I like the strong language used in this version. It says we are to strip off and throw aside every weight and the sin that so readily clings to and entangles us. Isn't that just the way sin feels? Sin traps us. It cleverly clings to us and pushes our buttons. Worse yet, it tangles us up, so we cannot run.

The New Testament in the Modern English translation puts it this way, "…Strip off everything that hinders us, as well as the sin which dogs our feet, and let us run the race that we have to run with patience, our eyes fixed on Jesus the source and the goal of our faith." Because you're reading this book, I know you've felt, at times, that sin dogs you and nips at your heels, so what should you do? Fix your eyes on Jesus, the source, and the goal of your faith. If you will look to Jesus, He will be the author and finisher of your faith and will help you finish strong.

RECEIVING A CROWN

We must realize that our finish line is not Heaven. Our finish line is the judgment seat of Christ. That's where we will receive our reward for the things we have done on the Earth; and, hopefully, will hear Jesus say, "Well done, good and faithful servant." It's unfortunate that Jesus won't be able to say that to everybody. Every born-again believer will spend eternity in Heaven, but that doesn't mean all will hear, "Well done!"

Years ago, I began to think a lot about this, about how the Lord had given me so much. He saved me. He delivered me. He healed me. He provided for me financially. He had given me a great life. God has done so much for me, and I'm grateful to Him for it all. Not only do I choose to obey Him, but I want to obey Him. With all my heart, I want to please Him. Besides our love freely given to Him, there is only one other thing we have to give to Him now and for all of eternity and that is our obedience.

There are other things we are to do like tithe, give offerings, help the poor, love God and people, fulfil the Great Commission of going into all the world to make disciples, baptizing, and teaching them to obey, read and study God's Word, and help in the church, but all these are wrapped up in one word: obedience.

You see, when I stand in front of Jesus at the judgment seat of Christ, eyeball to eyeball, He will ask me one question: Did you do what I asked you to do on the Earth? At that point, there are only two answers: "Yes" or "No." And most likely, those answering "No" would follow with, "Lord, let me tell You the reasons why I couldn't obey." I believe if anyone starts making excuses, He'll put His hand up and say, "Not now! I don't want to hear it," so I desperately want to be able to say, "Yes, Lord!" Don't you?

The Bible tells us that Jesus will give crowns to those of us who have obeyed Him and then, there will be a great worship service in Heaven. Notice, I said, "those of us." I've included myself. Because I've made up my mind that I will obey Him, and I will receive one of those crowns. Have you made up your mind?

If you say to me, "Do you think I'll get a crown some day?" Let me ask you this. Is obeying Jesus the most important thing in your life? If you answer, "Yes," then I believe you will receive a crown one day. That means you'll be among those who will have the privilege of removing your crown at this worship service and laying it at Jesus' feet. I think giving Jesus your crown will be the best thing you can do when it comes to all eternity.

Sadly, I've known people who have served God but are no longer serving Him today and have walked away from Him. Maybe it was because they felt they didn't get their prayers answered or maybe they didn't really understand faith. Maybe they didn't obtain their healing, or it could be a lot of other things. More often than not, however, they are no longer serving God because they fell into sin at some point. They are in what we call a "backslidden" condition, where they were born again and walked with God but, literally, slipped backward and walked away, or it could be that the person was never really born again, so their life was never really transformed.

I know one thing. Because you're reading this book, you love God and want to serve Him; and with each chapter you read, you're becoming more empowered with the truth that is able to make you free. So, let's all decide to run our race and strive for a crown we can lay at Jesus' feet.

Here's what the Apostle Paul tells us.

1 Corinthians 9:24-27

24 Know ye not that they which run in a race run all, but one receiveth the prize? So run, that ye may obtain.

25 And <u>every man that striveth for the mastery is temperate in all things</u>. Now they do it to obtain a corruptible crown; but we an incorruptible.

26 I therefore so run, not as uncertainly; so fight I, not as one that beateth the air:

27 But I keep under my body, and bring it into subjection: lest that by any means, when I have preached to others, I myself should be a castaway.

What's the prize that the Apostle Paul is talking about? It's a crown, the reward you receive at the end of your race. He says that the one who strives for the mastery is temperate in all things. The word "temperate" (a fruit of the Spirit) means to control your flesh and not overdue things. Does the scripture say in what things we are to be temperate? It does. It says "in all things."

Let me give you an example from a number of years ago. We had an athlete in our church who was a state champion wrestler. Even though he was only in the ninth grade at the time, no one would have messed with him. Do you know why? Because he trained and lifted weights; he was strong and had muscles. He ate right and worked hard because he was training for a title.

Likewise, you and I are also in training. We're in the event of our lives. We're not competing against each other, but we are running to finish our race, so we can receive an incorruptible crown. And just like a natural athlete, we, too, need to lift weights and develop our faith muscles by eating the right spiritual food, which is the Word of God and working hard in doing what God says to do. We also need to renew our mind and keep our body under control, so we can win our race.

That's why Paul likened his life to a race. Let's look at how the Amplified Classic says it.

> ## 1 Corinthians 9:25-27 (AMPC)
>
> **25 Now every athlete who goes into training conducts himself temperately and restricts himself in all things. They do it to win a wreath that will soon wither, but we [do it to receive a crown of eternal blessedness] that cannot wither.**
>
> **26 Therefore I do not run uncertainly (without definite aim). I do not box like one beating the air and striking without an adversary.**
>
> **27 But [like a boxer] I buffet my body [handle it roughly, discipline it by hardships] and subdue it, for fear that after proclaiming to others the Gospel and things pertaining to it, I myself should become unfit [not stand the test, be unapproved and rejected as a counterfeit].**

Paul was determined and really did have to fight. He said that he was a stern master of his body. Notice, it did not say that Paul asked God to control his body, nor did Paul ask a friend to keep his body under. That's what a lot of people want to do. They will pray to God and ask Him to keep their body under, or they will ask friends for help, and some friends may even try to help them do this, but I wonder how long they will remain friends doing that. Some people use the biggest excuse of all and say, "I couldn't help myself. It's not my fault." Or they'll fall back on, "The devil made me do it." Friend, these are lies and self-deception. The only one responsible for keeping your body under is You!

Too often, Christians like to blame the devil and evil spirits for things that are just the result of undisciplined flesh. I've heard it over and over again. A wife will say, "My husband gets so angry sometimes. He must be possessed with a demon." Most likely he's not. Most likely her husband just refuses to control his flesh. Let's give equal opportunity here. I've had husbands say to me, "My wife is so mean; she's evil. She must have a demon. I just know it." Most likely she doesn't. Most likely His wife just refuses to control her flesh.

Paul shared the secret to having a successful Christian life when he said, "I keep my body under and bring it into subjection." This man wrote two-thirds of the New Testament and took the gospel of Jesus Christ pretty much around the known world in his day. So, if Paul had to keep his body under to win the prize and not be a castaway, then that's what we need to do too.

No one reading this book wants to be a castaway. We all want to be overcomers. We all want to finish our course and complete our race. So, let's do it. Let's win the prize and receive our crown that we can lay at His feet! Let's leave sin behind and run our race! Let's go and sin no more!

Chapter
Fifteen
Questions

1. What was Jubilee?

2. What does it mean to be temperate?

3. What are some weights or sins in your life keeping you from running your race for God?

4. God wants us to conquer sin, but He also wants us to recover what sin has stolen from us. What are some things that have been stolen from you because of sin that you can trust the Lord to restore?

5. What weights can you lay aside that are slowing down your race?

6. What is our finish line?

Chapter
Fifteen
Confessions

✻   The Spirit of the Lord is in me and can come upon me to set me and others free. (Luke 4:18)

✻   I have been given authority over all the power of the enemy to stop anything the devil tries to do. (Luke 10:19)

✻   Whenever distress comes my way, I will encourage myself in the Lord, so He can show me what to do. (1 Samuel 30:6)

✻   Jubilee is mine, and I will get back everything the enemy has stolen from me. (Luke 4:18-19)

✻   I will lay aside anything that hinders me so I can run my race and finish what Jesus has given me to do. (Hebrews 12:1-2)

a prayer to overcome sin

The first step toward overcoming sin is to receive Jesus as your Lord and Savior. It will change you from the inside out and enable you to take hold of the supernatural tools you need to get free, stay free, and live free from sin. It all begins by praying this simple prayer aloud:

> **Dear Heavenly Father,**
>
> **Your Word says that whosoever shall call on the name of the Lord shall be saved (Acts 2:21).**
>
> **Romans 10:9-10 says if I confess with my mouth that Jesus is Lord and believe in my heart that Jesus was raised from the dead, I shall be saved, so I choose to do that right now.**
>
> **Jesus,**
>
> **I believe in You. I believe in my heart and confess with my mouth that You died on the cross for my sins, and that You were raised from the dead. I ask You to be my Lord and Savior. Thank You for forgiving me of all my sins. I believe I'm now a new creation in You. Old things have passed away and all things have become new in Jesus' name.**
>
> **Amen.**

If you prayed this prayer, you are now born again! You are now family in the kingdom of God, so please share the good news with us!

Email us at Cornerstone Word of Life Church office@cwol.org or call the church office at 256-461-7055. We would love to hear from you!

end notes

REFERENCES

1. Rick Renner, *Dressed to Kill,* (Tulsa, Oklahoma: Teach All Nations, A Division of Rick Renner Ministries, 2003), 131-132.

2. Rick Renner, *Sparkling Gems from the Greek,* (Tulsa, Oklahoma: Teach All Nations, A Division of Rick Renner Ministries, 2003), 514, 946, 490, 529.

3. Strong, James. The New Strong's Exhaustive Concordance of the Bible. Nashville: T. Nelson, 1990.

4. The Livingston Corporation, Life Application New Testament Commentary (Town: Tyndale House Publishers, Inc.,), as found in Word Search 8 Software.

5. W.E Vine, *Vine's Expository Dictionary of the Old and New Testament Words* (Nashville: Thomas Nelson, 1984), as found in PC Study Bible v.5.

All Confessions
In Biblical Order

✱   I will meditate on and be a doer of the Word of God, so that my way will be made prosperous, and I will have good success. (Joshua 1:8)

✱   Whenever distress comes my way, I will encourage myself in the Lord, so He can show me what to do. (1 Samuel 30:6)

✱   The joy of the Lord is my strength. (Nehemiah 8:10)

✱   I will not walk in the counsel of the ungodly, I will not get advice from sinners, and I will not sit in the seat of the scornful; but I will delight in the Lord, meditate on His Word, and be like a tree planted by the rivers of living water. (Psalm 1:1-3)

✱   I will spend time with God because in His presence is fullness of joy. (Psalm 16:11)

✱   Because I walk in meekness, I shall eat and be satisfied. (Psalm 22:26)

✱   As I walk in goodness, I am confident that I will see the goodness of the Lord. (Psalm 27:13)

All Confessions
In Biblical Order

✗   When I trust in the Lord and do good, I dwell in safety.
(Psalm 37:3)

✗   I have joy because I delight myself in the Lord.
(Psalm 37:4)

✗   The Lord will deliver me from every trap of the enemy.
(Psalm 91:3)

✗   The entrance of God's Word gives me light and
understanding. (Psalm 119:130)

✗   Because I love your Word, I walk in peace and do not
stumble. (Psalm 119:165)

✗   The Lord will perfect all that concerns me.
(Psalm 138:8)

✗   I will walk in gentleness because it is a kind answer
that will turn away wrath. (Proverbs 15:1)

✗   I choose joy because a merry heart does good like a
medicine. (Proverbs 17:22)

All Confessions
In Biblical Order

✳ I will overlook an offense because God's wisdom in me gives me patience. (Proverbs 19:11)

✳ Because I keep my eyes on Jesus, He will keep me in perfect peace. (Isaiah 26:3)

✳ As I walk in meekness, the joy of the Lord will increase in my life. (Isaiah 29:19)

✳ I will be gracious and show compassion to others because God is gracious to me. (Isaiah 30:18)

✳ I will, in gentleness, comfort others. (Isaiah 40:1-2)

✳ I will not fear for You are with me. I will not be dismayed for You are my God. I am strengthened and helped because God upholds me. (Isaiah 41:10)

✳ The Lord has made me righteous. He is holding my hand and is keeping me. He has opened my eyes and brought me out of prison. (Isaiah 42:6-7)

All Confessions
In Biblical Order

✻   I no longer sit in darkness because I have seen a great
     light. God's light has sprung up in me and removes
     all darkness and any shadow of death for me. (Matthew
     4:16)

✻   Because I walk in meekness, I am blessed and will
     inherit the Earth and will delight in an abundance of
     peace. (Matthew 5:5, Psalm 37:11)

✻   I will walk as Jesus walked, in humbleness of heart.
     (Matthew 11:29; Titus 3:1-2)

✻   I will be faithful with the things you give me, money,
     assignments, and whatever you say. I will be faithful
     so I can hear well done. (Matthew 25:21)

✻   The Spirit of the Lord is in me and can come upon me
     to set me and others free. (Luke 4:18)

✻   Jubilee is mine, and I will get back everything the
     enemy has stolen from me. (Luke 4:18-19)

✻   I have been given authority over all the power of the
     enemy to stop anything the devil tries to do.
     (Luke 10:19)

All Confessions
In Biblical Order

✗   I will be faithful in both the small and big things, and I will be faithful with money, so God will commit to me His true riches. (Luke 16:10-11)

✗   Your Word is spirit, and it is life, so I will read and speak Your Word to stay connected to You. (John 6:63)

✗   Because I continue in Your Word, I know the truth and it sets me free. (John 8:31-32)

✗   Who the Son sets free is free indeed, so I am free in Christ Jesus. (John 8:36)

✗   I walk in the same peace that Jesus did, so I will not be troubled or afraid. (John 14:27)

✗   I will cleanse and sanctify my mind with the washing of the Word. (John 15:3, 17:17)

✗   Jesus is the vine, and I am the branch, so I will stay vitally connected to the vine. (John 15:5)

✗   I will lead the unsaved and backslidden to repentance. (Romans 2:4)

All Confessions
In Biblical Order

✻   Because I am born again, I am in right standing with
    God. (Romans 3:24)

✻   Because of God's generosity freely given, He has
    made me right with Him and has restored me. (Romans
    3:24)

✻   I have the love of God because it has been poured out
    in my heart by the Holy Spirit. (Romans 5:5)

✻   I will not let sin reign in my body; I will not obey the
    lusts of my flesh. (Romans 6:12)

✻   I will not yield my body to wrongdoing but will yield
    my body to righteousness for the glory of God.
    (Romans 6:13)

✻   I have been set free from sin and have become a
    servant of righteousness. I walk in God's divine will,
    thoughts, and purposes. (Romans 6:18)

✻   Condemnation cannot live in me because I am in
    Christ Jesus and walk in the spirit and not the flesh.
    (Romans 8:1)

All Confessions
In Biblical Order

✳ **The same Spirit that raised Jesus from the dead dwells in me and is making my mortal body alive again.** (Romans 8:11)

✳ **I will live by the Spirit and put to death the things of my flesh.** (Romans 8:13)

✳ **I am more than a conqueror in Christ Jesus.** (Romans 8:37)

✳ **I will not be conformed to this world, but I will be transformed as I renew my mind with the Word of God so I can prove what is the perfect will of God.** (Romans 12:2)

✳ **I will cling to what is good, so that I can be good to others.** (Romans 12:9)

✳ **I will overcome evil with good.** (Romans 12:21)

✳ **I will clothe myself with the Lord Jesus Christ and make no provision for the lusts of my flesh.** (Romans 13:14)

All Confessions In Biblical Order

* I have the mind of Christ because I think His thoughts which I find in the Word of God. (1 Corinthians 2:16)

* I will remain faithful, so I can receive the true riches of God. (1 Corinthians 4:2)

* I will be faithful like Timothy so that God can send me to help and train others. (1 Corinthians 4:17)

* My body is the temple of the Holy Spirit who lives in me. I am not my own. I belong to God. (1 Corinthians 6:19)

* I will walk in temperance to obtain the prize at the end of my race, a crown that I can lay at Jesus' feet. (1 Corinthians 9:24-25, Revelations 4:10-11)

* I will fight by keeping my body under subjection, so I will not become a castaway. I will finish my course. (1 Corinthians 9:26-27)

* I shall discipline my body and bring it into subjection, so I can be a witness to others. (1 Corinthians 9:27)

All Confessions
In Biblical Order

✳   No matter what temptation comes, God is faithful and has made a way of escape for me. (1 Corinthians 10:13)

✳   God is not the author of confusion but of peace, so I will walk in peace. (1 Corinthians 14:33)

✳   I will not be deceived by hanging with those who practice evil because evil will cause corruption in me. (1 Corinthians 15:33)

✳   I will let all I do be done in love. (1 Corinthians 16:14)

✳   Because I am not ignorant of the devil's devices, I will win against the enemy every time by speaking the Word of God to that situation.
(2 Corinthians 2:11, 14)

✳   God always causes me to triumph in Christ.
(2 Corinthians 2:14)

✳   I purposely enter into God's presence to receive His fire that destroys any yokes of bondage and helps me keep my flesh under. (2 Corinthians 3:17)

All Confessions In Biblical Order

* Because I am born again, I am a new creation in Christ Jesus and old things have passed away.
  (2 Corinthians 5:17)

* I am the righteousness of God in Christ Jesus
  (2 Corinthians 5:21)

* I am seated in heavenly places, and I refuse to sin because it and the enemy are under my feet.
  (2 Corinthians 5:21, Ephesians 2:6, 1:22)

* I will cast down imaginations and every high thing that exalts itself against the Word of God.
  (2 Corinthians 10:5)

* I will not allow my flesh to dominate me in any area of my life; and because I walk in the spirit, I will not fulfill the lusts of my flesh. (Galatians 5:16)

* I will walk and live in the spirit. I will be responsive, controlled and guided by Him, so I will not gratify the cravings of my flesh. (Galatians 5:16)

* I will walk in patience because I know in due season I will reap if I do not faint. (Galatians 6:9)

All Confessions
In Biblical Order

✱   **God's Word floods me with light so I can know the hope He has called me to and how rich His glorious inheritance is to me. (Ephesians 1:18)**

✱   **Because I have been raised to sit in heavenly places with Christ Jesus, the devil is under my feet. (Ephesians 2:6, Ephesians 1:22)**

✱   **I am God's workmanship, created in Christ Jesus, and I shall walk in the good works He has ordained for me. (Ephesians 2:10)**

✱   **I will stay in unity as I walk in peace. (Ephesians 4:3)**

✱   **I will speak what is good and not what is evil for the benefit of those who listen. (Ephesians 4:29)**

✱   **I will be kind to others and quick to forgive because Christ has forgiven me. (Ephesians 4:32)**

✱   **I will be a follower of God and His Word because I am His child. (Ephesians 5:1)**

✱   **I will let my gentle spirit be known to all. (Philippians 4:5)**

All Confessions
In Biblical Order

✳   I will only think on those things that are true, noble, just, pure, lovely, and things that are of a good report. I will think on those things that have virtue, and things that are praiseworthy. These are the things I will meditate on. (Philippians 4:8)

✳   I can do all things through Jesus Christ who strengthens me. (Philippians 4:13)

✳   I will put on love which will produce perfect harmony. (Colossians 3:14)

✳   I will walk in a way that is holy and honorable and present my body as a living sacrifice to God every day. (1 Thessalonians 4:4, Romans 12:1)

✳   I will be joyful always because this is God's will for me. (1 Thessalonians 5:16-18)

✳   I will abstain from all appearances of evil. (1 Thessalonians 5:22)

✳   I will flee from all lusts and keep my heart pure. (2 Timothy 2:22)

All Confessions
In Biblical Order

✻   The Lord will deliver me from every evil work and keep me safe in His heavenly Kingdom (2 Timothy 4:18)

✻   I will live soberly and uprightly before God by denying ungodliness and worldly lusts. (Titus 2:12)

✻   The Word of God lives in me, and it divides between my soul and spirit and between my thoughts and God's thoughts. (Hebrews 4:12)

✻   Because I partake of the solid food of the Word of God, I am able to discern good from evil.
(Hebrews 5:14)

✻   I will lay aside anything that hinders me so I can run my race and finish what Jesus has given me to do.
(Hebrews 12:1-2)

✻   God corrects me because He love me. I will yield to His correction because it will produce the peaceable fruit of righteousness in me. (Hebrews 12:11)

✻   With patience, I will be quick to listen and slow to speak. (James 1:19)

All Confessions
In Biblical Order

✶   I will be swift to hear, slow to speak and slow to get angry because I am a doer of God's Word. (James 1:19, 22)

✶   I will walk in meekness in my conduct because those who do are considered wise and understanding. (James 3:13)

✶   I will obey God and His Word. I will not have illicit love affairs with the world. I will only be God's friend and not a friend of this world. (James 4:4)

✶   Because I am a temporary resident of the Earth, I will abstain from fleshly desires that war against my soul. (1 Peter 2:11)

✶   I will seek peace and pursue it. (1 Peter 3:11)

✶   God has given me everything that pertains to life and godliness, and it is mine as I grow in the knowledge of Him. (2 Peter 1:3)

✶   God has given me exceedingly great and precious promises, and I receive them as I walk in my new, divine nature. (2 Peter 1:4)

All Confessions
In Biblical Order

✳   I will add temperance to my faith so that I will not be barren but will produce much fruit. (2 Peter 1:6)

✳   I am born again and because I walk uprightly, God knows how to deliver me out of every temptation and evil work. I am delivered! (2 Peter 2:9)

✳   God is longsuffering with me, so I will be patient with others. (2 Peter 3:9)

✳   I will love others because God is love. (1 John 4:8)

✳   I will walk in love because perfect love casts out fear. (1 John 4:18)

✳   I will love others because God first loved me. (1 John 4:19)

about the author

Pastor Mark Garver is the founding and Senior Pastor of Cornerstone Word of Life Church since its inception in November of 1993. He is a 1990 graduate of RHEMA.

In addition to pastoring this thriving church, he holds minister's conferences and Holy Ghost Meetings in the Nations. He and his wife, Rhonda, founded Bible Institute, a two-year leadership training program which is operating at CWOL, online, and in a number of different nations. They also founded School of Ministry to train five-fold ministers of the Gospel.

For more books and information, feel free to visit:

GARVERMINISTRIES.ORG

Made in the USA
Columbia, SC
17 November 2024

46734586R10159